Lawsa Student Texts

Partnership

Lawsa Student Texts

Partnership

by

J J Henning BIur LLB   and   H J Delport BA LLB LLD
Attorney of the Supreme Court   Advocate of the Supreme Court
Professor of Law,   Professor of Law,
University of the Orange Free State   University of Port Elizabeth

An extract from
THE LAW OF SOUTH AFRICA
Volume 19

BUTTERWORTHS
DURBAN

Butterworths

Professional Publishers (Pty) Ltd
Reg No 87/03997/07

© 1984

Reprinted 1989

ISBN 0 409 04022 3

Durban
8 Walter Place, Waterval Park, Mayville
Durban 4091

Johannesburg
108 Elizabeth Avenue
Benmore 2010

Pretoria
Third Floor, Hatfield Forum, 1077 Arcadia Street, Hatfield
Pretoria 0083

Cape Town
3 Gardens Business Village, Hope Street
Cape Town 8001

Typeset and printed by Kohler Carton & Print (Natal)
The imprint Butterworths is used under licence

EDITORIAL NOTE

The material presented here is a reproduction of the title "Partnership" contained in volume 19 of *The Law of South Africa*. As the name indicates, the *Lawsa Student Texts* series is aimed solely at the needs of law students. Through the years it has become increasingly apparent that some titles in *The Law of South Africa*, notwithstanding the fact that this work contains a factual statement of the positive law applicable in the Republic of South Africa, are regularly consulted by students in order to gain the benefit of a concise and accurate exposition of the subject-matter of their studies in a wide variety of legal subjects. In presenting this reproduction, the basic aim is to provide for the needs of law students; these *Texts* are thus in no way to be regarded as substitutes for existing textbooks on the relevant subjects, but rather as *supplementary material* in which not only the existing law, but also substantiating information in the form of references to case law, statutes, textbooks, etc is reproduced.

In the light of the cost factor the text and footnotes of the original have been altered only minimally: additional material relevant to the subject, for example cases reported after the "cut-off" date in regard to the publication of the original text (viz 30 September 1982), has been inserted. An accurate reference to the law within the most recent period may further be ensured by making use of the keys to the *Cumulative Supplement* (1984 and further editions) to *The Law of South Africa* and *Current Law*.

A complete subject index and tables of statutes and cases, as well as an extract from the original bibliography of volume 19 of the *Law of South Africa*, which contains references to works pertaining solely to the subject of partnerships, are also provided.

T J SCOTT
Editor: *The Law of South Africa*

June 1984

PARTNERSHIP

by

J J HENNING and H J DELPORT

REFERENCES TO OTHER TITLES

for	agency and representation in general	.	.	.	*see*		AGENCY AND REPRESENTATION
for	arbitration	.	.	.	.	.	*see*	ARBITRATION
for	authority to contract on behalf of the partnership	.	*see also*		AGENCY AND REPRESENTATION
for	civil litigation .	.	.	.	.	*see also*	CIVIL PROCEDURE
for	civil relief (moratorium) to partners on military service	*see also*	DEFENCE
for	contractual capacity in general	.	.	.	*see*	CONTRACT
for	co-ownership .	.	.	.	.	*see also*	THINGS
for	criminal liability	.	.	.	.	*see also*	CRIMINAL LAW
for	criminal procedure	.	.	.	.	*see*	CRIMINAL PROCEDURE
for	delictual liability	.	.	.	.	*see also*	DELICT
for	dissolution of a partnership by a declaration of war	.	*see also*	WAR AND EMERGENCY
for	doctrine of the undisclosed principal	.	.	.	*see also*	AGENCY AND REPRESENTATION
for	estoppel and ostensible authority	.	.	.	*see also*	ESTOPPEL
for	general requirements of contracts	.	.	.	*see*	CONTRACT
for	joint-stock companies .	.	.	.	*see also*	COMPANIES
for	mental illness of a partner	.	.	.	*see also*	MENTAL HEALTH
for	passing-off	.	.	.	.	*see*	COMPETITION
for	registration and transfer of immovable property	.	*see*	DEEDS
for	sequestration .	.	.	.	.	*see also*	INSOLVENCY
for	taxation	.	.	.	.	*see*	REVENUE
for	transfer duty .	.	.	.	.	*see*	DEEDS

SELECTED LITERATURE

Bamford *Partnership and Voluntary Association*
Beinart "Capital in partnership" 1961 *Acta Juridica* 118
Delport *Gedingvoering tussen vennote*
De Villiers "Partnership" *SA Enyclopedia of Forms and Precedents* vol 13 136
De Wet and Yeats *SA Kontraktereg en Handelsreg*
Henning "Die Leeuevennootskap: Aspekte van deelname in wins en verlies deur vennote" 1980 *MB* 143
Joubert "Aspekte van die aanspreeklikheid van vennote" 1978 *THRHR* 291
Lindley *Law of Partnership*
Pothier *Treatise on the Contract of Partnership*

GENERAL DESCRIPTION AND BACKGROUND

361 Denotation and definition According to its context the word "partnership" is usually employed to denote either a contract of a particular kind[1] or the legal relationship arising from the contract;[2] or also a particular kind of association of persons[3] or a specific form of business organization;[4] or, for certain purposes, an entity or quasi-persona separate from the individual partners composing it.[5] In addition, being derived from the Latin noun "partiarius" (one who shares with another), it imports the inherent notion of participation among partners.[6] Using the second denotation, "partnership" may be defined as a legal relationship arising from a contract between two or more persons, usually not exceeding twenty,[7] each to contribute to a business or undertaking carried on in common, with the object of making and sharing profits.[8]

1 Note that this is the primary meaning of the word "partnership": De Groot *Inleiding* 3 21 1; Voet *Commentarius* 17 2 1; Pothier *Partnership* prel art 1; Van der Linden *Koopmans Handboek* 4 1 11; Van der Keessel *Prael* 3 21 1; *Ex parte Buttner Bros* 1930 CPD 138 146.

2 *Poppe, Russouw & Co v Kitching* (1888) 6 SC 307 314; *Ex parte Buttner Bros* supra; *Potchefstroom Dairies and Industries Co Ltd v Standard Fresh Milk Supply Co* 1913 TPD 506 513; *Michalow v Premier Milling Co Ltd* 1960 2 SA 59 (W) 61.

3 *Helpmekaar (Thusano) Taxi Diens v Nasionale Vervoerkommissie* 1978 1 SA 250 (O) 255; *Commissioner for Inland Revenue v Epstein* 1954 3 SA 689 (A) 699; *E S v Commissioner of Taxes* 1963 2 PH T27 (SR); De Wet and Yeats *Kontraktereg en Handelsreg* 377; and see Companies Act 61 of 1973 s 30(1); Hahlo *Company Law* 45.

4 See Van Wassenaer *Practyk Notariael* 2 171; Kersteman *Woordenboek* s v "compagnieschap"; Van der Keessel 3 22 2; *Commissioner of Taxes v Newfield* 1970 3 SA 422 (RA) 425; Wessels *History* 650 653-657; De Wet and Yeats 378. Cf Drake *Partnership* 1; Barrett and Seago *Partners and Partnerships* 1; Crane and Bromberg *Partnership* 137.

5 Barels *Advysen* 2 62; Insolvency Act 24 of 1936 ss 2 (definition of "debtor"), 3(2) 13 49 128; *Silbert & Co v Evans & Co* 1912 TPD 425 434; *Potchefstroom Dairies and Industries Co Ltd v Standard Fresh Milk Supply Co* supra 512 514; *Michalow v Premier Milling Co Ltd* supra 61–64; *Muller v Pienaar* 1968 3 SA 195 (A) 202; *Ex parte Cohen* 1974 4 SA 674 (W) 676; *Standard Bank of SA Ltd v Lombard* 1977 2 SA 808 (W) 813; *Gardee v Dhan-*

manta Holdings 1978 1 SA 1066 (N) 1068; *Strydom v Protea Eiendomsagente* 1979 2 SA 206 (T) 209–211; Hahlo and Kahn *Union of SA: Development of its Laws and Constitution* 702.

6 Pollock *Partnership* 9–11; Miller *Partnership* 7–8.

7 Companies Act 61 of 1973 s 30; *Suid-Westelike Tvlse Landbou-Koöp Bpk v Phambili African Traders Association* 1976 3 SA 687 (Tk).

8 For similar definitions, see Felicius *Tractatus de Societate* 1 1–4; De Groot 3 21 1; Van Leeuwen *RHR* 4 23 1, *Cens For* 1 4 23 1; Huber *HR* 3 11 1; Voet 17 2 1; Van der Keessel *Prael* 3 21, *Dictata* 3 26 1; Pothier art 1; Van der Linden *Koopmans Handboek* 4 1 11, *Notaris-Ambt* 5 23 6; *Poppe, Russouw & Co v Kitching* supra 310; *In re Cape of Good Hope Permanent Building Society* (1898) 15 SC 323 336; *Estate Davison v Auret* (1905) 22 SC 10 15; *Angehrn and Piel v Friedman* 1903 TH 267; *Uys v Le Roux* 1906 TS 429 433; *Joubert v Tarry & Co* 1915 TPD 277 280–281; *Mackay v Naylor* 1917 TPD 533 537; *Rhodesia Railways v Commissioner of Taxes* 1925 AD 438 464–465; *Lewis v Union Government* 1944 TPD 350 356; *Sacks v Commissioner for Inland Revenue* 1946 AD 31 40–43; *Isaacs v Isaacs* 1949 1 SA 952 (C) 956; *V (also known as L) v De Wet* 1953 1 SA 612 (O) 615; *Bester v Van Niekerk* 1960 2 SA 779 (A) 783–784; *Purdon v Muller* 1960 2 SA 785 (E) 792–793; 1961 2 SA 211 (A) 217; *S v Perth Dry Cleaners and Launderers (Pty) Ltd* 1964 1 SA 134 (T) 139; *Novick v Benjamin* 1972 2 SA 842 (A) 851; *Muhlmann v Muhlmann* 1981 4 SA 632 (W) 634. Cf the various definitions collected by Lindley *Partnership* 14–16; Miller 7; Crane and Bromberg 33–34.

362 Brief historical background Partnership, using the term in a very general way, is of great antiquity. Some of its primitive non-commercial forms have obvious origins in family arrangements and clan activities of the most ancient and elementary kind. As a profit-seeking and sharing device it must be as old as co-operative economic endeavour, starting with the first feeble stirrings of a rudimentary capitalistic system. Its use in various guises and forms was recorded long before the time of the Romans, pointing to the very remote origins of some of its underlying concepts. Thus, for instance, an essential element of modern partnership, the sharing of profits, appears in the agricultural portion of the Code of Hammurabi compiled about 1700 BC. Historically its course can be traced from the ancient civilizations of Mesopotamia to classical Greece and Rome and hence onward through medieval commercial practices and usury-evading devices, the Italian trading communities and far-reaching enterprises of the Renaissance to its present day position as one of the three most important forms of enterprise in the business world. Indeed some of the basic principles of partnership as a business organization seem to have changed astonishingly little in a period spanning more than four thousand years.[1]

Whatever the respective merits of the numerous and conflicting theories on the origin and development of various partnership concepts may be,[2] it seems sufficient to note that the Roman societas, the medieval commenda and the lex mercatoria left their imprint on the several types of partnership of modern law. This resulted from the study of, commentaries on and reception of the revived Roman law on the Continent from the twelfth century onwards, as well as the absorption of the practical principles of the lex mercatoria in the law of the time.[3]

The massive contribution of Roman partnership law,[4] distinguishing between various kinds of partnership[5] ranging from the societas omnium bonorum[6] — the earliest consensual descendant of the ercto non cito[7] — to the societas publicanorum — a highly sophisticated cross between societas and collegium and showing some corporate attributes[8] — can hardly be underestimated.[9] Present purposes do not require detailed discussion. Stated very briefly and generally, the contribution of the Roman law of partnership is especially marked, both in so far as the basic concept of partnership as a consensual contract of the utmost good faith as well as the relationship constituted by it between the partners inter se are concerned.[10]

Developments occasioned by commentators on the revived Roman law and the lex mercatoria include the acceptance of the doctrines of mutual agency and solidary liability for partnership obligations.[11] Equally important is the recognition in most, but not all, civil law jurisdictions of the so-called mercantile (entity) theory, viewing the partnership (external firm) as a persona separate and distinct from the partners composing it.[12]

The medieval commenda was in substance an arrangement by which a capitalist (commendator) entrusted capital to a trader (commendatarius) for employment in mercantile enterprises on the understanding that the commendator, while not in name a party to the enterprise and though entitled to a share of the profits, would not be liable for losses beyond the amount of his contribution. This concept of limiting the liability of non-managing investors spread from Italy into French commercial law, emerging as the *société en commandite*, the predecessor of the present day limited or commanditarian partnership.[13] From France it was incorporated into Roman-Dutch law[14] under its French name.[15]

---

1 Cf Barrett and Seago *Partners and Partnerships* 1–3; Crane and Bromberg *Partnership* 10; Little *Partnerships* 2; Sugarman *Partnership* 1–2; Goldschmidt *Universalgeschichte des Handelsrechts* 51–78; Hildesheimer *Das jüdische Gesellschaftsrecht* 11; Szlechter *Le Contract de*

Société en Babylone en Grece et à Rome 113–122; Holdsworth *History* vol 7 193; Heaton *History of Europe* 17–32; Schiffres 59 *Am Jur* par 2; Schmoller 1890 *Zeitschrift für Wirtschafts und Sozialwissenschaften* 93; Burns *Encyclopedia of the Social Sciences* vol 12 3; Salin *Encyclopedia of the Social Sciences* vol 15 195.

2 For various theories on the origins of consensual partnership, see Delport *Gedingvoering tussen Vennote* 9–13; as to limited partnerships, see Bates *Limited Partnership* 18–21; Bergstedt 1961 *Tulane Law Review* 816–818.

3 Barrett and Seago 3–14; Crane and Bromberg 11–12; Bates 18; Sugarman 1; Holdsworth 195–199; Story *Partnership* vii–ix; Goldschmidt 255–298; Lehmann *Lehrbuch des Handelsrechts* 225–236; Bauer *Unternehmung und Unternehmungsformen* 22–39; Schiffres 2; Burns 3; Bergstedt 817; Drake 1917 *Michigan Law Review* 609 616–617; Stein 1959 *Tulane Law Review* 595–606; Holdsworth 1916 *Juridical Review* 308; Mitchell 3 *Select Essays in Anglo-American Legal History* 143; Teetor 1962 *American Journal of Legal History* 178; Baker 1979 *Cambridge Law Journal* 295 299–300.

4 The main texts are Gaius *Inst* 3 148–154; *I* 3 25 1–9; *D* 17 2 1–84; *C* 4 37 1–7.

5 *D* 17 2 5, 7: Societas omnium bonorum; societas universorum quae ex quaestu veniunt; societas alicuius negotationis of which an important form was the societas publicanorum or societas vectigalium; societas rei unius; see Delport 9–10.

6 embracing all the property of the socii, both present and future: *I* 3 25 1; *D* 17 2 1, 3.

7 In its earliest form the ercto non cito was a consortium between sui heredes brought about at the death of the paterfamilias. As to the ercto non cito and the origins of the societas omnium bonorum, see Delport 6 10; Van Oven *Leerboek* 282; Daube 1938 *Cambridge Law Journal* 381; Wieacker *Societas Hausgemeinschaft und Erwerbsgesellschaft* 1 26; Watson *Obligations in the later Roman Republic* 126; Muirhead *Roman Law* 162; Arangio-Ruiz *La Societá in Diritto Romano* 3–30; Van Warmelo 1950 *THRHR* 218, 1957 *Tydschrift voor Rechtsgeschiedenis* 150 156; Levy 1934 *Zeitschrift der Savigny-Stiftung für Rechtsgeschichte (RA)* 258 289.

8 E g, it had perpetual succession: *D* 17 2 59. The question whether it had legal personality depends primarily on the interpretation inter alia, of *D* 3 4 pr and *D* 3 4 1. See Delport 17–19; Kniep *Societas Publicanorum* 37–46; Duff *Personality in Roman Private Law* 141; Buckland *Roman Law* 513; Crook *Law and Life of Rome* 234–236.

9 Story ix: "The Roman Law is an inexhaustible treasure of various and valuable learning; and the principles applicable to the law of partnership are stated with uncommon clearness … A slight glance at them will at once show the true origin of many of the general doctrines, incorporated into the modern jurisprudence of Continental Europe, as well as that of the common law."

10 The Roman law of partnership was concerned mostly with the relationship between the partners, being a consensual contract governing the obligations of the socii inter se. For the effect of the principle contained in *D* 17 2 63 pr, "societas ius quodammodo fraternitas in se habeat", see Delport 16–17; Buckland 508; Thomas *Roman Law* 304; Schulz *Classical Roman Law* 552; Van Oven 286; Daube 381. As to the various contributions of Roman partnership law in general, see Barrett and Seago 7–10; Goldschmidt 255–271; Stein 596; Holdsworth *History* 207; Buckland and McNair *Roman Law and Common Law* 300–307; Maine *Early History of Institutions* 234; Müller-Gugenberger *Gedächtnisschrift für Jurgen Rödig* 274–280.

11 Bergstedt 816; Drake 610–613; Stein 595–606; Goldschmidt 283; Lehmann 226.

12 Lehmann 236; Drake 613; Goldschmidt 292; Barrett and Seago 12–13. In contradistinction English law did, and for the most part it still does, refuse to recognize the entity theory. The aggregate or common-law theory of partnership — that there is no entity, only individuals — according no status to the firm, looks to the partners composing it; see Barrett and Seago 13–14; Crane and Bromberg 18–20; Lindley *Partnership* 30.

13 Lindley 823; Crane and Bromberg 143–144; Bergstedt 816–817; Bates 18; Holdsworth *History* 195–196; Goldschmidt 255–264; Wessels *History* 650–651; Van der Merwe *Juridiese Versekeringsbegrip* 70–76. This form of partnership did not take root in common-law jurisdictions and had to be introduced through legislation. For the several causes to which this peculiarity of English law is due, see Holdsworth 1916 *Juridical Review* 308 310–311; Lindley 824; Gower *Modern Company Law* 23.

14 Wessels 651; Bergstedt 816; Morice *English and Roman-Dutch Law* 193.

15 Van der Linden *Koopmans Handboek* 4 1 12 discusses it as "De Sociëteit, genaamd *en commendite*" [sic] and Van der Keessel *Prael* 3 21 7 as "de societatibus ad exemplum earum, que in Gallia vocantur *sociétés en commandite, contractis*".

363 Sources of law In the marked absence of a modern partnership code,[1] and apart from various enactments dealing with particular matters,[2] the law of partnership consists of South African common law,[3] derived mainly from Roman-Dutch law.[4]

Numerous Roman-Dutch authorities dealt with this subject,[5] but the treatise on the law of partnership of the great French jurist, Pothier,[6] was regarded as an authority of great weight in the Netherlands towards the end of the eighteenth century.[7] His treatise was translated into Dutch[8] and English[9] and has been regarded by the courts as an important authority in this branch of the law.[10]

The South African law and the English law of partnership are consistent with each other in some,[11] but not in all respects.[12] The latter may be useful as a guide,[13] but it is not binding[14] and should be approached with caution.[15]

1 Pre-Union statutes dealing exclusively with limited partnerships have all been repealed by the Pre-Union Statute Law Revision Act 36 of 1976. Sophisticated Western legal systems almost without exception have partnership and limited partnership codes and a case can certainly be made out for a modern partnership code in SA; see Naudé 1982 *MB* 5 13.

2 e g those relating to the lawfulness of the partnership agreement (see par 378 post); licensing (see par 380 post); the partnership name (see par 381 post); criminal procedure (see title CRIMINAL PROCEDURE); rules of court regulating civil litigation (see title CIVIL PROCEDURE); INSOLVENCY (see title INSOLVENCY); registration and transfer of immovable property (see title DEEDS); civil relief to partners on military service (see title DEFENCE). Other provisions are dealt with where relevant.

3 Cf *R v Goseb* 1956 2 SA 696 (SWA) 698; *Ex parte De Winnaar* 1959 1 SA 837 (N) 839; *R v Mlooi* 1925 AD 131 149; Van Zyl *Geskiedenis* 500.

4 in contradistinction to most other branches of our mercantile law; see De Wet and Yeats *Kontraktereg en Handelsreg* 378.

5 e g De Groot *Inleiding* 3 21; Vinnius *Inst* 3 26; Van Leeuwen *RHR* 4 23, *Cens For* 1 4 23; Huber *HR* 3 11; Voet *Commentarius* 17 2; Noodt *Operam Omniam ad D* 17 2; Van Bynkershoek *Obs Tum* 1137 1866 2757 2271 2557 3259; Pauw *Obs Tum Nov* 124 128 295 445; Kersteman *Woordenboek* s v "*societeit*" and "*compagnieschap*"; Boey *Woorden Tolk* s v "*societyt*"; Barels *Advysen* 2 58–65; Van der Keessel *Thes Sel* 698–706, *Dictata* 3 26,

Prael 3 21; Van der Linden *Koopmans Handboek* 4 1 11–14.

6 *Traité du Contrat de Société*.

7 *Robson v Theron* 1978 1 SA 841 (A) 852D-E; *Barker & Co v Blore* 1908 TS 1156 1159.

8 by Van der Linden under the title *Verhandeling van het Recht omtrent Sociëteiten of Compagnieschappen en Andere Gemeenschappen*.

9 by Tudor under the title *A treatise on the Contract of Partnership*.

10 *Robson v Theron* supra; *Barker & Co v Blore* supra.

11 *Gau v McDonald* (1874) 4 Buch 22 27; *Estate Davison v Auret* (1905) 22 SC 10 16; *Dickinson and Brown v Fisher's Executors* 1916 AD 374 394–395; *Wulfsohn v Taylor* 1928 TPD 99 103; *McLeod and Shearsmith v Shearsmith* 1938 TPD 87 91; *Oosthuizen v Swart* 1956 2 SA 687 (SWA) 692.

12 *Watermeyer v Kerdel's Trustees* (1834) 3 M 424 430–432; *Tyson v Rodger and Nicol* (1907) 10 HCG 139 155; *Fink v Fink* 1945 WLD 226 240–241; *Doyle v Fleet Motors PE (Pty) Ltd* 1971 3 SA 760 (A) 762; Morice *English and Roman-Dutch Law* 190–207; Henning 1980 *MB* 143 144 ns 19 20.

13 *Bester v Van Niekerk* 1960 2 SA 779 (A) 784; *Purdon v Muller* 1961 2 SA 211 (A) 231.

14 Cf *Trust Bank van Afrika Bpk v Eksteen* 1964 3 SA 402 (A) 410–411; Van Zyl 483–486; Henning 144. Recent appellate division decisions on partnership do not contain a single reference to English partnership law; see *Lee v Maraisdrift (Edms) Bpk* 1976 2 SA 536 (A); *Robson v Theron* supra; *Rodrigues v Alves* 1978 4 SA 834 (A).

15 De Wet and Yeats 378 n 8; Henning 144.

KINDS OF PARTNERSHIP

364 Introduction It is customary for writers on the law of partnership to categorize various kinds of partnership[1] and to distinguish between partners by using various qualifying terms.[2] Numerous classifications based on diverse divisions exist, resulting in terminology often both inconsistent and confusing.[3]

1 e g Nathan *Partnership and Private Companies* 26–33; De Wet and Yeats *Kontrakereg en Handelsreg* 380–381 417–419; Bamford *Partnership* 3–4 18–19 59–61; De Villiers *Encyclopedia of Forms and Precedents* vol 13 179–181; Wille *Principles* 472; Maasdorp *Institutes* vol 2 278–284; Lee and Honoré *Obligations* 135–136; Gibson *Mercantile and Company Law* 275–276; Wille and Millin *Mercantile Law* 410. Cf Story *Partnership* 122–138; Lindley *Partnership* 116–118; Barrett and Seago *Partners and Partnerships* 60–64.

2 e g managing partner, active partner, general partner, contracting partner, principal partner, known partner, ordinary partner, disclosed partner, special partner, partner *en commandite*, anonymous partner, silent partner, dormant partner, sleeping partner, secret partner, undisclosed partner, alien partner, ostensible partner, individual partner, original partner, retired partner, late partner, remaining partner, outgoing partner, incoming partner, existing partner, ex-partner, co-partner: De Wet and Yeats 393 418; Bamford 23 37 54 59–60; Lee and Honoré 135–136 142 144–146; Wille 472 475; Wille and Millin 412; Maasdorp 283 290–296; Nathan 27–32. Co-partner is a pompous legalism meaning nothing more than partner; see Crane and Bromberg *Partnership* 141–142 especially for a crisp explanation of various terms.

3 For apt illustrations, see Tudor ad Pothier *Partnership* 2 2 54; Story 122–135; *CJS* vol 68 par 1.

365 Divisions and distinctions In Roman-Dutch law various kinds of partnership[1] were distinguished with reference to, inter alia, duration,[2] method of formation,[3] extent of the contract,[4] kind of employment in which engaged[5] and extent of liability for partnership debts.[6] Terminology and classification varied, but one of the primary divisions made with reference to Roman law[7] was between universal and particular partnerships.[8] Under the first category Pothier[9] and also Van der Linden[10] included, and distinguished between, the societas universorum bonorum[11] and the societas universorum quae ex quaestu veniunt.[12] Particular partnerships again were of many kinds, for instance, partnerships in particular things or even in a single piece of property or undertaking only, partnerships for the exercise of some profession or art and commercial or trading partnerships.[13] The latter included partnerships trading in the name of all the partners in common, namely under a collective name or firm,[14] partnerships *en commandite*,[15] as well as anonymous and undisclosed partnerships.[16]

South African law accommodates partnerships of all sorts[17] satisfying the applicable requirements.[18] Various kinds and conditions of partners and partnership are recognized ranging, with reference to the extent of the contract,[19] from the universal[20] to the particular,[21] the ad hoc[22] or unius rei[23] and, with reference to liability for partnership debts, from the ordinary[24] to the extraordinary[25] and the latter from the *en commandite*[26] to the anonymous (silent).[27]

By and large the particular distinction between civil and commercial partnerships[28] prevalent in most civil law jurisdictions[29] does not obtain in South African law.[30] However, to some extent at least a difference between professional and trading partnerships is recognized by way of the non-applicability of certain statutory provisions to partnerships formed for the purpose of carrying on organized professions.[31]

The sharpest distinction is between ordinary and extraordinary partnerships. Commanditarian and anonymous (silent) partnerships attract special rules and are dealt with later.[32] Various aspects concerning universal partnerships are not free from doubt, requiring separate consideration.[33]

1 Note that *"amiraelschap"* (partnership for purposes of convoy or sailing partnership) and *"mede-rederschap"* (partnership in ships or shipping firm) were regarded as particular kinds of partnership: De Groot *Inleiding* 3 22 1: "Onder maetschap behoren amiraelschap ende mede-rederschap"; Voet *Commentarius* 17 2 5; Van der Keessel *Prael* 3 22 1;

3 23 1. "*Amiraelschap*" was defined as "*maetschap* van schepenen verscheide luiden toekomende tot verweering" and "*mederederschap*" as "*maetschap* van verscheide luiden, die een ofte meer schepen onder hun ghemeen zijnde tot ghemeene baet gebruicken": De Groot 3 22 2 and 3 23 1 respectively. The early chartered companies or "*compagnieën*" and the later "*naamloze vennootschap*" (joint stock or public company) were considered as particular types of partnership attracting special rules. For a discussion of the views of various Roman-Dutch authorities in this regard, see Van der Heijden *De Ontwikkeling van de Naamloze Vennootschap in Nederland voor de Codificatie* 51–55. For the comparable position in English law during this period, see Gower *Modern Company Law* 25–36; Cilliers and Benade *Company Law* 24 especially authorities referred to in ns 7 and 8.

2 Partnerships contracted without limitation or for a definite time or with a view to permanence, i e for the lifetime of the partners, though not for all eternity: De Groot 3 21 4; Voet 17 2 1; Van Leeuwen *Cens For* 1 4 23 2.

3 "Maatschap... door monde, door brieven, door bode": De Groot 3 21 4; express and implied partnerships distinguished: Voet 17 2 2; Van Leeuwen *Cens For* 1 4 23 3; Huber *HR* 3 11 6.

4 Partnerships of all property present and future, or of all gains or profits, or of all merchandise, contrasted to partnerships in a single piece of property or in a single transaction or venture only, in certain things or business, in some particular kind of profession, art, trade, commerce: De Groot 3 21 3; Van Leeuwen *RHR* 4 23 1, *Cens For* 1 4 23 2; Huber 3 11 2–5; Voet 17 2 4–5; Van der Keessel *Dictata* 3 26 2–3; Pothier *Partnership* 2 1 28, 2 2 63; Van der Linden *Koopmans Handboek* 4 1 12.

5 e g public or tax-farming partnerships, ship and convoy partnerships, private or ordinary partnerships, partnerships in some art, occupation, trade, handicraft, profession, commercial or trading partnerships: De Groot 3 21 9; 3 22 1; Van Leeuwen *Cens For* 1 4 23 31; Huber 3 11 2; Voet 17 2 3 5; Van der Keessel *Thes Sel* 707–710; Pothier 2 2 54–56; Van der Linden 4 1 12.

6 distinguishing between civil partnerships and commercial partnerships, i e partnerships not in trade and partnerships in trade. In partnerships not in trade (as well as universal partnerships) each of the partners was liable pro rata for partnership debts, each for his share only. In partnerships trading under a collective name (firm), each of the partners was liable in solidum, i e jointly and severally for partnership debts, but in the partnership *en commandite* and the undisclosed or silent partnership the partners *en commandite* and undisclosed or silent partners were not liable to creditors for partnership debts, but only to the principal or disclosed partner, the undisclosed or silent partner indefinitely and the partner *en commandite* only to the amount of his contribution: Pothier 6 1 96; 6 3 106; Decker ad Van Leeuwen *RHR* 4 23 1 n (b) (relying on Savary *Le Parfait Negociant* 381); Barels *Advysen* 2 59, 60; Van der Keessel *Thes Sel* 702–704, *Prael* 3 21 7; Van der Linden 4 1 13. For a discussion of the views of De Groot 3 1 31; Van Leeuwen *RHR* 5 3 11 and Voet 7 2 13, 16 (that partners in mercantile partnerships were only liable pro rata and that a partner was entitled to be freed from liability for partnership debts by abandoning his share), see *Lee v Maraisdrift (Edms) Bpk* 1976 2 SA 536 (A) 541; Van der Heijden 53; Joubert 1978 *THRHR* 291.

7 usually *D* 17 2 5 pr: "Societates contrahuntur sive universorum bonorum sive negotationis alicuius sive vectigalis sive etiam rei unius."

8 De Groot 3 21 3; Van Leeuwen *RHR* 4 23 1 and *Cens For* 1 4 23 2; Huber 3 11 2; Voet 17 2 4; Van der Keessel *Dictata* 3 26 2; Pothier 2 1 28; Van der Linden 4 1.

9 *Partnership* 2 1 28 341–346: "In our French law, besides those two kinds of partnerships, the conjugal community which is contracted between husband and wife, and that which is continued between the survivor of them and the heirs of the deceased, are universal partnerships of a different kind and governed by peculiar principles."

10 *Koopmans Handboek* 4 1 12. Classification and terminology varied; see De Groot 3 21 3; Voet 17 2 4, 5; Van Leeuwen *Cens For* 1 4 23 2; Huber 3 11 3.

11 Partnership of all property both present and future. For further comment, see par 367 post.

12 Partnership of everything acquired during its continuance from every kind of commerce, i e of all profits (acquests). For further comment, see par 367 post.

13 See ns 1 4–5 supra.

14 Pothier 2 3 57: "Partnership *en nom collectif* is that in which two or more traders enter into to carry on in common a certain commerce in name of all the partners"; Van der Linden 4 1 12: "b v op den naam van *N N en Compagnie*. Dit noem men de *firma* der Sociëteit" and 4 1 13 "Societeiten van koophandel die op eene *firma* gaan"; Barels 2 59, 60; Van der Keessel *Thes Sel* 703, *Prael* 3 21 7.

Compare the present day "vennootschap onder firma" of the Netherlands; see Mohr *Van
Maatschap, Vennootschap onder Firma en Commanditaire Vennootschap* 86–114.

15 Pothier 2 2 60; Van der Linden 4 1 12: "welke
een Koopman met een bijzonder persoon
aangaet, tot eenen handel, die alleen op naam
van den Koopman zal gedreven worden, en
waar toe de ander alleenlijk eene zekere
somme gelds inbrengt ... onder beding dat
hij een zeker aandeel in de winst trekken, en
in de verliezen dragen zal"; Decker ad Van
Leeuwen 4 23 1 n (b); Van der Keessel *Thes
Sel* 704, *Prael* 3 21 7. For further comment
see par 367 post.

16 Pothier 2 2 61: "The *anonymous or unknown*
partnership, which is also called *compte en
participation*, is that by which two or more
persons agree to take a share in a certain
business which shall be carried on by one or
other of them in his own name alone": Van
der Linden 4 1 12: "De *naamloze Societeit*".
Tudor ad Pothier 2 2 61 points out that Pothier treated the *société anonyme* and the *compte
en participation* as in effect the same. French
and Dutch law did and still do draw a clear
distinction between the *société anonyme*
("*naamloze vennootschap*") (joint-stock company or the more recent public company) on
the one hand and the *compte* or *société en participation* (previously "*handeling voor gemeene
rekening*", now "*stille maatschap*") (joint venture or silent partnership) on the other; see
Le Gall *French Company Law* 15–16 41–42;
Mohr 77–84; Maeijer *Vennootschapsrecht in
Beweging* 21–25. That Van der Linden 4 1 12
could not have been aware of the difference
appears from his definition of "*naamloze societeit*". This in turn led to the usage by SA
courts, legislators and writers of the term
"*naamlose vennootschap*" (anonymous part-
ship), indicating in its countries of origin a
public company, to describe a *silent* or undisclosed *partnership*. The continued usage in
modern SA law of this misnomer has never
been called in question. For further comment, see par 367 post.

17 For companies formed and registered in terms
of the Companies Act 61 of 1973 (sometimes
still described as "statutory partnerships" or
"incorporated partnerships": *Dadoo Ltd v
Krugersdorp Municipal Council* 1920 AD 530
573; Nathan *Partnership and Private Companies*
2; Gibson *Mercantile and Company Law* 285;
Maasdorp *Institutes* 278) and the contribution
and influence of partnership law in this regard, see title COMPANIES.

18 having regard to both the presence of Pothier's essentialia of partnership in a valid
agreement and the true intention of the
parties.

19 In *Bester v Van Niekerk* 1960 2 SA 779 (A)

784 Holmes AJA quoted as a matter of per-
suasive interest this passage from Lindley
Partnership (11th ed) 70–71: "It is customary ... to divide partnerships into universal ... and particular ... according to the
extent of the contract entered into by the
members. The classification is traceable to a
passage in the Digest ... and is not worth en-
larging upon, except for the purpose of distinguishing cases in which persons are
partners in some trade or business generally
from those in which they are partners in
some particular transaction or adventure only.
If persons who are not partners in other
business share the profits and loss, or the profits, of one particular transaction or adventure, they become partners as to that
transaction or adventure, but not as to anything else. For example if two solicitors who
are not partners, are jointly retained to conduct litigation in some particular case, and
they agree to share the profits accruing
therefrom, they become partners so far as the
business connected with that particular case
is concerned, but no further. So a partnership may be limited to the purchase and sale
of particular jewels, or to the working of
some particular patent, or to the working of
it in some particular place or district. In all
such cases as these, the rights and liabilities
of the partners are governed by the same
principles as those which apply to ordinary
partnership; but such rights and liabilities are
necessarily less extensive than those of persons who have entered into less limited contracts. The extent to which persons can be
considered partners depends entirely on the
agreement into which they have entered and
upon their conduct." Cf ns 4 8 supra.

20 See ns 11 and 12 supra.

21 See ns 4 and 19 supra and text to n 15 above.

22 Occasional partnership or partnership for a
specific occasion: *Enslin v Colonial Trust Corp
Ltd* 1923 CPD 358; *Hawkins v Fitzroy* (1831)
1 M 519.

23 Partnership in a single asset, transaction or
venture; see n 4 supra. Thus a joint venture
in respect of a single transaction can be a
partnership and there may be a partnership
in shares in a company or in an undivided
share in a partnership: *Bester v Van Niekerk*
supra 784–785; *Uys v Le Roux* 1906 TS 429;
Langermann v Carper 1905 TH 251; *Smith v
Robinson* (1889) 3 SAR 91; *Laughton v Griffin*
(1893) 14 NLR 84; *Grice & Co v James Perrott
Prince* (1890) 11 NLR 259; *Mackie Dunn and
Co v Tilley, Foggitt and Wilson* (1882) 1 HCG
423; *Agostino v Subat and Marinelli* (1914) 35
NLR 270; *Murray v Yates' Executors* 1916
EDL 293; *Du Toit v African Dairies Ltd* 1922
TPD 245; *De Kock and Kessel Ltd v Modern
Packaging (Pty) Ltd* 1943 WLD 216; *Munro v*

Ekerold 1949 1 SA 584 (SWA); *Stewart v Schwab* 1956 4 SA 791 (T); *Novick v Benjamin* 1972 2 SA 842 (A) 851; *Mattson v Yiannakis* 1976 4 SA 154 (W) 157; *Spie Batignolles Société Anonyme v Van Niekerk: in re Van Niekerk v SA Yster en Staal Industriële Koöp Bpk* 1980 2 SA 441 (NC) 444.

24 termed "ordinary" in contradistinction to "extraordinary", to indicate that each and every partner is liable towards third parties for partnership debts. For a further statement on terminology, see par 367 post.

25 See par 367 post.

26 See n 15 supra and par 367 post.

27 See n 16 supra and par 367 post.

28 For Roman-Dutch law, see n 6 supra.

29 The distinction between civil partnerships (e g *"maatschap"*, *"société civil"*, *"Gesellschaft des bürgerlichen Rechts"*) and commercial partnerships (e g *"vennootschap onder firma"*, *"société en nom collectif"*, *"offene Handelsgesellschaft"*) is of considerable significance on the Continent. A civil partnership is subject to the civil law as administered by the civil courts, and a commercial partnership is governed by the commercial law as administered by commercial courts. Whether a partnership is civil or commercial may in general be ascertained with reference to its objects, e g a normal trading partnership is considered to be commercial, but if the objects do not substantially involve trading operations, though involving gain or profit, then it will be regarded as a civil partnership: Lindley 25–28; *CJS* vol 68 par 1. This distinction is unknown to English law: Lindley 25.

30 probably due to the influence of English law. It has been repeatedly stated in SA law that a partnership consists of the carrying on of a business and, following *Smith v Anderson* (1880) 15 Ch 247 (CA) 258 that "business" is anything which occupies the time and attention of a man for the purpose of profit. "Business" is of wider import than "trade" — for the essential idea underlying "trade" is merely buying and selling — and includes an active occupation or profession: *Mullins and Meyer v Pearlman* 1917 TPD 639 647; *Modderfontein Deep Levels Ltd v Feinstein* 1920 TPD 288 290; *Platt v Commissioner for Inland Revenue* 1922 AD 42 50; *R v Silber* 1938 TPD 561 563; *SA Flour Millers' Mutual Association v Rutowitz Flour Mills Ltd* 1938 CPD 199 203; *R v Manson* 1938 TPD 63 64 65; *Standard General Insurance Co v Hennop* 1954 4 SA 560 (A) 561 564. Cf Companies Act 61 of 1973 s 30; Henochsberg *Companies Act* 59; English Partnership Act of 1890 (53 & 54 Vict c 39) ss 1(1) 45; Gibson 267; Lindley 10; Underhill *Partnership* 3–4.

31 e g the Companies Act 61 of 1973 s 30(2); Business Names Act 27 of 1960 definition of "business" as "any business of *trade*"; Licences Act 44 of 1962 sch 2 part II item 7 exemptions (1) and (5), item 10 exemption.

32 See par 367 post.

33 See par 366 post.

366 Universal partnerships In Roman and Roman-Dutch law universal partnerships were distinguished into two kinds:[1] firstly, those of all present and future property, termed societates universorum bonorum;[2] and secondly, those extending only to everything acquired from every kind of commerce, referred to as societates universorum quae ex quaestu veniunt.[3] The distinction between the archetype[4] of universal partnership, the societas omnium bonorum, and the universal partnership in commercial undertakings, namely the societas universorum quae ex quaestu veniunt, is still relevant. This is particularly so since the question whether and, if at all, in which instances universal partnerships of the first kind[5] are still recognized by South African law, is not free from all doubt.[6] According to one definition "the partnership *universorum bonorum* is that by which the contracting parties agree to put in common all their property, both present and future. It covers all their acquisitions whether from commercial undertakings or otherwise".[7] During its chequered career[8] in numerous guises, it has been described variously as: seemingly the oldest form of consensual societas;[9] a complete pooling of all assets from whatever source;[10] communal ownership by a group;[11] not really suitable to mercantile ventures, but rather to farming between relatives and close friends;[12] prohibited since olden times;[13] in great use, a partnership of brothers very well known to jurists and in custom;[14] the community of roturiers and even, sometimes, the nobles;[15] a partnership not being a trading venture, but rather a benefit society established for the advantage of its members,[16] nothing but a contract creating a community of property;[17] a fraternal association with a common goal rather than a commercial enterprise, an institution belonging to a bygone age;[18] an equitable remedy.[19]

Considerable reliance has been placed on an unsubstantiated remark by De Groot,[20] uncritically repeated by Voet,[21] that, excepting the customary community of property between spouses, the universal partnership of all future and present property was already of old prohibited in Holland.[22] However, certain other authorities, notably Pothier[23] and Van der Linden,[24] dealt with the partnership universorum bonorum at some length as being usual and valid, stressing the fact that such a partnership will not be held to have been entered into, unless it was clearly and expressly stipulated.[25] Indeed the more acceptable view seems to be that the partnership universorum bonorum, although then not of common occurrence,[26] was in fact *not* prohibited expressly either in Holland[27] or France[28] prior to the introduction of the French Code Civil[29] and the Wetboek Napoleon ingerigt voor het Koningrijk Holland[30] during the early nineteenth century, both then limiting its scope to merely that of all *present* property.[31] However, it seems that in South African law this controversy and hence the extent of recognition afforded to the partnership universorum bonorum still await final decision.[32]

It has readily been assumed that the community of property consequential to a putative marriage amounts to a tacit universal partnership subsisting as long as the "partners" remain in error.[33] This assumption has been described as an equitable solution[34] and the consequential "community of property" as a possible example of a partnership of all property in modern law.[35] But since the parties clearly intended marriage and not partnership, an essential requirement for the creation of a valid partnership is lacking.[36] Seen in proper perspective the ratio of the decision amounts to nothing more than a recognition of the Roman-Dutch law principle[37] that a putative marriage in community of property, although void, has the effect of entitling either spouse, acting in good faith, to enforce the rights of property which would have been competent to him or her if the marriage had been valid.[38] The use of the term universal partnership in this context thus does not seem to be necessary or conducive to greater clarity.[39]

It has frequently been said that a marriage in community of property creates a universal partnership in all goods between the spouses,[40] thus in effect continuing a practice not uncommon in Roman-Dutch law.[41] But in view of the various and numerous differences that have been listed,[42] it is obvious that it was never intended to equate or identify the marital community with the partnership universorum bonorum and that any effort to do so is not only historically incorrect but is also bound to fail.[43] Indeed there seems to be no reason for continuing the confusing and pointless practice of using the term universal partnership in connection with the marital community.[44]

Although the contrary has been suggested,[45] it appears that a partnership universorum bonorum, in so far as it may still be recognized by our law, may be entered into tacitly since "it would be contrary to well settled principles if it were to be said that a particular contract cannot be created tacitly; the principle is firmly established that any contract can be brought about by conduct".[46]

The second kind of universal partnership is that in commercial undertakings, the societas universorum quae ex quaestu veniunt,[47] also referred to as a partnership of general profits, or of all profits,[48] or merely as a general partnership.[49] It was accepted in Roman-Dutch law without any restrictions or averment of prohibition,[50] as is still the position in present South African law.[51] The parties thereby contract a partnership of all that they may acquire during its continuance from every kind of commercial activity. They are considered to enter into this kind of universal partnership when they declare that they contract with a view to creating a partnership without any further explanation,[52] or that they contract a partnership of all the profits which they may make from all sources.[53] In contradistinction to the societas universorum bonorum this kind of universal partnership is confined to profits alone. Whatever is acquired by inheritance, gift or legacy does not fall within it.[54] It may be entered into expressly or tacitly, that is, by implied consent and circumstance.[55]

1 Felicius *De Societate* 15 2, 26 9; De Groot *Inleiding* 3 21 3; Van Leeuwen *Cens For* 4 23 2; Huber *HR* 3 11 2; Voet *Commentarius* 17 2 4, 5; Van der Keessel *Dictata* 3 26 2; Pothier *Partnership* 2 1 28; Van der Linden *Koopmans Handboek* 4 1 12; *Isaacs v Isaacs* 1949 1 SA 952 (C) 955; *V (also known as L) v De Wet* 1953 1 SA 612 (O) 614; *Annabhay v Ramlall* 1960 3 SA 802 (D) 805; Story *Partnership* 123–124.

2 also referred to (in the singular as the societas omnium bonorum; societas totorum bonorum; societas universorum fortunarum. Gaius *Inst* 3 148; *I* 3 25 1; *D* 17 2 1; 17 2 3; 17 2 5 pr; 17 2 65; 17 2 73. In Roman law this partnership could be entered into only expressly: *D* 17 2 3, 7; see also n 8 infra.

3 *D* 17 2 7–13; 17 2 71. In Roman law these could be entered into expressly or tacitly: *D* 17 2 7. See also n 54 infra.

4 being seemingly the oldest and most comprehensive form of consensual universal partnership. Thus when the term "universal partnership" is used without qualification, it is usually a reference to this kind of universal partnership. Cf Voet 17 2 4; *Isaacs v Isaacs* supra 954–955: "[T]here is no such thing as a universal partnership in our Law in the circumstances such as those alleged ... the *societas universorum bonorum* or universal partnership"; Story 122–124; Nathan *Partnership and Private Companies* 27; *CJS* vol 68 par 1.

5 i e the partnership universorum bonorum.

6 See De Wet and Yeats *Kontraktereg en Handelsreg* 381 especially n 29; Bamford *Partnership* 18–19; Nathan 27.

7 *Isaacs v Isaacs* supra 955, using partially the description of Pothier 2 1 29. The latter is also used by Van der Linden 4 1 12 who adds (translation Morice): "It is not considered to have been the intention to enter into this sort of partnership, unless it has been positively expressed. ... [A]ll the property which each of the partners possesses at the time of entering on the partnership becomes from that moment the common property of the partnership, without any transfer being necessary. Everything is included in this partnership which comes to each of the partners under any title whatever, even by way of succession, gift or legacy. And there is no exception to this, except what comes to one of the partners on condition that it will not fall into the partnership, or what has been acquired by criminal or dishonest means. Such a partnership is liable for all the debts of each of the partners due at the time of entering into the partnership, as also for the debts which each of the partners is compelled to incur during the partnership, both for himself and for his wife and family. This, however, must not be extended to foolish expenditure, waste of money in gambling, debauchery, fines or penalties on account of crime, incurred by one of the partners."

8 The societas omnium bonorum is probably the oldest and certainly the most comprehensive form of consensual societas. Having its origin in the ancient consortium of sui heredes, it retained much of the nature and character of the earlier societas fratrum. Rules in the texts initially applicable to all societates, notably the societates beneficium competentiae, were long applied only to this form. It could only be entered into expressly. It is fairly obvious that it could be created for all persons having a community of interest with a view to their mutual advantage. This need not be pecuniary, i e it was not necessarily aimed at profit. Unsuitable for mercantile ventures, it was probably popular only when what was needed was agricultural rather than mercantile partnerships. It was soon superseded by other forms of partnership more suitable for business purposes and was no longer a common institution in post-classical times. However, it survived to enjoy unparalleled popularity in the Middle Ages. It was then that the idea of several persons associating themselves for the purpose not only of trade, but for mutual benefit, was considerably extended and that the foundations were laid for numerous associations, societies and guilds. In great use on the Continent in feudal times, these "fraternal partnerships" were very well known to jurists and in custom and were the vehicle of association of all classes. Particularly prevalent in agriculture, and thus known as "rustic partnerships", they may be described as not primarily trading ventures but rather benefit societies formed for the advantage of their members. The popularity and use of universal partnerships in this guise is attributed to the reason that a family by uniting its labours, revenues, gains and acquisitions became as it were a corporate body continually possessing its own patrimony by a species of survivorship, notwithstanding the death of individual members. Thus, not only undesirable consequences of the medieval maxim "mors omnia solvit" were avoided, but also the economic confusion and distress caused by dividing landed property into too small portions. As the necessities which gave

rise to these agricultural partnerships ceased to exist, their popularity waned. Universal partnerships were, however, sometimes still contracted for commercial and trading purposes, thus gradually developing a markedly moneyed character. Though then not of common occurrence, the drafters of the civil codes during the late eighteenth and early nineteenth centuries, fearing that a resurgence in its popularity would facilitate disorder in modern times and result in much fraud and litigation, limited its scope to all *present* property only. Thus in most civil law countries this kind of universal partnership comprises only all the *existing* property of the partners. It does not extend to property to be acquired by way of succession, donation or legacy and a stipulation to this effect is void. At present this kind of universal partnership is extremely rare and virtually non-existent, though courts in civil law jurisdictions have upheld or considered alleged universal partnerships in various instances during the nineteenth and even the present century. These instances, however, are not viewed as examples of true universal partnerships, but as equitable analogies for the purpose of overcoming various legal disabilities. For detailed discussion of the various aspects, see the authorities referred to in ns 9-19 infra. In Anglo-American law this kind of universal partnership seems possible, since there is no express prohibition against such partnerships, and partners in general may agree to contribute whatever they wish. (Gilmore *Handbook on the Law of Partnership* 104: "We can see no reason why parties should not be competent to form a universal partnership. There is nothing impractical in it, nor against morality or public policy.") This is not merely a theoretical possibility, since courts in common-law jurisdictions have upheld several associations and relationships closely resembling universal partnerships; see e g *Gray v Palmer* 9 Cal 616 640 (1858); *Goesele v Bimelar* 55 US (14 How) 589 (1852); *St Benedict Order v Steinhauser* 234 US 640 (1913); *Schwartz v Duss* 187 US 8 (1902); O'Neal 1949 *Louisiana Law Review* 476; Story 123. In modern Italy similar institutions are not uncommon; see Van Warmelo 1957 *Tijdschrift voor Rechtsgeschiedenis* 158 n 67.

9 Watson *Obligations in the later Roman Republic* 126-128; Thomas *Textbook of Roman Law* 300-301; Van Warmelo 147-165.
10 Thomas 300.
11 Burns *Encyclopedia of the Social Sciences* vol 12 3.
12 Watson 126.

13 De Groot 3 21 23.
14 Troplong *Commentaire du Contrat de Société* pars 256-259; Tudor ad Pothier *Partnership* 2 1 28-29.
15 ibid.
16 Wessels *History* 650; Morice *English and Roman-Dutch Law* 191.
17 O'Neal 474.
18 Van Wyk *Power to Dispose of Assets of Universal Martimonial Community of Property* 39.
19 e g O'Neal 476 relying on *Reynaud's Heirs v Peytarins Executors* 13 LA 121 (1839); *Lagarde v Daben* 155 LA 25, 98 So 774 (1924); *Succession of Arnold* 170 LA, 129 So 150 (1930); *Gray v Carter* 176 So 885 (LA App 1937).
20 3 21 3, but see ns 23-27 infra.
21 17 2 4 in fine, but prior to this casual reference to De Groot he discusses the societas omnium bonorum in some detail.
22 e g *Isaacs v Isaacs* supra 955; *V (also known as L) v De Wet* supra 616; *Annabhay v Ramlall* supra 805; Nathan 27; De Wet and Yeats *Kontraktereg en Handelsreg* (3d ed) 563 but see the more cautious approach adopted in the 4th ed 381; Bamford 19.
23 2 1 28-42; 4 2 79-81; 6 3 106 who discusses the societas universorum bonorum in detail, not merely with reference to Roman law but also particularly to prevailing French law, e g the Ordinance of Moulins arts 54 and 213, the Custom of Orleans art 80 and "many other customs". See especially Pothier 4 2 79-81.
24 4 1 12. Van der Linden ad Pothier *Societeiten of Compagnieschappen* 2 1 28-32 (ns on 233) repeatedly concurs with Pothier's discussion of the societas universorum bonorum, as being not only applicable to French, but also to Roman-Dutch law, e g: "Dit koomt met ons *Hollandsch* Recht volkomen overeen"; "Dit zelfd kan men ook zeggen van ons *Hollandsch* Recht". See also *V (also known as L) v De Wet* supra 614.
25 Van Leeuwen *RHR* 4 23 1-2, *Cens For* 4 23 2-4, 28-30; Huber 3 11 2-7; Van der Keessel *Dictata* 3 26 2, *Thes Sel* 216 706, but in *Prael* 3 21 2 he attempts somewhat unconvincingly and equivocally to explain De Groot's unsubstantiated remark that the societas omnium bonorum was prohibited in Holland; in fact, he seems to succeed only in underlining the fact that it was never *expressly* prohibited in Holland prior to codification; Boey *Woorden Tolk* s v "societyt"; see also n 27 infra; Voet 17 2 2; *V (also known as L) v De Wet* supra 614.
26 Van Brakel 1917 *Rechtsgeleerd Magazijn* 175-178; Troplong par 258; O'Neal 476.
27 See ns 24 and 25 supra. Schorer and Van Wyn *Dertig Rechtsgeleerde Vraagen* ad De Groot *In-*

leiding 3 21 3 points out that although community of property, except between husband and wife, was forbidden in *Zeeland*, their most pertinacious attempts to find a corresponding prohibition in *Holland* to substantiate De Groot's remark, were totally unsuccessful. Although *"gemeenschap van goedere"* was prohibited in Zeeland, the societas universorum bonorum was expressly allowed in Groningen by an ordinance permitting "societeiten van alle hebbende en toekomende goederen", an enactment of which particularly Van der Keessel *Prael* 3 21 2 seems to be totally unaware; see Fockema *Oud-Nederlandsch Burgerlijk Recht* 61. Van Brakel 175-178 provides additional proof that the universal partnership of all property was *not* prohibited in Holland: documentary evidence of a partnership omnium bonorum concluded in Holland by notarial deed, duly executed between two businessmen on 26 May 1642. To put the matter beyond reasonable doubt, further reference need only be made to the "Ontwerp Burgerlijk Wetboek van de Commissie — 1798" Book 4 Main Part XXI "Van Maatschap" art 3 and the "Ontwerp Burgerlijk Wetboek 1807-1808: Joannes van der Linden" Third Book Title 8 "Van Societeiten of Compagneschappen" art 3, both expressly providing for a universal partnership of all present and future property ("Societeit van alle de Goederen welke de deelgenoten reeds bezitten en bij vervolg verkrijgen zullen" (partnership of all property which the partners already have and will subsequently acquire), i e the partnership universorum bonorum).

28 Troplong par 263; Pothier 2 1 28-42; Domat *Civil Law in its Natural Order* (translation Strahan) pars 766-769; Planiol *Treatise on the Civil Law* (translation Louisiana State Law Institute) vol 2 par 1945; O'Neal 476.

29 art 1837. It was promulgated on 21 March 1804.

30 Code Napoleon adapte à la Hollande art 1613. Introduced during 1809 it was of short duration. On 1 March 1811 it was replaced by the French Code Civil; see Van Zyl *Geskiedenis* 416-417.

31 See sections referred to in ns 28 and 29 supra. In the Netherlands the present Burgerlijk Wetboek art 1658 acknowledges only the universal partnership of profit.

32 A decisive answer is not to be found in *Isaacs v Isaacs* supra 955; *V (also known as L) v De Wet* supra 614; *Bester v Van Niekerk* 1960 2 SA 779 (A) 784; *Annabhay v Ramlall* supra 805; *Langham v Milne* 1961 1 SA 811 (N) 814; *Ex parte Sutherland* 1968 3 SA 511 (W) 512F; *Muhlmann v Muhlmann* 1981 4 SA 632 (W); 1984 1 SA 413 (W); 1984 1 SA 97 (A). *Chiromo v Katsidzira* 1981 4 SA 746 (ZA). See also De Wet and Yeats 381 n 29 and Bam-

ford 19 n 21. It should be emphasized that this controversy was in fact not raised or dealt with in *Langham v Milne* supra in which the court was asked to find a universal partnership of this kind to have existed between two brothers, or in *Ex parte Sutherland* supra in which an order was granted declaring that a universal partnership in all property had existed between spouses married *out of* community of property, or in *Ally v Dinath* 1984 2 SA 451 (T) in which the court dismissed an exception to a claim for a declaration that a partnership universorum bonorum had existed between the parties who had lived together as man and wife for 15 years in an Islamic relationship. The same holds good for *Muhlmann v Muhlmann* 1981 4 SA 632 (W); 1984 1 SA 413 (W); 1984 1 SA 97 (A) although it should be pointed out that it appears that this kind of universal partnership was in fact not intended to be alleged or found to have existed between the parties who were married out of community of property.

33 *Mograbi v Mograbi* 1921 AD 274 275; see also *In re Rungabee v Veramoothoo* (1885) 6 NLR 152 153; *Ex parte L (also known as A)* 1947 3 SA 50 (C) 59-60; *Bam v Bhabha* 1947 4 SA 798 (A) 805; *Isaacs v Isaacs* supra 955; *Ratanee v Maharaj* 1950 2 SA 538 (D) 546; *V (also known as L) v De Wet* supra 614; *Annabhay v Ramlall* supra 805.

34 Yeats 1944 *THRHR* 148.

35 De Wet and Yeats 381 n 29.

36 See par 373 post.

37 Voet 23 2 89; *Ex parte L (also known as A)* supra 60.

38 See *Ex parte L (also known as A)* supra 59-60; *Ratanee v Maharaj* supra 547; *V (also known as L) v De Wet* supra 614; *Hare v Estate Hare* 1961 4 SA 42 (W) 45; *M v M* 1962 2 SA 114 (G) 117.

39 *Ex parte L (also known as A)* supra 59: "[T]he parties must be presumed to have intended a community of property amounting, as the Appellate Division for [the] purposes of the decision *assumed*, to an *universal partnership*" (italics supplied). See the criticism below on the use of the term "universal partnership" in connection with the marital community of property.

40 *Brider v Wills* (1886) 4 SC 282 284; *Chiwell v Carlyon* (1897) 14 SC 61 65; *Gillingham v Gillingham* 1904 TS 609 613; *Mograbi v Mograbi* supra 275; *Ex parte L (also known as A)* supra 59-60; *Isaacs v Isaacs* supra 955; *Ratanee v Maharaj* supra 546; *V (also known as L) v De Wet* supra 614; *Annabhay v Ramlall* supra 805; *Hare v Estate Hare* supra 44; *Thom v Worthmann* 1962 4 SA 83 (N) 88; *Ex parte Sutherland* supra 513. See also *Levy v Fleming* 1931 TPD 62 65.

41 e g Voet 17 2 4 and 23 2 80; De Groot 3 21 3,

10, 11; Van Leeuwen *Cens For* 4 23 5, *RHR* 4 23 3; Huber 3 11 7; Van der Keessel *Dictata* 3 26 3; *Holl Cons* 1 1; 1 19; 3 182; 3 203; 4 395; Pothier 2 1 28.

42 e g by De Groot 2 11 1–7; Voet 23 2 92; Huber 1 11 21; Van der Keessel *Thes Sel* 706, *Prael* 2 11 7; 3 21 10; *Holl Cons* 1 39; *Hare v Estate Hare* supra 44–45; Van Wyk *Power to Dispose of Assets of Universal Matrimonial Community of Property* 39.

43 *Ex parte Nathan Woolf* 1944 OPD 266 271 273 "[T]he idea of community, *societas*, partnership, arose only when the Romanists sought civil law vestments for a judicial figure whose origins they had forgotten"; *Estate Sayle v Commissioner for Inland Revenue* 1945 AD 388 394–395; *Oberholzer v Oberholzer* 1947 3 SA 294 (O) 296–297; *Hare v Estate Hare* supra 44–45; Van Wyk 39–40.

44 Van Wyk 40. It is interesting to note that the statement by Hahlo *Husband and Wife* (3d ed) 209 ("Community of property and of profit and loss results in a universal partnership of the spouses") has in the 4th ed 214 been amended to a more cautious: "Community of property and of profit and loss results in a universal *economic* partnership of the spouses" (italics supplied).

45 *Annabhay v Ramlall* supra 805 808. See also

V (also known as L) v De Wet supra 614.

46 *Ally v Dinath* supra 454.

47 See n 3 supra.

48 Van der Linden 4 1 12: "*sociëteit van algemeene winst*".

49 *Latham v Sher* 1974 4 SA 687 (W) 689H: "[T]he partnership was a general one involving all the business activities of the respective partners."

50 De Groot 3 21 3; Huber 3 11 5; Voet 17 2 5; Van Leeuwen *Cens For* 4 23 2; Van der Linden 4 1 12; Pothier 2 2 43–52; Van der Keessel *Dictata* 3 262.

51 *Isaacs v Isaacs* supra 955; *V (also known as L) v De Wet* supra 614; *Annabhay v Ramlall* supra 805; *Latham v Sher* supra 689–690.

52 Pothier 2 2 43; *Isaacs v Isaacs* supra 955; *V (also known as L) v De Wet* supra 614; *Annabhay v Ramlall* supra 805: "A *societas universorum quae ex quaestu veniunt* is one where the parties agree that all they may acquire during its continuance from any and every kind of commercial venture shall be partnership property."

53 Pothier 2 2 43.

54 Pothier 2 2 43; Van der Linden 4 1 12.

55 *Isaacs v Isaacs* supra 954; *V (also known as L) v De Wet* supra 615; *Annabhay v Ramlall* supra 805.

367 Extraordinary partnerships During the existence of an ordinary partnership all the partners are joint co-creditors and, for most practical purposes, joint co-debtors vis-à-vis outsiders. As soon as the partnership is dissolved the partners, though remaining co-creditors, are each liable for the full amount of a partnership debt, singuli in solidum.[1] In contradistinction, one feature common to all kinds of extraordinary partnership is that some of the members occupy the position of partners only in so far as their co-partners are concerned, but not vis-à-vis outsiders, that is, there is no vinculum iuris between them and the debtors and creditors of the partnership.[2] Thus the extraordinary partners are not liable to third parties for partnership debts as long as they do not act or are not held out to outsiders as ordinary partners, in which event they are liable as such.[3]

Prior to the introduction of the Pre-Union Statute Law Revision Act,[4] three kinds of extraordinary partnerships could be established. Two of these, the partnership *en commandite* and the anonymous (silent) partnership were known to Roman-Dutch law[5] and though not of frequent occurrence[6] may still be formed. The third kind, the limited partnership consisting of general partners and special partners, was introduced by statute in the Cape Province[7] and Natal[8] during the previous century. But it did not prove popular,[9] and the statutory provisions concerned[10] have been repealed.[11]

The anonymous or silent[12] partnership is created where parties agree to share the profits of a business which is to be carried on by one or some of the partners in his or their name alone, while the partners whose names are not disclosed remain the anonymous or silent partners,[13] sometimes also referred to as sleeping or dormant partners.[14] Although the anonymous or silent partner may be described as a partner, the essence of the arrangement is that this fact must be carefully concealed from the outside world.[15] He shares the risk of the undertaking with his co-partners and is liable to them for his pro rata share of partnership losses.[16] The partnership *en commandite* again is that which is to be carried on in the name of one or some of the partners and to which every partner whose name is not disclosed, called a commanditarian partner or partner *en commandite*, contributes a fixed sum of money on condition that he receives a certain share of the profit, if there is any, but that in the event of loss he is liable to his co-partners to the extent of the fixed amount of his agreed capital contribution only.[17]

It is clear that a partnership *en commandite* closely resembles an anonymous or silent partnership,[18] but that it is something more than that. There will be a partnership *en commandite* only if the special conditions mentioned are complied with. The two types differ in that the anonymous or silent partner is liable to his partners for his pro rata share of all partnership debts, whereas this liability of the commanditarian partner is limited to the amount of his agreed capital contribution.[19]

As far as resemblances between the two kinds of extraordinary partnership are concerned, a commanditarian partner and an anonymous or silent partner are similar in the following respects:

(a) They are undisclosed, which means that they are not held out to the world as partners.[20]

(b) They are not liable for partnership debts to creditors of the partnership, but only to their co-partners. The mere fact that outsiders become aware or are informed of the nature and terms of the partnership does not render them liable to partnership creditors. They only lose their protection against such liability if they have been held out to be or have acted as ordinary partners.[21] It has been said that the doctrine of the undisclosed principal[22] does not apply to these types of partnership[23] and thus cannot be utilized by a partnership creditor to hold either a commanditarian or an anonymous (silent) partner liable for partnership debts.[24]

(c) They may not participate actively in the business of the partnership.[25] However, mere interference per se in the partnership business, not amounting to holding out or acting as ordinary partners, does not render them liable to partnership creditors.[26] In Roman-Dutch law a partnership *en commandite* could validly be contracted on the condition that the managing partner, in carrying on the affairs of the partnership, avails himself of the advice and consent of the commanditarian partner.[27] It has, however, been stated that a clause in a partnership agreement that no risks shall be undertaken on account of the partnership unless with the consent of the partners, completely removes the partnership from the category of either *en commandite* or anonymous (silent) partnerships.[28]

(d) They cannot claim repayment of their contributions or payment of their share of the partnership profits in competition with the creditors of the partnership.[29]

Where doubt exists whether a particular partnership is an ordinary or extraordinary partnership, the court will always construe the deed of partnership in favour of its being an ordinary partnership, rather than in favour of its being an anonymous (silent) partnership or a partnership *en commandite*.[30] Although the contrary had been considered,[31] it was suggested that there is no apparent reason why extraordinary partnerships cannot be established otherwise than by express agreement.[32]

1 For the liability of partners for partnership debts, see below.

2 Pothier *Partnership* 2 2 63; cf De Villiers *Encyclopedia of Forms and Precedents* vol 13 (*Partnership*); De Wet and Yeats *Kontraktereg en Handelsreg* 418.

3 *Watermeyer v Kerdel's Trustees* (1834) 3 M 424; *Chapman v Gersigny* (1882) 3 NLR 112; *Brider v Wills* (1886) 4 SC 282; *Lamb Bros v Brenner & Co* (1886) 5 EDC 152; *Guardian Insurance and Trust Co v Lovemore's Executors* (1887) 5 SC 205; *Sellar Bros v Clark* (1893) 10 SC 168; *Geo Anderson v M Royce* (1895) 2 OR 266 277; *Green v Green and Hansen and Schrader* (1897) 12 EDC 68; *Murray v Findlay & Co* (1904) 21 SC 144; *Estate Davison v Auret* (1905) 22 SC 10; *S Butcher & Sons v Baranov Bros* (1905) 26 NLR 589; *Bale and Greene v Bennett* (1907) 28 NLR 361; *Tyson v Rodger and Nicol* (1907) 10 HCG 139; *Shapiro v*

Shapiro and Ketz's Trustee 1907 TS 472; *Bar-
ker & Co v Blore* 1908 TS 1156; *Le Voy v
Birch's Executors* 1913 AD 102; *Hall v Millin
and Hutton* 1915 SR 78; *Blumberg and Sulski v
Brown and Freitas* 1922 TPD 130; *Sabatelli v
St Andrew's Building Society* 1933 WLD 55;
Siegel and Frenkel v R 1943 SR 13; *Cohen v
Commissioner for Inland Revenue* 1948 4 SA 616
(T); *Venter v Naude* 1951 1 SA 156 (O); *Sacca
Ltd v Olivier* 1954 3 SA 136 (T); *Eaton and
Louw v Arcade Properties (Pty) Ltd* 1961 4 SA
233 (T). Cf *A Becker & Co (Pty) Ltd v Becker*
1981 3 SA 406 (A) 420-421.

4 36 of 1976.
5 Decker ad Van Leeuwen *RHR* 4 23 1 n (b);
Van der Keessel *Thes Sel* 704, *Prael* 3 21 7;
Pothier 2 2 60-63; 4 2 82; 6 2 102; Van der
Linden *Koopmans Handboek* 4 1 12, ad Pothier *Societeiten of Compagnieschappen* 6 1 96
note on 236; see also pars 362 and 365 ante.
6 Cf De Wet and Yeats 417 n 323.
7 The Special Partnerships' Limited Liability
Act 24 of 1861 (Cape) as amended by the
Special Partnerships' Limited Liability
Amendment Act 12 of 1906 (Cape).
8 The Special Partnerships Limited Liability
Act of 1864 (Law 1 of 1865 Natal).
9 Up to 1958, i e after nearly a century, only
70 limited partnerships had been registered
at the Cape Town office of the registrar of
deeds and 240 in Natal: Hahlo and Kahn
*Union of SA: Development of its Laws and Con-
stitution* 701 n 87. The limited partnership was
in effect merely a commanditarian partnership in a statutory guise, and according to De
Wet and Yeats 417 its introduction was un-
necessary and still another example of the
slavish imitation of English law. For a comprehensive discussion of the statutory provisions concerned, see De Villiers 180-182; Nathan *Partnership and Private Companies* 51-55.
10 See ns 6 and 7 supra.
11 by the Pre-Union Statute Law Revision Act
36 of 1976 s 1; but obviously not with retroactive effect; see Interpretation Act 33 of
1957 s 12(2); Smith *Insolvency* 69 n 83. In any
event the legislation concerned has certainly
not been repealed by the General Law
Amendment Act 70 of 1968 as is wrongly
indicated by Bamford *Partnership* 61 n 103.
In fact s 1 of the latter act only repealed so
much of the Registration of Firms Act 35 of
1906 (Natal) as was unrepealed. Cf De Wet
and Yeats 379 n 14 417 n 323.
12 The term "anonymous partnership" (*naamlose vennootskap*) being a translation of the
Dutch "*naamloze vennootschap*" and the French
"*société anonyme*" is a misnomer. In its countries of origin this term indicates and did in-

dicate the equivalent of the present SA public company and its English predecessor, the
joint-stock company. The modern equivalent in France and the Netherlands of the SA
so-called "anonymous partnership" is the
"*société en participation*" and the "*stille maatschap*" respectively, both usually translated
either as "silent partnership" or as "joint
venture". For a detailed statement, see par 365
ns 1 16 ante. As the term "anonymous partnership" has been consistently used by the
courts for "silent partnership" since *Watermeyer v Kerdel's Trustees* supra 430-437 as well
as in legislation still in force (see e g n 20 infra), this incorrect usage had of necessity also
to be maintained in the main text of this title,
but then it is immediately followed and
qualified by the more correct term "silent
partnership". For a lucid example of the correct usage of this term, see the Wetboek van
den Oranje-Vrijstaat: Hoofstuk C: De Wet
over de beperkte verantwoordelijkheid van
naamloze vennootschappen s 1: "De woorden '*naamloze vennootschap*' in deze wet zullen beteeken elke vennootschap waarvan het
kapitaal verdeeld is, of welke men overeen-
gekomen is in aandeelen te verdeelen, en zoo,
dat gezegde aandeelen getransporteerd kun-
nen worden zonder uitdrukkelijk verlof van
al de aandeelhouders, alsook elke vennootschap welke, bij hare daarstelling of door lat-
ere toelating, uit meer dan vijf-en-twintig
leden zal bestaan." This was in fact a direct
translation and careful reproduction of the
Cape Joint Stock Companies' Limited Liability Act 23 of 1861 which in turn was based
on the English Joint Stock Companies Act
of 1844 (7 & 8 Vict c 110) and Limited Liability Act of 1855 (18 & 19 Vict c 133). See
especially *In re Paarl Bank* (1891) 8 SC 131
136; *E Carstens ca C W Neebe* 1883 OFS 10 13.
13 Pothier 2 2 61; Van der Linden 4 1 12; *Watermeyer v Kerdel's Trustees* supra 432; *Lamb
Bros v Brenner & Co* supra 161; *Estate Davison
v Auret* supra 19-20; *Hall v Millin and Hutton*
supra 80; *Siegel and Frenkel v R* supra 15; *Sacca
Ltd v Olivier* supra 138; *Eaton and Louw v Arcade Properties (Pty) Ltd* supra 239.
14 e g *Lolly v Gilbert* (1830) 1 M 434; *Chapman
v Gersigny* supra 113; *Brider v Wills* supra 284;
Green v Green and Hansen and Schrader supra
75; *Murray v Findlay & Co* supra 147; *Shapiro
v Shapiro and Ketz's Trustee* supra 474; *Blumberg and Sulski v Brown and Freitas* supra 141;
Cohen v Commissioner for Inland Revenue supra
627; *Eaton and Louw v Arcade Properties (Pty)
Ltd* supra 239.
15 *Lamb Bros v Brenner & Co* supra; *Siegel and
Frenkel v R* supra 15; *Eaton and Louw v Arcade*

Properties (Pty) Ltd supra 239.

16 Pothier 2 2 63; Van der Linden 4 1 12; *Lamb Bros v Brenner & Co* supra 161 165; *Guardian Insurance and Trust Co v Lovemore's Executors* supra 212; *Estate Davison v Auret* supra 18-20; *Le Voy v Birch's Executors* supra 107; *Eaton and Louw v Arcade Properties (Pty) Ltd* supra 240.

17 Decker ad Van Leeuwen *RHR* 4 23 1 n (b); Van der Keessel *Thes Sel* 704, *Prael* 3 21 7; Pothier 2 2 60; Van der Linden 4 1 12; *Watermeyer v Kerdel's Trustees* supra 433; *Lamb Bros v Brenner & Co* supra 161; *Estate Davison v Auret* supra 19; *S Butcher & Sons v Baranov Bros* supra 592-593; *Du Toit v African Dairies Ltd* 1922 TPD 245 247; *Venter v Naude* supra 162; *Eaton and Louw v Arcade Properties (Pty) Ltd* 240.

18 *Eaton and Louw v Arcade Properties (Pty) Ltd* supra 240.

19 Pothier 2 2 63; Van der Linden 4 1 12; *Lamb Bros v Brenner & Co* supra 165; *Estate Davison v Auret* supra 18-20; *S Butcher & Sons v Baranov Bros* supra 592-593 603-604; *Venter v Naude* supra 162; *Eaton and Louw v Arcade Properties (Pty) Ltd* supra 240. Cf Nathan *Common Law* vol 2 940.

20 Thus in terms of the Business Names Act 27 of 1960 ss 1 and 3 the names and particulars of a "special partner", defined as an anonymous partner in an anonymous partnership and a partner *en commandite* in a partnership *en commandite*, need not be disclosed in any trade catalogue, trade circular, business letter, order for goods or statement of account.

21 Pothier 6 2 102; Van der Linden 4 1 13; Van der Keessel *Thes Sel* 704, *Prael* 3 21 7; *Watermeyer v Kerdel's Trustees* supra 432; *Chapman v Gersigny* supra 113; *Lamb Bros v Brenner & Co* supra 165; *Guardian Insurance and Trust*

Co v Lovemore's Executors supra 212; *Murray v Findlay & Co* supra 147; *Estate Davison v Auret* supra 20; *S Butcher & Sons v Baranov Bros* supra 604; *Bale and Greene v Bennett* supra 380; *Blumberg and Sulski v Brown and Freitas* supra 141; *Cohen v Commissioner for Inland Revenue* supra 627; *Venter v Naude* supra 162; *Sacca Ltd v Olivier* supra 138.

22 For a statement on this doctrine, see title AGENCY.

23 For the vexed question whether this doctrine ought to be applied to partnerships in general, see *Karstein v Moribe* 1982 2 SA 282 (T) 293.

24 *Eaton and Louw v Arcade Properties (Pty) Ltd* supra 240; Hahlo and Kahn 701; De Villiers 180.

25 Decker ad Van Leeuwen 4 23 1 n (b); *Barker & Co v Blore* supra; *Sabatelli v St Andrew's Building Society* supra 57; *Eaton and Louw v Arcade Properties (Pty) Ltd* supra 239.

26 Van der Keessel *Thes Sel* 704; *Hall v Millin and Hutton* supra 80-81; *Siegel and Frenkel v R* supra 15; *Sacca Ltd v Olivier* supra 138.

27 Van der Keessel *Prael* 3 21 7.

28 *Barker & Co v Blore* supra 1158.

29 *Watermeyer v Kerdel's Trustees* supra 436; *Sellar Bros v Clark* supra 171; *Tyson v Rodger and Nicol* supra 154-155; *Sabatelli v St Andrew's Building Society* supra 58; *Siegel and Frenkel v R* supra 15; *Venter v Naude* supra 165.

30 *Barker & Co v Blore* supra 1158; *S Butcher & Sons v Baranov Bros* supra 593; *Eaton and Louw v Arcade Properties (Pty) Ltd* supra 240.

31 *S Butcher & Sons v Baranov Bros* supra 593: "I have discovered no authority to show that a partnership *en commandite* can be inferred. It is, as the definition shows, the result of an express agreement."

32 Bamford 60.

ESTABLISHMENT OF PARTNERSHIP

368 Introduction A partnership is established by means of a valid agreement which embodies the basic essentialia of a partnership and which is entered into with the true intention of creating a partnership.[1]

Common-law authorities do not deal with the establishment of a partnership in great detail. Apart from a brief reference to certain specific essentialia, and a cursory discussion of particular aspects thereof, little further attention is given to the matter.[2] The statement of the law by some authorities is insufficient.[3] In addition there appears to be some discrepancy amongst Roman-Dutch law authorities regarding the exact requirements for a valid partnership.[4] The result is that the courts have often in the past referred to English law for guidance in this respect.[5]

1 The various essentialia and the required intention to establish a partnership are dealt with

under the abovementioned heading. The requirements in respect of the partnership agreement as such are dealt with below.

2 See Voet *Commentarius* 17 2 1; De Groot *Inleiding* 3 21 1–3; Noodt *Opera Omnia* 17 2 (pro socio); Van Leeuwen *RHR* 4 23 1–2; Huber *HR* 3 11 1–4; Van der Keessel *Dictata* 3 26 1; Van der Linden *Koopmans Handboek* 4 1 11.

3 *Estate Davison v Auret* (1905) 22 SC 10 referring to Voet 17 2 1; see also *Angehrn and Piel v Friedman* 1903 TH 267 277, describing common-law definitions of partnership as indefinite.

4 In *Estate Davison v Auret* supra the court compared Pothier *Partnership* 1 3 8 and Voet 17 2 1 and pointed out that "Voet says no-

thing about putting anything into a common stock, or about the parties having to account to each other, and that Pothier says nothing about sharing of losses". The court nevertheless found that, upon closer examination, there appears to be no "substantial difference" between these two authorities. Further discrepancies are to be found in the authorities' exposition regarding the nature of individual essentialia; see below.

5 See e g *Dickinson and Brown v Fisher's Executors* 1916 AD 374 394; *Purdon v Muller* 1961 2 SA 211 (A).

ESSENTIALIA

369 Basic statement South African courts have accepted Pothier's formulation[1] of the essentialia of partnership as a correct statement of the law. According to the oft quoted case of *Joubert v Tarry & Co*,[2] these essentials are fourfold: "First that each of the partners brings something into the partnership, or binds himself to bring something into it, whether it be money, or his labour or skill. The second essential is that the business should be carried on for the joint benefit of both parties. The third is that the object should be to make a profit. Finally the contract between the parties should be a legitimate contract ... Where all these four essentials are present, in the absence of something showing that the contract between the parties is not an agreement of partnership, the court must come to the conclusion that it is a partnership."

This statement of the law has been confirmed by the courts on a number of occasions.[3] Although the appellate division has taken notice of certain criticism in this respect,[4] the prevailing viewpoint is that it is now too late to call the above-mentioned exposition into question.[5] It has been said that no substantial grounds for doing so exist in any event, for whatever theoretical deficiencies it may or may not have, the law as stated affords a sound practical guide in order to ascertain whether a partnership has been established.[6]

The appellate division has accepted that the requirement that the contract should be legitimate, is strictly speaking not a particular essentiale of a partnership, but a common requirement of all contracts.[7] It is therefore not necessary to perpetuate a reference to this requirement.

1 Pothier *Partnership* 1 3 8–14.

2 1915 TPD 277.

3 *Blumberg and Sulski v Brown and Freitas* 1922 TPD 130; *Rhodesia Railways v Commissioner of Taxes* 1925 AD 438; *Wulfsohn v Taylor* 1928 TPD 99; *Lewis v Union Government* 1944 TPD 350; *Isaacs v Isaacs* 1949 1 SA 952 (C); *Blismas v Dardagan* 1951 1 SA 140 (SR); *V (also known as L) v De Wet* 1953 1 SA 612 (O); *Morewear Industries (Rhodesia) Ltd v Industrial Exporters Ltd* 1954 4 SA 213 (SR); *Bester v Van Niekerk* 1960 2 SA 779 (A); *Purdon v Muller* 1961 2 SA 211 (A); *S v Perth Dry Cleaners and Launderers (Pty) Ltd* 1964 1 SA 134 (T); *Novick v Benjamin* 1972 2 SA 842 (A).

4 *Purdon v Muller* supra, where reference was made to the criticisms by De Wet and Yeats

Kontraktereg en Handelsreg 2d ed 515, and Van den Heever *Partiarian Agricultural Lease* 23. Both these authors contend that the summary in *Joubert v Tarry & Co* supra is unsatisfactory since the concluding remarks indicate that other essentialia in addition to the four mentioned should be present before a partnership can be established. Van den Heever suggests that one such essential is the necessity of a "mutual mandate" between the partners.

5 *Purdon v Muller* supra 218.

6 *Purdon v Muller* supra 218.

7 *Bester v Van Niekerk* supra quoting with approval *Delyannis v Kapousousoglu* 1942 2 PH A40 (W); see also *Purdon v Muller* supra.

370 Nature and scope

(a) *Contribution by each partner*

Each partner must make some contribution to the partnership. A trader who shares the profit in his business with a person who makes no contribution to the business, makes a donation to the latter, and no partnership is thereby created.[1] The required contribution may either be money, food, skill, labour or its equivalent.[2] The contribution can be corporeal or incorporeal[3] (e g shares), and need not be money in specie but only money's worth.[4] Movable or immovable property can be contributed,[5] either in itself or merely its use.[6] If property is contributed in itself, the general rule is that ownership therein must be transferred to the partnership unless the parties have agreed otherwise.[7]

The contributions of the respective partners must be capable of being valued,[8] but need not be of the same character, equal value or same quantity.[9] A partner can contribute all his assets or only certain specific items.[10] These items can either be contributed singly, or in combination, such as money and labour.[11] If labour is contributed, it is not required that it should be exclusively made available to the partnership, but a wife who works in her husband's business is not a partner if her contribution consists of no more than the rendering of ordinary services normally expected of a wife in her position.[12]

The contribution must be subjected to the risks of the business. A party who remains entitled to a return of his contribution, whatever the fortunes of the business, cannot be a partner.[13] Where the use of property only is contributed, the property itself is naturally not subjected to the risks of the enterprise.

In Roman law a contribution was deemed to be invalid if it originally came into possession of the partner unlawfully.[14] The point is not dealt with by Roman-Dutch law authorities and has not yet been raised in South African courts.

A partner's contribution must be placed at the disposal of the partnership.[15]

(b) *Business to be carried on for the joint benefit of the parties*

This requirement entails two separate essentialia:

(i) *Business to be carried on in common* The English Partnership Act of 1890[16] requires, for the establishment of a partnership, inter alia the "carrying on [of] a business in common". Neither Pothier, nor other Roman-Dutch law authorities on partnership expressly mention this essentiale. Pothier[17] merely states that there should be an "intérêt commun" (common interest). It has, however, been held that " 'carrying on business in common' in the English definition and Pothier's requisite of 'gemeen belang' connote the same idea".[18] That a partnership consists of the carrying on of a business, has been stated repeatedly.[19]

A business is "anything which occupies the time and attention and labour of a man for the purpose of profit".[20] For partnership purposes the business need not be of a continuous nature: a joint venture in a single transaction can constitute a valid partnership.[21] More than one business can be carried on by the same partnership and these businesses need not be of the same nature.[22]

The business must be carried on *in common*.[23] This means in the first place that a business arrangement by which each party can act independently of the others and in his sole interest, cannot be a partnership.[24] Thus, a partnership is not established where each party is free to deal with or to dispose of his total interest in the business when and how he desires.[25] In the second place, carrying on a business in common implies that each party should be engaged as a principal in the venture and not merely as an agent or employee of the others.[26] This does not mean, however, that each party should have a share in the management of the partnership, for it is clear that a partnership can be formed on the basis that only one partner is clothed with management responsibilities.[27]

In South African law a partnership is constituted by means of an agreement to carry on business. It is therefore not required that the partners actually commence with business before the partnership is established.[28]

(ii) *Joint benefit of all parties* This requirement implies, in the first place, that a partnership cannot be formed if each party is entitled to obtain an individual benefit from the business. Thus, for example, an investment in shares cannot be a partnership if the object is not to make a profit jointly, but that each party, individually, should obtain half of the shares for his exclusive advantage.[29]

The second implication of this requirement is that a partnership cannot exist where the benefit obtained is not a joint one but a benefit to one or some parties only. In practical terms it means that each partner is to share in the gains or profits. A partnership cannot therefore be established on the basis that one "partner" is to receive all the profits whilst the others have to bear all the loss.[30] This does not mean that the respective shares have to be equal in value.[31] A partner can be given a conditional share in the profits, for example, that he would be entitled to a share in the profits only after certain projections have been met.[32]

From the fact that the benefit must be a joint benefit, it follows that a partnership cannot exist where the benefit obtained is to no party's advantage.[33]

(c) *Profit as object*

It is essential that a partnership should have as its object the making of gain or profits.[34] Social clubs, sports clubs and welfare or charitable institutions are therefore not partnerships.[35] The business must be capable of making profits,[36] but it is not required that it should be distinctly clear that profits will actually ensue. A speculative venture can therefore be a partnership.[37]

The making of profits must be the immediate aim of the parties. Thus an agreement to form a company and to become directors of the company cannot be a partnership, even though the parties intend that the ultimate aim is to make profits through the company.[38] It is furthermore required that the parties should actually intend to make profits. A partnership therefore cannot exist where the making of profits is an incidental possibility and not the main aim of the venture.[39]

Partners must aim to make profits and to divide them.[40] A partnership is therefore not established where the aim is merely the acquisition and not the ultimate sharing of profits.[41] The profits to be shared are the net profits, namely the difference between gross return and expenditures.[42]

1 Vinnius *Inst* 3 26 pr. A brief reference to this requirement is also made by Van der Keessel *Thes Sel* 705, *Dictata* 3 26 1. Van der Linden *Koopmans Handboek* 4 1 11 merely reiterates Pothier *Partnership* 1 3 8.

2 *Poppe, Russouw & Co v Kitching* (1888) 6 SC 307 314; *Uys v Le Roux* 1906 TS 429 433. It has been said with reference to German law that a contribution includes "everything which may aid in the achievement of the common goal" and as such an obligation to refrain from doing something (e g not to sell in a certain area), or the mere signing of the partnership agreement by a party with a good personal credit, would also be valid contributions: Heenen *International Encyclopedia of Comparative Law* vol 13 s 27.

3 Voet *Commentarius* 17 2 6.

4 See *Laughton v Griffin* (1893) 14 NLR 84 102, where a guarantee given by a surety for the repayment of an overdraft was in the particular circumstances regarded as a sufficient contribution. In *Morewear Industries (Rhodesia) Ltd v Industrial Exporters Ltd* 1954 4 SA 213 (SR) 216 the sale of goods to a partnership below the market price or at cost was held to be a valid contribution to a partnership.

5 *Oosthuizen v Swart* 1956 2 SA 687 (SWA).
6 Pothier 1 1 3; *Gau v McDonald* (1874) 4 Buch 22; *SA Loan Mortgage and Mercantile Agency v Cape of Good Hope Bank and Littlejohn* (1888) 6 SC 163 186–187; *Whiteaway's Estate v Commissioner for Inland Revenue* 1938 TPD 482 485; *Fortune v Versluis* 1962 1 SA 343 (A); *Muller v Pienaar* 1970 2 SA 385 (C) 390. This distinction is important in assessing the extent of partnership assets.
7 See par 395 post.
8 Pothier 1 3 10.
9 Pothier 1 3 9; Huber *HR* 3 11 14.
10 *Poppe, Russouw & Co v Kitching* supra. A societas omnium bonorum is formed if partners contribute all their assets, both past and future. A societas particularis (singularis) results when only single items are contributed; see par 367 ante.
11 D 17 2 5 1; 17 2 52 2; 17 2 71; Vinnius 3 26 pr; Huber 3 11 14.
12 Cf *V (also known as L) v De Wet* 1953 1 SA 612 (O) 615H; Hahlo *Husband and Wife* 4th ed 290.
13 *Bale and Greene v Bennett* (1907) 28 NLR 361; *Hart v Pickles* 1909 TH 244; *Wulfsohn v Taylor* 1928 TPD 99; *S v Perth Dry Cleaners and Launderers (Pty) Ltd* 1964 1 SA 134 (T). It seems to follow from this requirement that a partner cannot secure his capital contribution to the firm by means of a mortgage bond over the assets of the firm; see *Bale and Greene v Bennett*. Van der Keessel *Prael* 3 21 5 considers an agreement by which a "partner" is under all circumstances guaranteed repayment of his capital not only as contrary to the nature of partnership, but also void because it is in effect an usurious loan. See further par 367 ante.
14 D 17 2 52 16–18; 17 2 53; Pothier 1 3 10.
15 See par 392 post.
16 (53 & 54 Vict c 39) s 1(1).
17 1 3 11. According to De Wet and Yeats *Kontraktereg en Handelsreg* 386 this requirement entails that each partner must be a rightful claimant of the common partnership funds. This view has not yet found direct support in case law; on the contrary, it has been held that a partner need not necessarily share in the goodwill of the partnership (which is part of the partnership funds), although this arrangement is unusual: *Blismas v Dardagan* 1951 1 SA 140 (SR). The "common interest" requirement is not repeated by other common-law authorities, apart from Van der Linden 4 1 10, who follows Pothier 1 3 11 with the statement that "societeit voor het gemeen belang van *beide* partijen werde aan-

gegaan" (italics supplied).
18 *Wulfsohn v Taylor* supra 103.
19 Cf *Poppe, Russouw & Co v Kitching* (supra 314, where mention is made of a "lawful commerce or business"; *Uys v Le Roux* supra 433: "there should be the intention to carry on some business or undertaking"; *Joubert v Tarry & Co* 1915 TPD 277 281 282: "partaking in joint business"; *Mackay v Naylor* 1917 TPD 533 537: "partnership involves carrying on a business or venture in common".
20 *Standard General Insurance Co v Hennop* 1954 4 SA 560 (A) 565.
21 *Enslin v Colonial Trust Corp Ltd* 1923 CPD 358; *Bester v Van Niekerk* 1960 2 SA 779 (A).
22 See *Bate v Hunt* (1883) 2 SC 179 181.
23 *Wulfsohn v Taylor* supra; *Mackay v Naylor* supra.
24 See Burgess and Morse *Partnership Law and Practice* 4: "Although the participators may make different contributions, those contributions must relate to the same business. Thus although different persons may collaborate and contribute to a common project that collaboration will not make them partners in any legal sense."
25 *Chisholm v Alderson's Trustee* (1885) 2 BAC 34 42; *Langermann v Carper* 1905 TH 251 259; *Oblowitz v Oblowitz* 1953 4 SA 426 (C) 433.
26 *Tyson v Rodger and Nicol* (1907) 10 HCG 139 154: "There is a great difference between saying a contract or a business is carried on so as to produce a benefit to a party, and saying it is carried on on his behalf, that is, as a contract or business in which he is one of the principals engaged." The partnership should therefore not be carried on merely to *benefit* the partners, but it should be carried on on all the partners' *behalf* as principals. In *Wulfsohn v Taylor* supra the court referred with approval to *Baddeley v Consolidated Bank* (1888) 38 Ch 238 (CA) 247, where it was stated that the question concerning the existence of a partnership is "whether the parties have both of them such an interest in the business that one of them can be considered agent of the other and also principal".
27 Voet 17 2 13.
28 English law is apparently on a different footing. Lindley *Partnership* 14th ed 16 states that "it is the carrying on of a business, not an agreement to carry it on, which is the test of a partnership".
29 *Novick v Benjamin* 1972 2 SA 842 (A) 851. In *Henwood & Co v Westlake and Coles* (1887) 5 SC 341 two workmen who had agreed to erect a building for a third party were held not to be in partnership because, although

profit had been intended, they were separately paid for their work. Cf *Langermann v
Carper* supra; *R v Milne and Erleigh* (7) 1951
1 SA 791 (A) 831.

30 Such an agreement constitutes the so-called
societas leonina which is not a valid partnership: *D* 17 2 29 2; Pothier 1 3 13; Voet
17 2 8; De Groot *Inleiding* 3 21 5; Van Leeuwen *RHR* 4 23 1; Huber 3 11 9; Vinnius 3 16
pr; Van der Keessel *Dictata* 3 26 9; Van der
Linden 4 1 11; *Gau v McDonald* supra; *Poppe,
Russouw & Co v Kitching* supra; *Estate Davison
v Auret* (1905) 22 SC 10. It is still an open
question whether the insertion of such a
clause in a partnership agreement has the effect that no partnership is formed, or whether
the clause itself is merely void, thus leaving
the partners to share profits in terms of common-law principles. Continental authorities
favour both these viewpoints; see Henning
1980 *MB* 143 146. There is also authority in
certain legal systems that although the presence of a so-called "leonine clause" stands in
the way of a partnership, the clause itself (and
the contract) is valid as a donation agreement: Henning 147.

31 See par 397 post.

32 Pothier 1 3 13. The condition must be
reasonable, for where it is clear that attain-
ment of the projection is too remote a possibility, the contract will be deemed to be a
leonine partnership: Henning 147.

33 See par 371 post.

34 See the authorities quoted in par 369 n 3 ante.
It has not yet been directly decided in SA
courts whether *gain* (other than profits) can
be the aim of a partnership and, if so, what
type of gain would qualify. Common-law
authorities generally require lucrum or
quaestus to be the aim of partnership: Voet
17 2 1; Kersteman *Woordenboek* s v "societeit"; Van Leeuwen 4 23 1; Van der Keessel
Dictata 3 26 1; Vinnius 3 26 pr. Both lucrum
and quaestus are wide enough to incorporate
both profits and other gains. De Groot 3 21 1
states that the aim of partnership is "gemeene baat te trekken". Van der Linden 4 1 11
describes the aim as "winst of voordeel te
doen". This corresponds with Pothier 1 3 12.
In *Isaacs v Isaacs* 1949 1 SA 952 (C) 956 an
object "to provide for the livelihood and
comfort of the parties, and that of their chil-
dren, including the proper education and up-
bringing of the latter" was held to be
equivalent to making a profit and thus sufficient for partnership purposes. The concept "profit" is not defined in the English
Partnership Act of 1890 (53 & 54 Vict c 39), but

there is authority for the proposition that a
transaction entered into for a fiscal motive,
namely tax avoidance, can be a partnership,
unless the trading elements in the transaction is "predominantly an artificial structure
remote from trading": *Newstead (Inspector of
Taxes) v Frost* 1979 2 All ER 129 (CA); 1980
1 All ER 363 (HL); and see Burgess and
Morse 5. There is faint SA authority to the
same effect; see *Meyerowitz v Commissioner for
Inland Revenue* 1963 3 SA 863 (A) 873. According to Dutch law a pecuniary profit motive is not strictly required: the achievement
of another material gain would suffice, such
as a joint exercise for the purpose of saving
costs. See Henning 147 n 63; Heenen *International Encyclopedia of Comparative Law* vol
13 s 21. See *Ally v Dinath* 1984 2 SA 451 (T)
where it was stated that this is also the position in South African law.

35 *In re Panmure Club* (1886) 5 EDC 170; *Re
The Cape Town Club* (1902) 19 SC 420. A
building society is not a partnership: *In re
Cape of Good Hope Permanent Building Society*
(1898) 15 SC 323.

36 *S v Perth Dry Cleaners and Launderers (Pty)
Ltd* supra. Where it is clear that an existing
partnership cannot make any profits in the
future, the partnership can be dissolved by
means of a court order: *Curtis and Curtis v
Beart* 1909 TH 141; *Armstrong v Wallwork*
1913 CPD 978.

37 Cf *Smith v Robinson* (1889) 3 SAR 91; *Laughton v Griffin* supra.

38 *Mackie Dunn & Co v Tilley, Foggitt and Wilson*
(1883) 1 HCG 423; *P J Joubert v Voss Bros*
1893 H 202; *Poppe, Russouw & Co v Kitching*
supra. If the intention to form a company is
abolished, however, and the parties agree to
carry on without being associated in company form, such arrangement can constitute
a partnership: *Ford v Abercrombie* 1904 TS 878.

39 Van der Keessel *Dictata* 3 26 1.

40 Kersteman s v "societeit"; Van der Linden
4 1 11. Van Leeuwen 4 23 1 merely states that
profits should be in commune, an opinion
shared by Vinnius 3 26 pr and Voet 17 2 1.
Sharing or division of profits was stated as a
requirement in *Poppe, Russouw & Co v Kitching* supra; *Uys v Le Roux* supra 433; *Estate
Davison v Auret* supra 16.

41 Lindley 1 3 suggests that a partnership can also
exist where the parties agree to make profits
in order to hand it over to a charitable institution. It is difficult to see, however, how
this arrangement could be to the joint benefit
of the parties.

42 See the authorities quoted in par 371 post.

371 Additional essentialia

(a) *Mandate between partners*

It has been held in an early case that there must exist a mandate between the contracting parties before it can be said that the particular contract is a partnership.[1] This view which has found academic support,[2] has been referred to in a number of subsequent cases,[3] but it has never been expressly confirmed that such mandate is an additional requirement for a partnership to those requirements stated above.[4]

(b) *Sharing of losses*

It has been stated in some cases that a partnership consists of the sharing of profits *and losses*.[5] This view is generally supported by common-law authorities.[6] The sharing of losses must, however, be taken as a reference to a sharing of gross losses, for it is clear that the sharing of net losses is not an essential for a valid partnership.[7] The sharing of profits and losses therefore implies that a partner must at all events share in the losses "so far, at least, as they constitute a charge upon, and diminution or deduction from the profits".[8] An agreement by which gross returns are shared without mutual responsibility in respect of expenses or advances is therefore not a partnership.[9]

1 *Blumberg and Sulski v Brown and Freitas* 1922 TPD 130 138. Reliance was placed on Pothier *Pandectae* 17 2 Introd as authority for the following statement: "Before we can say there is a partnership we must be sure that there exists a mandate between the contracting parties. This mandate need not be expressed. It may be implied but it must exist." The court accepted that evidence of the mandate can be found in the fact that the parties share in profit and loss: where losses are taken into account it implies that the one partner is responsible for what the other partner does in incurring the loss. If the one partner simply takes half of the produce, there is no implied mandate to the other that the latter can pledge the credit of the former.

2 Van den Heever *Partiarian Agricultural Lease* 27–29; Gibson *Mercantile and Company Law* 268 n 11.

3 *Venter v Naude* 1951 1 SA 156 (O); *Morewear Industries (Rhodesia) Ltd v Industrial Exporters Ltd* 1954 4 SA 213 (SR). In *Oblowitz v Oblowitz* 1953 4 SA 426 (C) 433 the court remarked that "one co-owner is not as such the agent of the others, whereas a partner is". See too *Bain v Barclays Bank Ltd* 1937 SR 191; *Wulfsohn v Taylor* 1928 TPD 99 102 n 4 infra.

4 It was stated in *Wulfsohn v Taylor* supra that the test put forward in *Blumberg's* case supra flows from Pothier's requirements for partnership as enumerated in *Joubert v Tarry & Co* 1915 TPD 277 (see par 369 ante) and that a mutual mandate will be found to be present if these requirements are met. The court furthermore pointed out that Pothier's second essential, viz that there should be a common interest, imports the idea of a mandate, and is equivalent to saying that a business should be carried on in common.

The idea of a "mutual mandate" between partners is rejected by De Wet and Yeats *Kontraktereg en Handelsreg* 385. These authors contend that a mutual mandate is merely a naturale of a partnership because a partner can be contractually limited or excluded from being an agent of the partnership. It is questionable, however, whether *Blumberg's* case did in fact imply that every partner should be the agent of the partnership: it appears as if the court merely meant to convey that the partner who has the authority to act as agent must do so in a capacity of both principal and agent. The principle underlying the mandate between the parties is therefore simply that each partner must be involved as a principal in the partnership affairs; see par 370 ante.

5 *Gau v McDonald* (1874) 4 Buch 22 28; *Smith v Robinson* (1889) 3 SAR 91; *Poppe, Russouw & Co v Kitching* (1888) 6 SC 307; *Uys v Le Roux* 1906 TS 429. In *Langermann v Carper* 1905 TH 251 259 sharing of profits and losses was said to be "the very essence" of partnership.

6 Huber *HR* 3 11 1; *Prael* 3 26 1; Noodt *Opera Omnia* 17 2 1; Voet *Commentarius* 17 2 1. The principle is usually expressed in the dictum "societas est communio lucri et damni".

7 De Groot *Inleiding* 3 21 5; Voet 17 2 8; Huber *HR* 3 11 3; Van der Keessel *Prael* 3 21 5; *Dictata* 3 26 9; Van der Linden *Koopmans Handboek* 4 1 11; *Tyson v Rodger and Nicol* (1907) 10 HCG 139 147; *Geo Anderson v M Royce* (1895) 2 OR 266 271; *Hart v Pickles* 1909 TH 244 250; *Dickinson and Brown v Fisher's Executors* 1916 AD 374 394; *Blumberg and Sulski v Brown and Freitas* supra; *Purdon v Muller*

1961 2 SA 211 (A); See also *Estate Davison v Auret* (1905) 22 SC 10 17; Henning 1980 *MB* 143 148.

8 Story *Partnership* s 21, quoted with approval in *Blumberg's* case supra.

9 *Granger & Co's Estate v Anglo-African Trading Co Ltd* 1913 SR 13 19; *Mackay v Naylor* 1917 TPD 533 537; *Du Preez v Steenkamp* 1926 TPD 362.

INTENTION TO ESTABLISH PARTNERSHIP

372 General In order to create a valid partnership it must, in addition to the presence of the partnership essentialia in an agreement, be clear that the parties to the contract did in fact intend to establish a partnership.[1] What is required is a clear intention to be partners.[2] Where this intention is absent no partnership can come into being, even though the agreement may contain the required essentialia of partnership.[3]

1 "It seems clear from authority that in order to determine whether a particular agreement does or does not constitute a partnership it is not sufficient to enquire whether the alleged partner does or does not enjoy a share of the profits, the fact that he receives a share is not conclusive, the real intention of the parties as deduced from the whole agreement must be looked to": *Deary v Deputy Commissioner of Inland Revenue* 1920 CPD 541 547. See also *De Villiers v Smith* 1930 CPD 219 221–222: "[E]ven if [the agreement] contains all the essentials of a partnership agreement as laid down in *Joubert v Tarry & Co* it does not follow that the Court is bound to construe it as a partnership agreement. It was pointed out by Wessels, JP, in the case of *Blumberg & Sulski v Brown & Freitas* (1922) TPD 130 that the Court was not bound to draw such a conclusion. He said at p 136: '... The Court [in *Joubert v Tarry & Co*] came to the conclusion that [the agreement] was in fact a partnership not only because it contained all the elements of a *prima facie* partnership, but because the parties intended a partnership.' " See further *Alfred Knox v Charles Lloyd and Samuel Nathan* (1890) 11 NLR 182; *S Butcher & Sons v Baranov Bros* (1905) 26 NLR 589; *Estate Davison v Auret* (1905) 22 SC 10; *Joubert v Tarry & Co* 1915 TPD 277; *Dickinson and Brown v Fisher's Executors* 1916 AD 374 382; *Els v Bruce* 1923 EDL 381; *Isaacs v Isaacs* 1949 1 SA 952 (C); *Blismas v Dardagan* 1951 1 SA 140 (SR) 146; *Purdon v Muller* 1961 2 SA 211 (A) 218 221.

2 Van der Keessel *Prael* 3 21 1; Vinnius *Inst* 3 26 pr. In Roman law this intention was expressed as affectio societatis (D 17 2 33) or animus contrahendae societatis (D 17 2 44); see Delport *Gedingvoering tussen Vennote* 15.

3 See the authorities in n 1 supra in conjunction with par 379 post.

373 Construing the intention The presence of the essentialia of partnership in an agreement is prima facie proof of an intention to create a partnership.[1] Upon such proof a court will find a partnership established unless such a conclusion is negatived by a contrary intention disclosed on a correct construction of the agreement between the parties read in the light of all other admissible evidence.[2] It must therefore be clear that the prima facie intention evidenced by the presence of the essentialia of partnership in an agreement, is in fact the true or real intention of the parties.[3]

In ascertaining the real intention of the parties, a court will take all admissible evidence into account.[4] Each case depends on the terms of the particular agreement[5] and other surrounding facts,[6] such as the conduct of the parties;[7] the circumstances under which the contract was made;[8] the aim of the transaction;[9] and the express intention or statements of the parties.[10] Such expressed intention will, however, be given effect only if it in fact corresponds with the real intention of the parties.[11] Generally speaking a court will nevertheless, as between the parties themselves, give as much effect to the express statements of the contracting parties regarding their intention as is possible. Thus, where a contract expressly states that the parties are not partners, one of them will not be entitled to claim that a partnership exists contrary to his own solemn declaration, unless the express declaration was intended as a mere blind to deceive creditors.[12] Similarly, where the contract expressly states that the parties are partners, a court will, as between the parties, construe it as a partnership if possible, even though that construction is in doubt.[13] Such a provision will not, however, be decisive as against third parties.[14]

A court will not give effect to any simulated intention,[15] and it is thus possible that a partnership may be found to exist even though this is expressly denied by the parties,[16] or they give their contract a different name, such as lease.[17] Similarly, a court will not hold that a partnership is established where it is clear that this was not the real intention of the parties, even though they expressly called their agreement a partnership.[18]

In construing the real intention of the parties, the agreement as a whole must be looked at.[19] The fact that profits are shared is a strong indication that a partnership exists, but this is not in itself conclusive.[20]

The requirement that the parties must intend to establish a partnership does not necessarily imply that the parties must be subjectively aware of the fact that a partnership has been created by their contract. Where the parties intend to establish something which is in law a partnership, a partnership legally exists even though the parties did not at the time of conclusion of the contract know that this would be the legal consequence of their agreement.[21]

1 *Estate Davison v Auret* (1905) 22 SC 10; *Uys v Le Roux* 1906 TS 429 433; *Blumberg and Sulski v Brown and Freitas* 1922 TPD 130; *Isaacs v Isaacs* 1949 1 SA 952 (C); *V (also known as L) v De Wet* 1953 1 SA 612 (O); *Purdon v Muller* 1961 2 SA 211 (A).

2 *Blumberg and Sulski v Brown and Freitas* supra; *Rhodesia Railways v Commissioner of Taxes* 1925 AD 438; *Isaacs v Isaacs* supra; *V (also known as L) v De Wet* supra; *Morewear Industries (Rhodesia) Ltd v Industrial Exporters Ltd* 1954 4 SA 213 (SR); *Purdon v Muller* supra; *S v Perth Dry Cleaners and Launderers (Pty) Ltd* 1964 1 SA 134 (T).

3 ibid. This is a particularly important requirement when a partnership is created with fiscal motives in mind; see Gillooly 1981 *DR* 383.

4 *Purdon v Muller* supra; *Levin v Barclays Bank DCO* 1968 2 SA 45 (A).

5 *Purdon v Muller* supra.

6 See *Blismas v Dardagan* 1951 1 SA 140 (SR).

7 *Smith & Co v Oertel* (1863) 5 S 16; *Alfred Knox v Charles Lloyd and Samuel Nathan* (1890) 11 NLR 182; *Feitelberg v Kaplan and Kaplan* 1913 WLD 48; *Els v Bruce* 1923 EDL 381; *Fink v Fink* 1945 WLD 226.

8 *S v Perth Dry Cleaners and Launderers (Pty) Ltd* supra.

9 *S v Perth Dry Cleaners and Launderers (Pty) Ltd* supra. See too *Meyerowitz v Commissioner for Inland Revenue* 1963 3 SA 863 (A) 873, where the court found an arrangement between a taxpayer and certain trusts to avoid the payment of tax an abnormal structure and not a partnership.

10 *Le Voy v Birch's Executors* 1913 AD 102; *Dickinson and Brown v Fisher's Executors* 1916 AD 374; *Blismas v Dardagan* supra.

11 *Estate Davison v Auret* supra; *Joubert v Tarry & Co* 1915 TPD 277; *Deary v Deputy Commissioner of Inland Revenue* 1920 CPD 541; *Els v Bruce* supra; *Blismas v Dardagan* supra; *Purdon v Muller* supra; *S v Perth Dry Cleaners and Launderers (Pty) Ltd* supra.

12 *Le Voy v Birch's Executors* supra.

13 *Dickinson and Brown v Fisher's Executors* supra.

14 Cf *Le Voy v Birch's Executors* supra. It was pointed out in *Levin v Barclays Bank DCO* supra that where an outsider disputes the nature of the particular agreement, his own conception of the business arrangement between the parties to the contract becomes a relevant consideration.

15 *S v Perth Dry Cleaners and Launderers (Pty) Ltd* supra.

16 *Smith & Co v Oertel* supra.

17 *Estate Davison v Auret* supra; *Joubert v Tarry & Co* supra.

18 *S v Perth Dry Cleaners and Launderers (Pty) Ltd* supra.

19 *Els v Bruce* supra; *Lewis v Union Government* 1944 TPD 350.

20 *Smith & Co v Oertel* supra; *Rogers v Forder & Co* (1882) 3 NLR 8; *Estate Davison v Auret* supra; *Hart v Pickles* 1909 TH 244 250; *Deary v Deputy Commissioner of Inland Revenue* supra; *Dickinson and Brown v Fisher's Executors* supra.

21 *Turrell v Argo* 1976 2 PH A35 (N). See too *Delyannis v Kapousousoglu* 1942 2 PH A40 (W).

DETERMINING EXISTENCE OF PARTNERSHIP

374 General In determining whether a particular contract gives rise to a partnership, regard must be had to both the presence of the essentialia of partnership in the agreement and the true intention of the parties. In the absence of the essentialia no partnership can come into being, even though the creation of it may have been the serious intention of the contracting parties.[1] Such an agreement may nevertheless constitute a valid agreement, differing only in nature from a partnership, provided the requirements for a valid contract are complied with.[2]

The mere fact that a contract contains the essentialia of partnership does not necessarily mean that no other legal relationship than partnership is created by it. Upon a proper construction of the true intention of the parties it may well appear that, notwithstanding the presence of the essentialia in the agreement, a contract other than partnership has been created.[3] In the ultimate analysis it is therefore always a matter of construction of the agreement, to ascertain whether a particular agreement gives rise to a partnership or not.[4] Such construction may at times pose some difficulties,[5] and it is often a question of some nicety whether or not a specific contract bears the characteristics of a partnership.[6]

1 *Guardian Assurance and Trust Co v Lovemore's Executors* (1887) 5 SC 205 213; *Dickinson and Brown v Fisher's Executors* 1916 AD 374; *Els v Bruce* 1923 EDL 381 387; *Lewis v Union Government* 1944 TPD 350.
2 *Dickinson and Brown v Fisher's Executors* supra.
3 *Blumberg and Sulski v Brown and Freitas* 1922 TPD 130; *Truter v Hancke* 1923 CPD 43; *De Villiers v Smith* 1930 CPD 219; *Blismas v Dardagan* 1951 1 SA 140 (SR).
4 *Purdon v Muller* 1961 2 SA 211 (A).
5 *Purdon v Muller* supra.
6 *Priest v Charles* 1935 AD 147.

375 Partnership distinguished from other legal relationships Although each case must depend on its own merits, the courts have in the past laid down certain broad guide lines for distinguishing between a partnership and the following legal relationships:

(a) *Co-ownership*

Co-ownership cannot be equated with partnership, the latter being a term of wider ambit. Partners may well be co-owners of the property owned by the partners, but the converse does not apply in the absence of evidence clearly establishing this.[1] In certain circumstances, however, the fact that the parties are co-owners may be one factor indicating that a partnership exists.[2] The mere acquisition of a share in co-ownership does not, however, per se establish a partnership.[3]

Generally speaking, and excluding all exceptional cases, the principal difference between co-ownership and partnership are the following:[4]

(i) Co-ownership is not necessarily the result of agreement, while partnership is.

(ii) Co-ownership does not necessarily involve community of profit and loss, while partnership does.

(iii) One co-owner can without the consent of the others alienate his interest in the property jointly owned, whereas a partner cannot.

(iv) One co-owner is not as such the agent of the others, whereas a partner is.

(v) Co-ownership need not exist for the sale for gain or profit, whereas that element is fundamental to the legal conception of a partnership.

Whether a given relationship between two persons amounts either to co-ownership or to partnership may nevertheless be a complicated question. Thus, where co-owners of property employ it with a view to profit and divide the profit obtained by its employment, the difference between the two legal concepts may become extremely obscure.[5] The fact that each co-owner is perfectly free to deal with and dispose of his interest in the joint property would, however, be sufficient proof that no partnership exists.[6]

(b) *Loan*

A person can advance money to a firm on the understanding that interest on the advance is to be calculated with reference to a share in the profits of the business.[7] It is also possible, although unusual, that an agreement is made by which a person's share in the profits of a business is to be calculated with reference to interest charged on capital contributed to the firm.[8] These agreements contain the essentialia of partnership, but the difficulty is to ascertain whether in fact they represent a partnership agreement or a loan agreement.[9]

The English Partnership Act of 1890[10] provides that "the advance of money by way of loan to a person engaged or about to engage in any business on a contract with that person that the lender shall receive . . . a share of the profits arising from carrying on the business, does not of itself make the lender a partner with the person or persons carrying on the business or liable as such". It has been held that this is also the position in South Africa.[11] A partnership is therefore not necessarily created where an advance is made to a firm on the understanding that it will be recouped by means of a share in the profits.[12]

It is clear that a partnership cannot be formed unless a party's contribution to the enterprise is subjected to the risks of the venture. Thus, where a party advances capital to a business upon the basis that the full amount plus interest must be returned to him at a later stage, whatever the fortunes of the business, the agreement is one of loan and not partnership.[13] However, the mere fact that a party is entitled to the return of the full amount of the principal sum contributed by him is not always conclusive. Where a partner contributes the use of capital to the business he remains entitled to the return of the full amount, and only the interest on it will be subjected to the risks of the business.[14] Similarly, where both capital and services are contributed by a party, the agreement is not necessarily a loan merely because the capital plus interest is to be repaid in full, for it is clear that a partner may also lend money to the firm.[15] In such cases all other surrounding facts must be considered in order to ascertain the true nature of the agreement.[16]

(c) *Master and servant*

A person who works in a business in return for a share in the profits can either be a partner in the business or merely an employee.[17] The problem of distinguishing between an employee and a partner has arisen where parties have attempted to cloak their contract of service as a partnership in order to evade statutory provisions regarding the protection of employees.[18] It has also arisen in cases of the so-called "ploughing contracts" according to which a landowner makes his land available to another who agrees to cultivate it at his own expense and to hand over to the owner a share of the produce.[19] The problem frequently comes to light where a person is simply appointed manager of a going concern in return for a share in the profits of the business.[20]

It is clear that a servant can be given a share in the profits of a business as an inducement to industrious work. This fact does not, however, convert the service agreement into one of partnership.[21] It is likewise clear that a person who has a say in the management of the business is not necessarily a partner.[22] However, an agreement which states that the manager will serve the other party, or that he is taken into employment, constitutes a strong indication that a partnership is not created, for the conception of service is foreign to the relationship of partners.[23] Similarly, it is an indication that a partnership is not established if the manager is to obey the other party's instructions[24] or his share in the profits is described as "payment" for his services.[25] It has also been said that it is more likely that a contract of employment rather than partnership is created where the contract can be cancelled by either the manager or the other party at short notice after its conclusion.[26]

On the other hand, it is contrary to the nature of a contract of employment that the employee should be entitled to compensation for his interest in the business after cancellation of the contract. If a contract contains such a provision the inference can be drawn that a partnership and not a relationship of master and servant has been created.[27] It has also been held that it is strange for a party to contend that he is employed in the capacity as manager where the contract on which he relies nowhere describes him as a manager.[28]

(d) *Lease*

A contract in terms of which one party is to supply the other with particular movable or immovable property upon the understanding that the first mentioned party is entitled to a share in the profits or produce made from the use of the property, can prima facie be either a partnership or a lease.[29] The main test in these cases is whether a community of profit and loss exists. Where gross returns and no losses are shared the contract is not one of partnership, for in the case of partnership sharing of net profits is required.[30]

There is authority to the effect that a colonus partiarius is not a partner but a lessee.[31]

(e) *Syndicates and joint ventures*

In order to determine whether a given contract is a partnership, the name which the parties have given to the contract is not conclusive.[32] Thus a syndicate[33] and a joint venture[34] can be a partnership, provided the requirements in respect of a partnership are complied with. Where these requirements are not fulfilled, however, a partnership is not created. In this sense syndicates, joint ventures and joint contractors are forms of commercial association distinct from partnership.[35]

1 *Oblowitz v Oblowitz* 1953 4 SA 426 (C) 433; and see too *Tshabalala v Tshabalala* 1921 AD 311. Common-law authorities experienced some difficulty in distinguishing between co-ownership and partnership, the communis opinio being that co-owners are not partners in the absence of affectio societatis; see Delport *Gedingvoering tussen Vennote* 15.

2 *Buckingham v Doyle* 1961 3 SA 384 (T) 389; see further *Muller v Pienaar* 1970 2 SA 385 (C) 390; *Eensaam Syndicate v Moore* 1919 OPD 107.

3 *Langermann v Carper* 1905 TH 251 259. For co-ownership in general, see title THINGS.

4 *Oblowitz v Oblowitz* supra, quoting with approval Lindley *Partnership* 11th ed 34, and stating that this statement is consistent with Roman-Dutch law.

5 ibid; and cf *Novick v Benjamin* 1972 3 SA 842 (A) 851.

6 *Chisholm v Alderson's Trustee* (1885) 2 BAC 34 42; *Langermann v Carper* supra.

7 See *Geo Anderson v M Royce* (1895) 2 OR 266; *Watermeyer v Kerdel's Trustees* (1834) 3 M 424; *Estate Davison v Auret* (1905) 22 SC 10; *Tyson v Rodger and Nicol* (1907) 10 HCG 139; *Bale and Greene v Bennett* (1907) 28 NLR 361;

Deary v Deputy Commissioner of Inland Revenue 1920 CPD 541; *Wulfsohn v Taylor* 1928 TPD 99.

8 *Dickinson and Brown v Fisher's Executors* 1916 AD 374 383.

9 A partnership may be entered into to attempt to disguise an usurious loan; see Pothier *Partnership* 1 5 22; *Estate Davison v Auret* supra 16.

10 (53 & 54 Vict c 39) s 2(3)(d).

11 *Geo Anderson v M Royce* supra; *Bale and Greene v Bennett* supra, referring with approval to *Watermeyer v Kerdel's Trustees* supra and *S Butcher & Sons v Baranov Bros* (1905) 26 NLR 589. See too *Estate Davison v Auret* supra.

12 *Bale and Greene v Bennett* supra; *Hancock v Cole* 1909 CTR 1034.

13 *Bale and Greene v Bennett* supra 382; *Wulfsohn v Taylor* supra 103; *S v Perth Dry Cleaners and Launderers (Pty) Ltd* 1964 1 SA 134 (T). It may even be a contract of master and servant: *Hart v Pickles* 1909 TH 244.

14 Pothier 1 5 22.

15 *Commissioner for Inland Revenue v Estate Whiteaway* 1933 TPD 486; *Schlemmer v Viljoen* 1958 2 SA 280 (T) 287.

16 Cf *Deary v Deputy Commissioner of Inland Re-*

venue supra. For loan in general, see title LOAN.

17 See *R v Thesen* (1888) 6 SC 68; *Hart v Pickles* supra; *Feitelberg v Kaplan and Kaplan* 1913 WLD 48; *Els v Bruce* 1923 EDL 381; *Strachan v Prinsloo* 1925 TPD 709; *De Villiers v Smith* 1930 CPD 219; *Venter v Livni* 1950 1 SA 524 (T); *Blismas v Dardagan* 1951 1 SA 140 (SR); *Purdon v Muller* 1961 2 SA 211 (A); *S v Perth Dry Cleaners and Launderers (Pty) Ltd* supra.

18 *S v Perth Dry Cleaners and Launderers (Pty) Ltd* supra. See also Labour Relations Act 28 of 1956 s 71.

19 *Strachan v Prinsloo* supra.

20 *Smith & Co v Oertel* (1863) 5 S 16; *R v Thesen* supra; *De Villiers v Smith* supra.

21 *Venter v Livni* supra.

22 *Le Voy v Birch's Executors* 1913 AD 102. Cf *Feitelberg v Kaplan and Kaplan* supra, where an auctioneer who had received a share in profits but had no say in the management of the business and had no other authority, was held to be an employee.

23 *Hart v Pickles* supra; *Blismas v Dardagan* supra.

24 *Els v Bruce* supra; see also *Harrington v Fester* 1980 4 SA 424 (C) 434.

25 *De Villiers v Smith* supra.

26 *Hart v Pickles* supra; see too *Els v Bruce* supra 387 and the Labour Relations Act 28 of 1956 s 71.

27 *Purdon v Muller* supra.

28 *Purdon v Muller* supra.

29 Cf *Mackay v Naylor* 1917 TPD 533; *Blumberg and Sulski v Brown and Freitas* 1922 TPD 130; *Kunze v Steytler* 1932 EDL 4. In *Joubert v Tarry & Co* 1915 TPD 277 a contract of this nature was found to be a partnership even though it was described by the parties as a lease. For lease generally, see title LEASE.

30 *Du Preez v Steenkamp* 1926 TPD 362 364; see par 370(c) ante.

31 In Roman law this type of lease was described as a quasi societas: *D* 19 2 25 6. Voet *Commentarius* 19 2 8 states that it is more akin to a partnership than a lease. In *Oosthuizen v Oosthuizen* 1903 TS 688 it was held obiter that the colonus partiarius is something between a lessee and a partner. In *Blumberg's* case supra the partiarian agricultural lease was described as sui generis "partaking in some respects of a lease and in other respects of a partnership". In *Du Preez v Steenkamp* supra Greenberg J made it clear, however, that the colonus partiarius is a lessee and not a partner, and this view was confirmed in *Stevens v Van Rensburg* 1948 4 SA 779 (T) and (apparently) in *Britz v Ashton Municipality* 1975 4 SA 842 (C). For an extensive review of the authorities, see Roberts 1942 *SALJ* 236; Van den Heever *Partiarian Agricultural Lease* 20 et seq.

32 See par 373 ante.

33 *In re The Venus Syndicate: ex parte Thring and Middleton* (1891) 12 NLR 222; *Laughton v Griffin* (1893) 14 NLR 84; *Olifants Tin "B" Syndicate v De Jager* 1912 TPD 305; cf too *Eensaam Syndicate v Moore* supra.

34 See *Trimble and Bennett v Goldberg* 1906 TS 1002; *Joubert v Tarry & Co* supra.

35 See in respect of joint contractors: *Henwood & Co v Westlake and Coles* (1887) 5 SC 341; joint ventures: *Guardian Insurance and Trust Co v Lovemore's Executors* (1887) 5 SC 205; *Uys v Le Roux* 1906 TS 429 432; *Henry Fell v Thomas Goodwill* (1884) 5 NLR 265; *Bale and Greene v Bennett* supra; *R v Bowen* 1967 3 SA 236 (R).

376 General indicia to be considered In determining whether a particular agreement constitutes a partnership or not, the courts have in the past considered certain facts as important indicia in this regard. Thus it has been held that the fact that the parties operate on a common banking account is a strong indication that their legal relationship is one of partners.[1] Similarly, although the sharing of net losses is not an essentiale of a partnership, the fact that the parties have expressly agreed to share such losses strengthens an inference that a partnership exists between the parties.[2] On the other hand, it has been held that where the goodwill of a business remains vested in one party, it is an important feature in showing that a partnership does not exist, for although the goodwill need not necessarily be vested in a partnership, it is generally regarded as a partnership asset and one would at least expect it to vest in the partnership pro tempore.[3] Furthermore, the fact that the contract is so arranged that neither party risks anything in so far as his contribution to the capital of the partnership is concerned, is also an indication that a partnership has not been established.[4]

1 See *Joubert v Tarry & Co* 1915 TPD 277; *Levin v Barclays Bank DCO* 1968 2 SA 45 (A); *Har-* *rington v Fester* 1980 4 SA 424 (C) 434. Cheques made out to a firm, which are sub-

sequently endorsed by the firm and the alleged partners, constitute prima facie proof of the existence of a partnership: *Taylor v Budd* 1932 AD 326.

2 *Hart v Pickles* 1909 TH 244 250; *Purdon v Muller* 1960 2 SA 785 (E).

3 *Blismas v Dardagan* 1951 1 SA 140 (SR); *S v Perth Dry Cleaners and Launderers (Pty) Ltd* 1964 1 SA 134 (T).

4 *S v Perth Dry Cleaners and Launderers (Pty) Ltd* supra and cf *Wulfsohn v Taylor* 1928 TPD 99. See also pars 369 375(b) ante.

PARTNERSHIP AGREEMENT

377 General As stated above[1] a partnership is established by means of a valid agreement which embodies the basic essentialia of partnership and which is entered into with the true intention of creating a partnership. The conclusion of such an agreement between the parties being a prerequisite for the constitution of a partnership[2] it follows that a partnership cannot be imposed on persons in any manner, for example, by means of a joint bequest in terms of a will[3] or by means of a joint donation.[4] A third party can similarly not be imposed on an existing partnership as a partner unless all the parties agree to the admission of such party as a partner.[5]

A partnership agreement is an ordinary contract which must comply with all the general requirements in respect of the conclusion of contracts.[6] If a person has been induced to enter into a partnership agreement through a misrepresentation, he can claim rescission of the agreement.[7]

Being an ordinary contract, a partnership can be entered into conditionally.[8]

Being a bilateral contract, the terms of a partnership agreement cannot be varied without the consent of all partners.[9]

1 See par 368 ante.
2 *Oblowitz v Oblowitz* 1953 4 SA 426 (C).
3 De Groot *Inleiding* 3 21 2; Voet *Commentarius* 17 2 2; Huber *HR* 3 11 8; Van der Keessel *Dictata* 3 26 1; *Ex parte Naggs* 1904 CTR 20; *Ex parte Grobler* 1916 TPD 414; *Ex parte Coetzer* 1942 CPD 205. A person also cannot be compelled to become or remain a partner against his wish: *Ex parte Grobler*; *Flanagan v Flanagan* (1913) 34 NLR 452.
4 Vinnius *Inst* 3 26 pr; Van der Keessel *Prael* 3 21 1.
5 See par 379 post; cf *Ex parte Federal Supply and The Cold Storage Association* 1906 CTR 698.
6 See title CONTRACT.
7 *Farmers' Co-op Ltd v Wrightson* 1928 SR 10; *Roux v Ashburner* 1927 EDL 182. Damages might also be recoverable in a case of fraudulent misrepresentation. Where the contract

was concluded as a result of a negligent misrepresentation it has been held that damages in such a case are not recoverable: *Latham v Sher* 1974 4 SA 687 (W). The contrary view has, however, also been expressed: *Kern Trust (Edms) Bpk v Hurter* 1981 3 SA 607 (C). Rescission of a partnership on the grounds of misrepresentation does not have retrospective effect to the date of its commencement: if the partnership has commenced with business, creditors of the partnership are entitled to look to the partners and the assets of the partnership for payment (*Farmers' Co-op Ltd v Wrightson* 12) and the partnership must be liquidated in the normal manner: *Brighton v Clift* 1970 4 SA 247 (R).
8 See par 384 post.
9 *Lockhart v De Beer's Mining Co* (1886) 4 HCG 85 94.

378 Lawfulness Being an ordinary contract, a partnership agreement must be lawful. This means that both the conclusion and the business of the partnership must not be prohibited by law or be contrary to good morals or public policy.[2]

Legislation which affects the conclusion or carrying on of particular partnerships include the following:

(a) In terms of section 30(1) of the Companies Act[3] a partnership may not consist of more than 20 persons. Where the number exceeds 20 the partnership automatically terminates, and it does not revive if and when the membership drops to below 21.[4] A new partnership can, however, be formed expressly or tacitly in such a case.[5]

Section 30(2) of the Companies Act allows the minister of industries, commerce and tourism to exempt organized professions from the provisions of section 30(1) by means of a notice in the *Gazette* to this effect. At present six professions have thus been exempted, namely attorneys, notaries and conveyancers,[6] accountants and auditors,[7] professional engineers,[8] quantity surveyors,[9] pharmacists[10] and stockbrokers.[11]

(b) Professional persons and persons following certain occupations are statutorily prohibited from concluding partnerships under certain circumstances. Examples include the following:

(i) a registered accountant and auditor cannot conclude a partnership with any person who is not also a registered accountant and auditor;[12]

(ii) an advocate may not practice in partnership with any person other than a practising advocate;[13]

(iii) persons cannot practise in partnership as architects[14] or as quantity surveyors[15] unless each person is a properly qualified architect or quantity surveyor. The same holds true in respect of pharmacists,[16] attorneys,[17] nurses,[18] dentists and medical practitioners,[19] and veterinarians;[20]

(iv) a claimholder may not work a claim in partnership with any person who is not the holder of a digger's certificate;[21]

(v) homeopaths, naturopaths, osteopaths and herbalists may not practise their profession in partnership, unless the name of each of the partners appears in the register kept for this purpose by the department of health and welfare.[22] Chiropractors may only practise in partnership if the names of the partners appear in a list kept by the department of health and welfare.[23]

(c) A partnership between a dentist and a dental technician which involves the business of a dental technician is prohibited.[24] A partnership whose business involves work done by a dental technician is void, unless all the partners are either dentists or dental technicians.[25]

(d) In terms of section 2(1)(a) of the Gambling Act[26] the establishment of a partnership with the object of conducting a lottery or a sports pool is prohibited.

(e) A partnership between persons of different race is illegal if it involves the occupation of premises in an area which is not statutorily designated for occupation by persons belonging to the specific race group in question, unless the necessary consent for occupation is obtained.[27]

(f) A partnership may not hold out or advertise to carry on the business of an estate agency unless all the partners acting as estate agents are in possession of valid fidelity fund certificates issued in terms of the Estate Agents Act.[28]

(g) Partnerships carrying on the business of stockbrokers must comply with the provisions of the Stock Exchange Control Act.[29]

(h) In terms of the Agricultural Produce Agency Sales Act[30] a partnership may only carry on the business of a commission agent if each partner is registered as such under that act.

Apart from these statutory prohibitions, a partnership is also unlawful (and therefore void) if the subject-matter or object of its business conflicts with the common law or if it is against public policy or good morals. Whether this is so, is essentially a question of fact in each individual case. Thus, an association which is formed with the object to stifle competition is not a partnership,[31] neither is an association with an object to swindle, steal, conduct immoral acts, or carry on usury.[32] A partnership between bookmakers is not unlawful,[33] and neither is a partnership between a man and a woman who live together in adultery and conduct business for their joint benefit.[34] A partnership formed for purposes of gambling is unlawful[35] but not a partnership in the purchase of shares,[36] lottery tickets[37] or investment in jackpot permutations.[38]

It should be kept in mind that a partnership is not *necessarily* unlawful merely because its business may possibly be performed in a manner contrary to law. There is a presumption that partners intend to act lawfully, and where partners stand to embark on business and the possibility exists that the business may be conducted either in a lawful or unlawful manner, the partnership will not be void except on proof that the partners actually intended to perform the business unlawfully.[39] The partnership will naturally be unlawful if the partners had in fact embarked upon business in the unlawful manner.[40]

When the conclusion of a partnership or its business as such is unlawful, the partnership is void and has no legal effect. A party to the invalid agreement cannot claim that the other party contribute acquired assets to the "partnership", or that the latter party make a contribution towards the sharing of losses.[41] Where one "partner" has performed in terms of the unlawful contract, he is entitled to recover his performance,[42] subject, however, to the so-called par delictum rule.[43] In terms of this rule, a "partner" who is in pari delicto cannot recover what he has parted with pursuant to the illegal contract. This is nevertheless not a rigid rule, and a court may come to the relief of a plaintiff where such a course is necessary to prevent injustice or to satisfy the requirements of public policy.[44] There are no fixed rules as to when a court will relax the par delictum rule, and each case must be decided on its own facts. The fact that one "partner" may as a result of the illegal contract be enriched at the expense of the other "partner" can serve as a ground for relief, but relief would usually be refused if the granting of it would in effect amount to an enforcement of the illegal agreement in an indirect way.[45] Relief has been granted to a "co-partner" to recover the purchase price of a share in an illegal partnership from the other "partner", where it was clear that the agreement had been terminated and that the parties were no longer conducting business.[46]

It is an open question whether a partnership is also unlawful, and therefore void, if only one partner in the firm carries on his business in contravention of a particular statute. It has been held that where a partner discovers that his co-partner contravenes a statute, he may repudiate the agreement, or continue it while insisting on the cessation of the unlawful practice. If, however, he fails to take either of these courses, and after a long period agrees to a dissolution of the partnership, he cannot set up the illegal conduct of his erstwhile partner as justification for the retention of partnership assets.[47]

A partnership's business may be lawful initially, but can become unlawful at a later stage. In such an event the partnership terminates ipso iure.[48]

A court will, as in the case of all unlawful contracts, raise the unlawfulness of a partnership agreement mero motu, where such appears from the nature of the partnership business or other evidence before the court.[49]

1 See generally the title CONTRACT.
2 Voet *Commentarius* 17 2 7; Pothier *Partnership* 1 3 14; *Maciver v Stevenson* (1921) 42 NLR 357; *Brown v Vlok* 1925 AD 56; *Momple v Momple* (1927) 48 NLR 374; *Langham v Milne* 1962 4 SA 574 (N); *Bester v Van Niekerk* 1960 2 SA 779 (A); *Karstein v Moribe* 1982 2 SA 282 (T).
3 61 of 1973.
4 *SA Flour Millers' Mutual Association v Rutowitz Flour Mills Ltd* 1938 CPD 199. See too *R v Twala* 1952 2 SA 599 (A); *Opperman v Taylor's All African Services* 1958 4 SA 696 (C); *Suid-Westelike Tvlse Landbou-Koöp Bpk v*

Phambili African Traders Association 1976 3 SA 687 (Tk); *Wakefield v ASA Seeds (Pvt) Ltd* 1976 4 SA 806 (R).
5 *SA Flour Millers' Mutual Association v Rutowitz Flour Mills Ltd* supra.
6 GN R57 of 11 January 1974 *Gazette* 4138.
7 GN R54 of 11 January 1974 *Gazette* 4138.
8 GN R1813 of 26 September 1975 *Gazette* 4856.
9 GN R2391 of 19 December 1975 *Gazette* 4932.
10 GN R1194 of 13 June 1980 *Gazette* 7068.
11 GN R89 of 22 January 1982 *Gazette* 7996. In terms of s 3(1) of the Stock Exchange

Control Act 7 of 1947 40 persons or more may form an association to carry on the business of a stock exchange, notwithstanding the provisions of the Companies Act 61 of 1973. For purposes of this section a partnership is reckoned as one person.

12 Public Accountants' and Auditors' Act 51 of 1951 s 30(1)(c). See too s 30(1)(g) and (h) which respectively prohibit a registered accountant from being engaged in public practice whilst he has been suspended from practice, and from being engaged in public practice without having the required professional indemnity insurance.

13 Admission of Advocates Act 74 of 1964 s 9(2).

14 Architects' Act 35 of 1970 ss 22–23.

15 Quantity Surveyors' Act 36 of 1970 ss 22–23.

16 Pharmacy Act 53 of 1974 s 29.

17 Attorneys Act 53 of 1979 s 83(1). See too s 83(4) which prohibits an attorney to practise as a partner if he has been struck off the roll, and s 83(10) which makes it a criminal offence for an attorney to practise as a partner in a firm without having a fidelity certificate.

18 Nursing Act 50 of 1978 s 27.

19 See the Medical, Dental and Supplementary Health Service Professions Act 56 of 1974.

20 Veterinary Act 16 of 1933.

21 Precious Stones Act 73 of 1964 s 49.

22 Homeopaths, Naturopaths, Osteopaths and Herbalists Act 52 of 1974 s 2; see too ss 5 8.

23 Chiropractors Act 76 of 1971 s 1.

24 Dental Technicians Act 19 of 1979 s 32(1).

25 s 32(3).

26 51 of 1965.

27 See inter alia the Group Areas Act 36 of 1966 s 17, and in this respect *Osman v Reis* 1976 3 SA 710 (C); the Black Land Act 27 of 1913 s 1; the Bophuthatswana Land Control Act 39 of 1979 s 12 and in this respect *Karstein v Moribe* supra.

28 112 of 1976 s 26. This prohibition does not refer to an attorney who performs acts as an estate agent in connection with his activities as a practising attorney; see the definition of

estate agent in s 1 of the act. See also *Rogut v Rogut* 1982 3 SA 928 (A).

29 7 of 1947.

30 12 of 1975.

31 Van der Keessel *Prael* 3 21 3; *Ex parte Federal Supply and The Cold Storage Association* 1906 CTR 698.

32 Voet 17 2 7; Pothier 1 3 14; *Langham v Milne* 1962 4 SA 574 (N); *S v Bloxam* 1971 2 SA 488 (W) 495.

33 *Goldstein v Nochemowitz* 1914 OPD 95; *Whittet v O'Connor* (1918) 39 NLR 376. Contra: *H Woolman v N Glensnick* (1905) 26 NLR 379.

34 *V (also known as L) v De Wet* 1953 1 SA 612 (O); and see the authorities cited in par 379 n 7 post. A partnership with an alien enemy is unlawful.

35 *Laughton v Griffin* (1893) 14 NLR 84 105.

36 *Smith v Robinson* (1889) 3 SAR 91; *Laughton v Griffin* supra 91.

37 *Bishop v Conrath* 1947 2 SA 800 (T); *Garth v Lai* 1961 2 SA 15 (W).

38 *Mattson v Yiannakis* 1976 4 SA 154 (W).

39 See *Claasen v African Batignolles Construction (Pty) Ltd* 1954 1 SA 552 (O) 553 quoted with approval in *Karstein v Moribe* supra 291.

40 *Karstein v Moribe* supra 291; see too *Reynolds v Kinsey* 1959 4 SA 50 (FC).

41 Voet 17 2 7; 17 2 57. This follows from the general rule of contract: "ex turpi causa non oritur actio."

42 The action used is the condictio ob turpem vel iniustam causam; see title CONTRACT.

43 In pari delicto potior est conditio defendentis (possidentis).

44 *Jajbhay v Cassim* 1939 AD 537; and see title CONTRACT.

45 *Osman v Reis* supra.

46 *Osman v Reis* supra.

47 *Brown v Vlok* supra.

48 See *Enseleit v Enseleit* 1952 2 SA 385 (T).

49 *Flanagan v Flanagan* (1914) 35 NLR 27 36; *Momple v Momple* supra 377; see generally the title CONTRACT.

379 Parties to partnership contract

(a) *Capacity*

The general principles relating to contractual capacity apply to persons entering into a partnership.[1] As such, a person cannot become a member of a partnership unless he has the capacity to enter into a partnership agreement.[2] A minor would therefore as a general rule not be able to conclude a partnership agreement unless he is assisted by his natural guardian. A woman married in community of property would likewise be precluded from entering into a partnership agreement, unless she is assisted by her husband, or she carries on business as a public trader and the partnership agreement falls within the scope of her business as a public trader.[3] A partnership may conclude a partnership agreement with another partnership, or even with a natural person.[4] Similarly, a company may enter into a partnership with another company, a natural person, or an existing partnership.[5] A partnership may be established between a husband and wife,[6] as well as between two persons living together as husband and wife.[7] An unrehabilitated insolvent is as a general rule incapable of entering into a partnership, unless he has the permission of his trustee.[8]

As stated above, a partnership between certain persons is unlawful and therefore void.[9]

(b) *Number of partners*

From the fact that a partnership is constituted by means of a bilateral contract, it follows that a partnership must consist of at least two members.[10] In terms of section 30(1) of the Companies Act[11] a partnership may have a maximum of 20 members only, unless it is a professional partnership which has been exempted from this maximum in terms of section 30(2).[12]

(c) *Partners by estoppel*

A person cannot be a member of a partnership unless an agreement to this effect exists between all the partners in the firm. Where, however, partners in an existing partnership represent to third parties that a non-partner is in fact a member of the partnership, the partners may under certain circumstances, as far as the third parties are concerned, be estopped from denying that the non-partner was a partner in the firm. Similarly, although a person cannot be compelled to be a partner against his wishes, a person (who is not a partner in a firm) may, as far as third parties are concerned, be estopped from denying that he is a partner if he by word or conduct represents himself to be a partner, or knowingly allows himself to be represented as a partner.[13] The application of the estoppel doctrine does not, however, have the effect that the non-partner is recognized as a partner *vis-à-vis* the true partners.

(d) *Sub-partnerships*

A partner may without the consent of his co-partners enter into a partnership agreement with an outsider in respect of his own share in the partnership. This is referred to as a sub-partnership.[14] The outsider cannot, however, become a member of the partnership without the consent of all the co-partners.[15]

(e) *Change in membership*

A new member can only be admitted to an existing partnership by means of a contract between the old members and the new member.[16] Such a contract can be established by means of an agreement between the incoming partner and all the existing partners, or by means of an agreement between the incoming partner and one or more existing partners duly authorized to act in this respect on behalf of the partnership.[17] The admission of a new partner to a partnership has the legal effect that the original partnership terminates and that a new partnership is created.[18] Strictly speaking it is therefore not possible to increase the membership of a partnership without dissolving it.[19] Similarly, a partnership terminates if a partner should retire.[20]

1 For a full statement regarding contractual capacity in general, see title CONTRACT.

2 Voet *Commentarius* 17 2 1; Van Leeuwen *RHR* 1 4 23, 27.

3 *SA Incorporated Merchants' Protection Agency Ltd v Kruger* 1947 3 SA 304 (T); for a married woman as public trader, see title MARRIAGE.

4 *Tedder v Greig* 1912 AD 73.

5 *Pavie v The French Bakery Co Ld* 1903 TH 5 9; *Rhodesia Railways v Commissioner of Taxes* 1925 AD 438 465; *Welverdiend Diamonds v H & B Syndicate* 1928 1 PH A39 (W); *SA Leather Co (Pty) Ltd v Main Clothing Manufacturers (Pty) Ltd* 1958 2 SA 118 (O).

6 *Silver v Silver* 1934 NPD 396; *Fink v Fink* 1945 WLD 226; *Bredenkamp v Comax Wholesalers (Pty) Ltd* 1965 1 PH B11 (C); *Sher v Sadowitz* 1970 1 SA 193 (C).

7 *Isaacs v Isaacs* 1949 1 SA 952 (C); *V (also known as L) v De Wet* 1953 1 SA 612 (O); see also *Annabhay v Ramlall* 1960 3 SA 802 (D).

8 See the Insolvency Act 24 of 1936 s 23(2)–(3)

and cf *Stein Bros v Chanani* 1930 WLD 119; *Priest v Charles* 1935 AD 147; and *George v Lewe* 1935 AD 249, which were decided in terms of s 21 of the Insolvency Act 32 of 1916.

9 See par 378 ante.

10 Naturally a partnership can be carried on by one partner only, but the notion of a partnership having a "sole partner" is legally unfounded.

11 61 of 1973.

12 See par 378 ante.

13 *J Geikie v W Bailey and J T Button* (1882) 3 NLR 196; *Herron v Trustee of Torque Electrical Engineering Co* (1905) 22 SC 432; *S Butcher & Sons v Baranov Bros* (1905) 26 NLR 589; *Wilson and Spurgin v Burt* 1906 CTR 922; *Dyer and Dyer v Hartwanger* 1915 EDL 398; *Jelliman v SA Manufacturing Co* 1923 CPD 215; *Bain v Barclays Bank* (*DC&O*) *Ltd* 1937 SR 191; *Van Dyk v Conradie* 1963 2 SA 413 (C); *Boonzaier v Kiley* 1981 2 SA 618 (W) 619. For the general principles of estoppel, see title ESTOPPEL.

14 *Grice & Co v James Perrott Prince* (1890) 11 NLR 259; see too *Murray v Yates' Executors* 1916 EDL 293.

15 At common law the rule was expressed in the maxim "socii mei socius, meus socius non est": *D* 17 2 20; Pothier *Partnership* 5 2 91.

16 Voet 17 2 24; *Grice & Co v James Perrott Prince* supra; *Wagstaff and Elston v Carter and Talbot* 1909 TS 121.

17 *Wagstaff and Elston v Carter and Talbot* supra. The admission can also be ratified if no authority existed: ibid.

18 For the liability of the incoming partner for the debts of the old partnership, see par 422 post.

19 It seems possible, however, that partners, upon establishment of the partnership, can agree with a third party that he would be admitted to the partnership at a later stage. In such an event it could well be argued that the original partnership does not have to terminate when the new partner is admitted.

20 See par 419 post.

380 Formalities, registration and licensing No formalities are prescribed for the conclusion of a partnership agreement, and the contract may thus be concluded in writing, orally or even tacitly, that is, implied by conduct.[1] Parties may naturally agree on certain formalities inter se, and in such an event the partnership will only be established once these formalities have been complied with. Thus, when the parties agree that the partnership will only be established upon a written contract having been executed and signed, the partnership will accordingly be established only upon fulfilment of this formality.[2]

A partnership need not be registered.[3] Partnerships carrying on certain trades must be licensed.[4]

1 De Groot *Inleiding* 3 21 4; Voet *Commentarius* 17 2 2; *Grice & Co v James Perrott Prince* (1890) 11 NLR 259; *S Butcher & Sons v Baranov Bros* (1905) 26 NLR 589; *Angehrn and Piel v Friedman* 1903 TH 267; *Fink v Fink* 1945 WLD 226; *Isaacs v Isaacs* 1949 1 SA 952 (C).

2 See *Onkruyd v Haupt* (1846) 2 M 225; *Hadingham v Carruthers* 1911 SR 33. See also par 383 n 4 post; and cf *Shapiro v Roth* 1911 WLD 43.

3 The Registration of Firms Act 35 of 1906 (Natal) and The Registration of Businesses Act 36 of 1909 (Tvl) formerly required the registration of certain partnerships in Natal and the Transvaal respectively. These acts were repealed by the General Law Amendment Act 70 of 1968 and the Revenue Laws

Amendment Act 89 of 1972 (s 14) respectively. The Special Partnerships' Limited Liability Act 24 of 1861 (Cape) and The Special Partnerships Limited Liability Act 1 of 1864 (Law 1 of 1865 Natal) required the registration of partnerships in which the liability of the partners were limited to a specific sum. These acts were repealed by the Pre-Union Statute Law Revision Act 36 of 1976.

4 See generally the Licences Act 44 of 1962. A partnership carrying on the business of a nursing agency must be licensed in terms of the Nursing Act 50 of 1978. On the effect of practising in partnership without a licence, see *Momple v Momple* (1927) 48 NLR 374; *Hammerschlag v Dingle Hotel and Store* 1925 GWL 24 30.

381 Partnership name A partnership is as a general rule free to use any name. There are, however, certain common-law restrictions (notably those relating to passing-off)[1] and statutory provisions (in particular the Business Names Act)[2] in this respect. A partnership may not use a name or description which signifies some connection between the partnership and a stock exchange in the Republic, when in fact no such connection exits.[3] A registered accountant may not practise under a firm name or title unless certain information appears on every letterhead bearing the firm's name.[4] A partnership may not describe its business activities as that of a "pharmacy" or a "chemist shop" or "drug store" or any other similar term, unless all the partners are registered pharmacists.[5]

1 See title COMPETITION.
2 27 of 1960; see Bräsler 1979 *MB* 116.
3 Stock Exchange Control Act 7 of 1947 s 2A.

4 Public Accountants' and Auditors' Act 51 of 1951 s 30(1)(d).
5 Pharmacy Act 53 of 1974 s 29.

382 Preparation of partnership contract The Attorneys Act[1] provides that only an attorney, notary or conveyancer may for gain, fees or reward draw up any agreement deed or writing relating to the creation or dissolution of any partnership or any variation of its terms. Stamp duties are payable in respect of the drafting of a partnership agreement.[2]

1 53 of 1979 s 83(8)(a)(iv).
2 Stamp Duties Act 77 of 1968 s 3.

COMMENCEMENT OF PARTNERSHIP

383 General A partnership is established as soon as the parties have reached consensus on the essentialia of partnership and concluded the agreement with the real intention of becoming partners.[1] From this it follows that the business need not necessarily be embarked upon before the partnership is constituted, although, naturally, this would be strong proof of the parties' real intention to constitute a partnership.[2] It furthermore follows that an inchoate agreement or mere preliminary negotiations cannot establish a partnership, even if this is coupled with payment of money in anticipation of the partnership.[3] On the other hand, where consensus has been reached and the parties have the intention to constitute a partnership, a partnership is actually established even though the parties may view the later signing of a written agreement as the actual starting point of their agreement and regard their interim activities as provisional pending the conclusion of such an agreement.[4] Where, however, the drafting and signing of a written agreement is looked upon as an essential requirement for the establishment of the partnership, the partnership will in fact only commence if this formality is complied with.[5]

1 *S Butcher & Sons v Baranov Bros* (1905) 26 NLR 589 597.
2 Pothier *Partnership* 1 2 5 states that a partnership is complete as soon as the parties have each agreed to bring something in common, although they may not at that time have actually contributed their quota. See also par

370 n 27 ante and cf *Lampakis v Dimitri* 1937 TPD 138.
3 *S Butcher & Sons v Baranov Bros* supra.
4 *Delyannis v Kapousousoglu* 1942 2 PH A40 (W); *Eaton and Louw v Arcade Properties (Pty) Ltd* 1961 4 SA 233 (T) 238.
5 See the authorities quoted in par 380 n 2 ante.

384 Partnership subject to condition The actual establishment of a partnership can be made subject to a condition.[1] The parties may naturally also agree that the contract would only be operative from a certain date.[2] In such cases the partnership is only established once the condition is fulfilled or the agreed date has arrived.[3]

A partnership cannot be created retrospectively.[4]

1 Voet *Commentarius* 17 2 1; Pothier *Partnership* 3 1 64; *Shapiro v Roth* 1911 WLD 43.
2 Pothier 3 1 64.
3 *Poppe, Russouw & Co v Kitching* (1888) 6 SC 307 314; cf *Ruston v Bacon* 1903 TS 251; *Gold-*

berg v Di Meo 1960 3 SA 136 (N).
4 *S Butcher & Sons v Baranov Bros* (1905) 26 NLR 589 597. Cf, however, *Eaton and Louw v Arcade Properties (Pty) Ltd* 1961 4 SA 233 (T) 238E.

385 Agreements to enter into partnership A partnership agreement must be clearly distinguished from an agreement to enter into a partnership agreement. The latter is a perfectly competent arrangement to make, but it does not mean that a partnership agreement actually comes into existence at the time of conclusion of the first agreement.[1] It is essentially a question of fact whether a partnership agreement or an agreement to enter into a partnership has been concluded.[2]

1 *Craik v Robertson* 1902 CTR 691 697; *S Butcher & Sons v Baranov Bros* (1905) 26 NLR 589; *Gilbert v Cameron* 1963 2 PH A36 (SR); *Harrington v Fester* 1980 4 SA 424 (C) 426 434.

2 ibid; see also *Lampakis v Dimitri* 1937 TPD 138, where a partnership agreement was actually concluded although business had not commenced.

LEGAL NATURE OF PARTNERSHIP

386 Two theories The respective merits of the entity and aggregate theories of the nature of partnership and consequently the extent to which courts and legislators have treated or should regard the partnership as a legal entity or merely as a collection of individuals has been a matter of considerable debate and dispute both in common and civil law jurisdictions.[1] Some controversy still remains,[2] also in South African law.[3]

Ultimately the entity theory has its origin in the mercantile concept of the partnership (firm) as a body or entity separate and apart from the members composing it and having rights and obligations distinct from those of its members.[4] For this reason it is also known as the mercantile theory.[5] It has been adopted by code or judicial usage in most, but not all civil law jurisdictions[6] with the practical result, stated very briefly and generally, that a commercial partnership has its own name and domicile and the capacity to sue and be sued, to own property, to carry on business and to incur attendant rights and obligations.[7] It should be emphasized that the impression often conveyed that all civil law jurisdictions have always treated all kinds of partnership as a legal persona, is far from accurate.[8] There are very important exceptions.[9]

English law and hence most other common-law jurisdictions did, and for the most part still do, refuse to recognize the partnership as an entity distinct from the members composing it.[10] Speaking generally the partnership (firm) is treated as merely an aggregate or collection of individuals. The aggregate theory, so closely associated with the common law that it is often called the common-law theory of partnership ignoring the partnership (firm), looks to the partners composing it.[11] The partners are the owners of partnership property and the rights and liabilities of the partnership are their rights and liabilities. Any change of partners destroys the identity of the partnership. A partner may be the debtor/creditor of his partners, but he cannot be the debtor/creditor of his partnership or be employed by it, inasmuch as a person cannot contract with himself. This non-recognition of the firm as a legal entity is one of the most marked differences between partnerships and incorporated companies.[12]

That neither the aggregate nor the entity theory can always be followed in all situations has been recognized in many instances. Courts and legislators in aggregate jurisdictions have to some extent adopted the mercantile view, treating the partnership as an entity for certain purposes.[13] Courts in entity jurisdictions similarly disregard the entity theory under exceptional circumstances to achieve desired results.[14] Thus it has been shown that a considerable number of the supposed differences between the aggregate and entity theories are merely verbal.[15] However, the application of two distinct concepts of partnership in the same legal system may and did in turn lead to some confusion and uncertainty as to the precise legal nature of a partnership in particular circumstances.[16] Hence it is submitted that a clear appreciation of these two distinct theories and their different sources remains important for a better understanding of the legal nature of partnership in the various sophisticated Western legal systems,[17] and this includes South African law.[18]

1 Crane and Bromberg *Partnership* 20; Barrett and Seago *Partners and Partnership* 12–13; Lindley *Partnership* 29–31; Miller *Partnership* 14–16; Cooke *Corporation, Trust and Company* 184–185; Crane 1915 *Harvard Law Review* 762; Lewis 1916 *Harvard Law Review* 158 291; Drake 1917 *Michigan Law Review* 609; O'Neal 1949 *Louisiana Law Review* 450; Ribbens 1978 *Codicillus* 7 18.

2 Jensen 1963 *Vanderbilt Law Review* 377; O'Neal 451; Van Schilfgaarde and Van Solinge *De Vennootschap volgens het Ontwerp BW* 14–17; Heenen *International Encyclopedia of Comparative Law* vol 13 8–14.

3 e g *Spaeth v Schneider* 1960 2 SA 629 (SWA) 631; *Michalow v Premier Milling Co Ltd* 1960 2 SA 59 (W) 63; *Muller v Pienaar* 1968 3 SA 195 (A) 202–203; *Standard Bank of SA Ltd v Lombard* 1977 2 SA 808 (W) 813; *Strydom v Protea Eiendomsagente* 1979 2 SA 206 (T) 209–211; De Wet and Yeats *Kontraktereg en Handelsreg* 391 408 525–526; Hahlo and Kahn *Union of SA: Development of its Laws and Constitution* 702.

4 Barrett and Seago 12; Crane and Bromberg 19; O'Neal 451; Crane 764. According to Lewis 617: "So far as precedents are concerned there is no warrant for the entity theory in the classical Roman law and its existence ... seems to be due to a false analogy of the unit entity of the juristic person and the composite entity of partnership."

5 Crane and Bromberg 19; Lindley 29: "Commercial men and accountants are apt to look upon the firm in the light which lawyers look upon a corporation, i e as a body distinct from the members composing it, and having rights and obligations distinct from those of its members. Hence in keeping partnership accounts, the firm is made debtor to each partner for what he brings into the common stock, and each partner is made debtor to the firm for all that he takes out of that stock. In the mercantile view, partners are never indebted to each other in respect of partnership transactions, but are always either debtors to or creditors of the firm."

6 Crane and Bromberg 18; Crane 764–765; O'Neal 452; Heenen 8. The commercial partnership is treated as a separate legal entity in notably France, Belgium, Spain, Scot-

land, Louisiana and in all Latin-American countries whose codifications are based on either that of Spain or France.

7 O'Neal 452; Meyer 1971 *Tulane Law Review* 347. For other tendencies, see Lindley 29.

8 O'Neal 452 warning against undue reliance on American texts such as Burdick *Partnership* 3d ed 82–83; Gilmore *Handbook on the Law of Partnership* 117.

9 e g in a considerable number of civil law jurisdictions on the Continent, notably Germany, Italy and the Netherlands, partnerships are at present not granted a separate legal identity. See O'Neal 452; Heenen 8–11; and, as to Scotland, especially Miller 16: "[The] separate entity of the firm is explicit; but ... that entity is different in its legal consequences from the juristic *persona* of an incorporated association."

10 Crane and Bromberg 18–19; Barrett and Seago 13; O'Neal 450–451; Heenen 14–17; Lindley 29–30.

11 ibid.

12 Lindley 30. For the consequences in English law of the non-recognition of the partnership in the mercantile sense, see Lindley 31–52.

13 Crane and Bromberg 25–29; Lindley 30; O'Neal 451.

14 To prevent an injustice or fraud courts have accordingly not hesitated to "disregard the fictional entity of the partnership and regard the members as individuals": O'Neal 472.

15 O'Neal 472.

16 See Crane and Bromberg 20–25; Barrett and Seago 13–14.

17 See Heenen 8–14.

18 See e g *Executors of Paterson v Webster, Steel & Co* (1881) 1 SC 350 355–356: "The real question ... [is] whether the firm should be looked upon as a body distinct from the members comprising it, or whether, ignoring the firm, the law should not look merely to the partners comprising the firm. There can be no doubt that, as a general principle, the Court can only recognise the members of which the firm consists ... *[I] do not wish to be understood as laying down that a contract may not be made with a firm as a firm if this be clearly the intention of the parties*" (italics supplied).

387 Brief historical background In Roman law the societas was treated as a consensual contract which governed the obligations between the socii themselves.[1] The leading title on partnership in the *Digest* deals almost exclusively with the relations of the socii inter se.[2] As a result of the undeveloped state of the Roman law of agency and subject to some qualifications, the societas was virtually non-existent as against third parties, the socii alone being important.[3] Hence the societas was not regarded as a persona or corpus or universitas,[4] with the possible exception of the societas publicanorum.[5]

During the later Middle Ages and especially from the twelfth century onwards, various factors contributed towards the development of partnership law, particularly as regards the external relationship towards third parties.[6] In Italy the commercial partnership trading with capital contributed by the partners under a collective name or firm became common practice. Stated very briefly and generally the concept of the partnership as a group with a collective name and a common legally binding signature soon led to various distinctions between the individual partners and the firm (partnership) and ultimately resulted in the recognition of the firm (partnership) as a separate legal entity. This notion of the firm came into the general legal theory and practice of most Roman derivative systems on the Continent during the sixteenth and seventeenth centuries.[7]

The extent to which the various new developments and concepts were received and recognized in Roman-Dutch law has been and still is a matter of some doubt, due to conflicting authorities.[8] In this regard some Roman-Dutch authorities often relied on by the courts have been criticized for their failure to appreciate new developments, particularly in the sphere of mercantile law as well as for their uncritical reliance on and unimaginative repetition of Roman law concepts then already outmoded.[9]

At least one authority described a partnership as a legal person, an entity in itself, separate from the partners as individuals.[10] However, it appears that partnerships were as a general rule not considered to be legal personae.[11] Certain commercial "partnerships",[12] at present better described as chartered companies,[13] were viewed as corporate bodies.[14] These companies cannot be considered as the equivalent of the present day partnership, but were the forerunners of the *"naamloze vennootschap"* in the Netherlands.[15] The latter at present corresponds to the South African and English public company.[16] However, although all that follows is not free from some doubt,[17] it seems that in certain instances the mercantile view of partnership was adopted, in the sense that a distinction was made between the partnership creditors and the creditors of the individual partners.[18] Partnership creditors had preference over partnership assets. Hence a partner's individual creditors could not lay claim to his share in the partnership assets in prejudice to the creditors of the partnership. They were not entitled to attach or seize partnership assets for the private debts of a partner, although private creditors were entitled to the net share of a partner due to him out of that which remained after all the partnership debts were subtracted.[19] If a merchant carried on business at different places with different partners, none of his several partnerships could be held liable or the assets of one seized for the debts of his other partnerships.[20] A partnership debtor could not set off a debt owing to him by an individual partner, nor a private debtor a debt owing to him by the partnership.[21] In addition a partner could be convicted of theft of partnership property.[22]

1 Schulz *Classical Roman Law* '549; Kaser *Roman Private Law* (translation Dannenbring) 226; Lee *Elements of Roman Law* 324; Sohm *Institutes* (translation Ledlie) 406; Thomas *Roman Law* 300; Buckland *Roman Law* 510; Watson *Obligations in the later Roman Republic* 125; De Zulueta *Institutes of Gaius* vol 2 179; Van Oven *Romeinsch Privaatrecht* 288.
2 D 17 2; see par 362 ns 4 7 10 ante.

3 Van Oven 281; De Zulueta 179–180; Buckland 510; Stein 1959 *Tulane Law Review* 595–596; Thomas 302; Lee 324; Kaser 226; Schulz 551.
4 Schulz 550; Kaser 226; Lee 324; Thomas 303; Buckland 510; Watson 135; De Zulueta 179; Van Oven 280; Delport *Gedingvoering tussen Vennote* 17; Corbett 1887 *Law Magazine and Review* 223; Duff *Personality in Roman Private*

Law 144.

5 depending upon the interpretation of, inter alia, D 3 4 pr, 1; see Duff 141-147 159-161; Corbett 223; Delport 17-19; Watson 135; Buckland 513; Lee 324; Crook *Law and Life of Rome* 234-236; Kniep *Societas Publicanorum* 37-46.

6 Holdsworth 1916 *Juridical Review* 312-313. See par 362 ante.

7 For detailed discussion, see Holdsworth 312-313; Cooke *Corporation, Trust and Company* 48-49 184-185; Drake 1917 *Michigan Law Review* 616-617; Mitchell *Select Essays in Anglo-American Legal History* vol 3 187-192; Stein 598-603; Lehmann *Lehrbuch des Handelsrechts* 230-232; Goldschmidt *Universalgeschichte des Handelsrechts* 256-271; see par 362 ante especially ns 9-12.

8 Lichtenauer *Geschiedenis van de Wetenschap van het Handelsrecht in Nederland tot 1809* 81-127 164; Van der Heijden *De Ontwikkeling van de Naamloze Vennootschap in Nederland vóór de Codificatie* 3-6; Kohler 1907 *Zeitschrift für das Gesammte Handelsrecht* 293-300. See especially as to the various conflicting views with regard to the liability for partnership debts, *Lee v Maraisdrif (Edms) Bpk* 1976 2 SA 536 (A) 541-542; Joubert 1978 *THRHR* 292-296; De Wet and Yeats *Kontrakbreg en Handelsreg* 404 n 212; Stein 603; Fockema *Oud-Nederlandsch Burgerlijk Recht* vol 2 73-75.

9 especially De Groot *Inleiding* and Voet *Commentarius*; Lichtenauer 55-59 97-102 108-109; Van der Heijden 52; Henning 1980 *MB* 144 n 19; see Van der Linden *Koopmans Handboek* 4 1 1-9.

10 Barels *Advysen* 2 62: "Als zynde in Rechten en Practyque notoir dat eene Compagnie is een *corpus mysticum* (een verbeeld lichaem) of een lichaem op zich zelven, geheel en al verschillende van de Compagnons in hun particulier" (signed by Jan van Ende en A van Ende, Amsterdam, 15 November 1707) and 2 86: "[D]at de societeit van C en A, is een

corpus mysticum, (een verbeeld lichaem) en zulks dan ook voor een ander persoon moet worden geconsidereerd, als A particulier" (signed by A van Ende, 25 September 1716, Amsterdam).

11 Kohler 293; Andreae vol 2 75: "[A]an rechtspersoonlijkheid schijnt dus niet te denken"; Van der Heijden 28-29; cf Lichtenauer 164.

12 e g "de Vereenigde Oost-Indische Compagnie", "de West-Indische Compagnie".

13 See par 365 n 1 ante; Lichtenauer 166.

14 Huber *HR* 1 3 11 31; Van der Heijden 29 106; Lichtenauer 167.

15 Lichtenauer 165; Van der Heijden 41-83; and see Voet 17 2 5, 13; Huber 1 3 11 31; Van der Linden 4 1 5.

16 See pars 365 ns 1 16 and 367 n 12 ante.

17 Cf *Standard Bank v Wentzel and Lombard* 1904 TS 828; *Grassis and Shrewe v Lewis* 1910 TS 533; *Liquidators of the Durban Roodepoort Mynpacht Syndicate v Blankfield* 1922 TPD 173; *Spaeth v Schneider* 1960 2 SA 629 (SWA); De Wet and Yeats 408 n 239.

18 For detailed discussion of the various authorities, see Kohler 293-300; cf *Silbert & Co v Evans & Co* 1912 TPD 425 432-433 439: "Now the first principle that joint creditors must look to the joint estate, and creditors of the individual partners to the separate estate is clearly a principle of the Civil Law as understood in Holland."

19 Kersteman *Woordenboek* s v "societeit" (517-518): "*Quod bona Societatis non sunt bona socii*, dat de goederen van de Societeit niet zyn de goederen van een Compagnon"; *Holl Cons* 2 235, 4 6; Barels 2 62; Van der Keessel *Prael* 3 21 7; Voet 2 4 55. For a detailed discussion, see Kohler 293-300; Fockema 75.

20 Van der Keessel 3 21 7. Cf Voet 14 4 6-8.

21 Van Leeuwen *Cens For* 1 4 36 24; Voet 16 2 10; Pothier *ad Pandectae* 16 2 17 n (2): "quia societas facit ut quodammodo videantur una persona."

22 Voet 17 2 28.

388 General rule From an early date the courts, with a few notable exceptions[1] — and it would seem mainly with reference to English law[2] — treat the partnership merely as a group or association of individuals having in law no existence apart from its members,[3] thus in effect and in the main adhering firmly to the aggregate theory of the nature of partnership.[4] In addition a partnership was and is statutorily prohibited from being a body corporate. No association of persons formed after 31 December 1939 for the purpose of carrying on any business that has for its object the acquisition of gain by the association or by its individual members, can be a body corporate, unless it is registered as a company under the Companies Act[5] or is formed in pursuance of some other law or was before 31 May 1962 formed in pursuance to Letters Patent or Royal Charter.[6]

Hence there is now no doubt that the basic principle or general rule is that a partnership is not a legal entity or persona separate from its members; it has no existence in itself distinct from the partners composing it, although there are certain exceptions or quasi-exceptions.[7] The rights and duties of the partnership are the rights and duties of the partners, and its property is owned in common by the partners in undivided shares.[8] If two or more individuals in their capacities as partners enter into an agreement with another person, the identity of the partners is synonymous with the identity of the individuals entering into the agreement. Evidence that they entered into the agreement as partners is only evidence as to the relationship between the two or more individuals — a relationship established by contract between the two or more individuals.[9] As in English law, this non-recognition of the firm (partnership) in the mercantile sense of the word is one of the most marked differences between partnerships and incorporated companies.[10]

1 See par 371 ante; cf e g *Robertson and Osmond Executors of Naude v Executrix of Ziervogel* (1833) 3 M 354 358; *Still v Norton* (1838) 2 M 211; *De Vries en Marais v Hollins* (1882) 1 SAR 25 26; *Standard Bank v Wentzel and Lombard* 1904 TS 828 838; *Ehrig and Weyer v Transatlantic Fire Insurance Co* 1905 TS 557 560: "[A] firm may for some purposes be treated as having a separate identity"; *Pretoria Hypothec Mpy v M and D Golombick* 1906 TH 51 52; *Silbert & Co v Evans & Co* 1912 TPD 425 434 441; *Potchefstroom Dairies and Industries Co Ltd v Standard Fresh Milk Supply Co* 1913 TPD 506 512; *Estate Brown v Brown* 1923 EDL 291 295; *Rees v Feldman* 1927 TPD 884 888; *Liquidators of the Durban Roodepoort Mynpacht Syndicate v Blankfield* 1922 TPD 173 176; *Ex parte Buttner Bros* 1930 CPD 138 140; *Whitaker v Whitaker and Rowe* 1931 EDL 122; *Mahomed v Karp Bros* 1938 TPD 112 113; *Michalow v Premier Milling Co Ltd* 1960 2 SA 59 (W); *Standard Bank of SA Ltd v Lombard* 1977 2 SA 808 (W) 813G.

2 *Executors of Paterson v Webster, Steel & Co* (1881) 1 SC 350 356; *Ehrig and Weyer v Transatlantic Fire Insurance Co* supra 560: "Both by English law and our own a firm has no separate *persona*." The first reported decision since Union where reliance was placed pertinently on Roman-Dutch law for authority that a partnership is *not* a legal persona seems to be *Harding and Parker v John Pierce & Co* 1919 OPD 113; but see also *Silbert & Co v Evans & Co* supra 423 441–442.

3 *Jacobson v Norton* (1841) 2 M 218; *Norton's Trustees v Norden's Trustees* (1848) 3 M 330; *Bate v Hunt* (1883) 2 SC 179; *J J Venter, J J Joubert, A L de Wet v den Kerkeraad der Gereformeerde Kerk te Bethulie* 1879 OFS 4 5; *Ehrig and Weyer v Transatlantic Fire Insurance Co* supra; *Executors of Paterson v Webster, Steel & Co* supra 355; *Standard Bank v Wentzel and Lombard* supra 833–835 838; *Grassis and Shrewe v Lewis* 1910 TPD 533 538; *Silbert & Co v Evans & Co* supra 434 444; *R v Shamosewitz*

and *Schatz* 1915 AD 682 693; *Stern & Co v De Waal* 1915 TPD 60 65; *Ebrahim & Co v Hassen* 1916 EDL 340 342; *Harding and Parker v John Pierce & Co* supra 118; *Sliom v Wallach's Printing and Publishing Co Ltd* 1925 TPD 650 656; *R v Levy* 1929 AD 312 322; *Parker v Rand Motor Transport Co* 1930 AD 353 357–358; *Solomon v Law Society of the Cape of Good Hope* 1934 AD 401 410; *Palmer v The Attorney-General* 1934 TPD 50 51; *R v Hewertson (1)* 1937 CPD 5 22; *McLeod and Shearsmith v Shearsmith* 1938 TPD 87 92; *Kaplan v Turner* 1941 SWA 29; *Baldinger v Broomberg* 1949 3 SA 258 (C) 268; *Shingadia Bros v Shingadia* 1958 1 SA 582 (FC) 586; *Commissioner for Inland Revenue v Epstein* 1954 3 SA 689 (A) 699; *Goldberg v Di Meo* 1960 3 SA 136 (N) 142; *Michalow v Premier Milling Co Ltd* supra 61; *Muller v Pienaar* 1968 3 SA 195 (A) 202–203; *Abro v Softex Mattress (Pty) Ltd* 1973 2 SA 346 (D) 351; *Ex parte Cohen* 1974 4 SA 674 (W) 675; *Standard Bank of SA Ltd v Lombard* supra 813; *Strydom v Protea Eiendomsagente* 1979 2 SA 206 (T) 209; *Spie Batignolles Société Anonyme v Van Niekerk: in re Van Niekerk v SA Yster en Staal Industriële Korp Bpk* 1980 2 SA 441 (NC) 446.

4 See par 386 ante.

5 61 of 1973.

6 Companies Act 46 of 1926 s 4bis; Companies Act 61 of 1973 s 31. See *Helpmekaar (Thusano) Taxi Diens v Nasionale Vervoerkommissie* 1978 1 SA 250 (O) 255; De Villiers *Encyclopedia of Forms and Precedents* vol 13 144; Cilliers and Benade *Company Law* 6–7.

7 *Muller v Pienaar* supra 202–203; *Ex parte Cohen* supra 675; *Strydom v Protea Eiendomsagente* supra 209; *Standard Bank of SA Ltd v Lombard* supra 813; *Lombard v Standard Bank of SA Ltd* 1977 2 SA 806 (T) 807D; see ns 1–2 supra and par 389 post.

8 *Sacks v Commissioner for Inland Revenue* 1946 AD 31 40; *Muller v Pienaar* supra; *Strydom v Protea Eiendomsagente* supra.

9 *Muller v Pienaar* supra 203; *Strydom v Protea*

Eiendomsagente supra 211; but see also par   10 *Muller v Pienaar* supra 202; Lindley *Partnership*
389 post.   31; see par 386 ante.

389 Exceptions or quasi-exceptions There are certain exceptions or quasi-exceptions
to the general rule stated above,[1] amounting to some appreciation of the mercantile
concept of the nature of partnership.[2] In more vivid terms the effect of these exceptions
or quasi-exceptions is that "a kind of juristic ghost" materializes where they apply.[3]

The first and foremost exception is afforded by the law of insolvency.[4] A considerable
time before the introduction of the present Insolvency Act,[5] and even prior to that of its
immediate predecessor,[6] the estate of a partnership was considered as constituting an
entirely different persona from the private estates of the individual partners,[7] as well as
to be a iuris persona distinct from the partners.[8] Hence the estate of a partnership could
be perfectly solvent, though one of the private estates had been sequestrated;[9] judgment
could be given against the estate of a dissolved partnership;[10] and such an estate, if insolvent
at the time of dissolution of the partnership, could subsequently be sequestrated.[11] Nevertheless the present Insolvency Act[12] has "plainly intended to alter the common law and
to treat the partnership as having a separate estate and as being in the same position as
any other debtor".[13] At common law the partnership is not a separate persona and *ultimately*
the partners are personally liable for partnership debts.[14] Keeping this in mind, the
practicable though wholly artificial scheme for dealing with insolvent partnerships,
embodied in the Insolvency Act,[15] may be described as a radical departure from the
common-law position, since it retains the partnership estate as a separate estate from the
estates of the individual partners and precludes partnership creditors from preferring
their claims against the individual estates.[16] Initially at least partnership creditors have
to look for payment to the partnership estate only.[17] Private creditors of the individual
partners are similarly precluded from proving claims against the partnership estate.[18]
The trustee of the partnership estate is only entitled to the residue, if any, of a partner's
estate after all the claims of the private creditors of the partner have been paid in full,
if that residue is required to pay the partnership's debts.[19] Similarly, the trustee of a
partner's estate is entitled to the residue, if any, in the partnership estate after the claims
of partnership creditors have been paid in full, so far as that partner would have been
entitled to it, if his estate had not been sequestrated.[20] In accordance with this arrangement
separate accounts must be framed in the estate of the partnership and that of each individual
partner.[21] This scheme is more than a mere theoretical modification of common law,[22]
necessitating the hypothesis that third parties dealing with and granting credit to a
partnership do so in reliance only on the assets of the partnership and that throughout
their dealings with the partnership they have looked on it as a separate entity. It is a
fiction "indispensable in justifying the provisions operating against partnership creditors".[23] Since the moment a partnership is sequestrated the partnership creditors are
primarily confined to the partnership assets and automatically deprived of recourse against
the partners individually, the partnership estate is treated, for purposes of insolvency
law, "as a separate entity as soon and as long as its liabilities exceed the value of its assets".[24]
Otherwise partnership creditors would be deprived of the safeguards against preferences
which are extended to all other types of creditors.[25] Since the protection of creditors of
the partnership estate as a separate entity is the overriding factor, an exception is admitted
on the general rule that a partner may not prove against his partnership in competition
with partnership creditors and that similarly the partnership may not prove against the
insolvent estate of a partner,[26] in the case of two partnerships having some, but not all,
partners in common.[27] When a certain trade is carried on by A, B and C in partnership
(the major firm), and A and B, also in partnership (the minor firm), carry on a business
altogether separate from that of the major firm, upon insolvency of the minor firm the
major firm may prove a claim against the insolvent estate of the minor firm in competition

with its separate creditors, provided that the debt from the minor to the major firm arises bona fide in the ordinary course of business in respect of the distinct trades.[28] It seems that upon insolvency of the major firm, the minor firm cannot prove against the insolvent estate of the major firm for a similar debt by the major to the minor firm, although this question may perhaps be regarded as still open.[29] It has been suggested that the treatment of the various estates as separate entities should be carried through consistently, with the consequence that one partnership should be allowed to prove against the insolvent estate of another irrespective of the composition of the two partnerships, even though they may have exactly the same partners.[30] Although previously the practice was to grant its rehabilitation,[31] a partnership whose estate has been sequestrated cannot at present be rehabilitated.[32]

Implicit in the decision[33] of allowing the major firm to prove against the insolvent estate of the minor firm, is the recognition of the validity of the underlying contract between two partnerships having common, though not the same, partners; furthermore, a partnership may conclude a partnership agreement with another partnership.[34] But an attempt of two partnerships, having the same partners and not being separately conducted, to contract with each other is stillborn, since they are the same persona and there must be two parties to a contract: a person cannot contract with himself.[35] The position may be different where the two partnerships are quite distinct from one another, e g if they carry on business with distinct capitals and separate books on separate premises, and the business of the one is not mixed up with that of the other.[36]

Another exception is considered to exist in matters of civil practice and procedure, where the existence of the partnership as a separate entity is to some extent recognized, albeit not as an entity endowed with legal personality.[37] During the subsistence of a partnership a partnership creditor is obliged to sue all the partners together for payment of a partnership debt.[38] Judgment must be taken against the partnership, not against the partners individually, and execution must first be levied on the partnership assets and these be exhausted before the assets of the individual partners may be attached in execution for the remainder of the judgment debt.[39] Furthermore, a partnership may sue or be sued in its own name.[40] If so sued and judgment is taken against a partnership without the name of any of the partners being disclosed, execution may issue only against the property of the partnership. The assets of a partner who has not been served, who has not appeared, who has not been adjudged to be a partner and whose name has not been disclosed as partner under the court rules[41] cannot without further proceedings be attached in execution of a judgment against the partnership.[42] Where a partner is entitled to a moratorium suspending all civil legal remedies against him, then, in the absence of an express statutory provision to the contrary, the result is that all civil remedies against the partnership are also suspended.[43] If only some, but not all the partners are on military service and hence only some are entitled to a suspension of all or certain civil legal remedies against them under the Moratorium Act,[44] civil proceedings may be instituted against the partnership.[45] If judgment is obtained against the partnership, execution may be levied on the partnership property and after it is exhausted on the separate property of the individual non-serving partners, but not on the separate property of a serving partner.[46] A partnership which had been dissolved after the accrual of the cause of action but before the issue of summons, may nevertheless be sued in its name at the date of the accrual of the cause of action.[47] The court also refused to exercise its discretion to order payments by instalments in terms of Supreme Court rule 45(12)(j) in respect of a partnership debt against a partner in circumstances where both the partnership and the partner prima facie appeared to be insolvent, because apart from other considerations, such an order would probably not be in line with current trends concerning partnerships in insolvency.[48] It therefore appears that for purposes of civil proceedings against a partnership, a partnership creditor is compelled to treat the partnership as an entity.[49]

Another exception is considered to exist in the case where a third person is sued by the partnership. He cannot set off a debt owed to him by one of the partners individually. Similarly, when an individual partner claims, a debt owing by the partnership cannot be set off.[50]

Whether or not a partnership can be considered "a person" for purposes of a particular statutory provision, is a matter of interpretation.[51]

There may well be other instances where for certain purposes the mercantile view of the nature of partnership prevails and the partnership is recognized and appreciated as a separate entity.[52]

1 See par 388 ante.

2 See par 386 ante.

3 *Strydom v Protea Eiendomsagente* 1979 2 SA 206 (T) 209F; Hahlo and Kahn *Union of SA: Development of its Laws and Constitution* 702: "The firm as such is without substance, a kind of juristic ghost which comes nearest to materialising in the statutory provisions for the separation of partnership estates."

4 ibid.

5 24 of 1936.

6 Insolvency Act 32 of 1916.

7 *De Vries en Marais v Hollins* (1882) 1 SAR 25 26. It may be of some interest to note that this judgment was handed down before the introduction of the Tvl law on insolvency, i e Wet 13 van 1895 der Zuid-Afrikaansche Republiek. See also *Pretoria Hypothec Mpy v M and D Golombick* 1906 TH 51 52.

8 *Blumberg and Her v Shapiro and Ketz* 1907 TH 65 66. But see contra for purposes of criminal proceedings, *R v Shamosewitz and Schatz* 1915 AD 682 686 693.

9 *De Vries en Marais v Hollins* supra.

10 *Pretoria Hypothec Mpy v M and D Golombick* supra.

11 *Blumberg and Her v Shapiro and Ketz* supra; and see *Essakow v Gundelfinger* 1928 TPD 308 313; *Stellenbosch Farmers' Winery Ltd v Pretorius* 1970 3 SA 234 (SWA).

12 24 of 1936.

13 *Michalow v Premier Milling Co Ltd* 1960 2 SA 59 (W) 63; *Cassim v The Master* 1962 4 SA 601 (D) 606; *Ex parte Fernandez* 1965 3 SA 726 (O) 728; *Stellenbosch Farmers' Winery Ltd v Pretorius* supra; *Ex parte Cohen* 1974 4 SA 674 (W) 677; *Gardee v Dhanmanta Holdings* 1978 1 SA 1066 (N) 1067–1068; *Strydom v Protea Eiendomsagente* supra 209; *Ferela (Pty) Ltd v Craigie* 1980 3 SA 167 (W) 169A; see also the title INSOLVENCY.

14 See par 388 ante; *Michalow v Premier Milling Co Ltd* supra; *Ex parte Cohen* supra.

15 s 2 (definition of "debtor"); ss 3(2) 13 49 92(5) 128.

16 *Michalow v Premier Milling Co Ltd* supra; *Ex parte Cohen* supra. But see also *Silbert & Co v Evans & Co* 1912 TPD 425 439: "Now the first principle that joint creditors must look to the joint estate, and creditors of the individual partners to the separate estate is clearly a principle of the Civil Law as understood in Holland." As to the position in Roman-Dutch law, see par 387 ante.

17 s 49; *Michalow v Premier Milling Co Ltd* supra; *Ex parte Cohen* supra; *Strydom v Protea Eiendomsagente* supra.

18 ibid.

19 ibid.

20 ibid.

21 s 92(5).

22 *Michalow v Premier Milling Co Ltd* supra 62: "An example illustrates the possible extent of its practical effect. A partnership having no assets and one or more creditors is sequestrated; the partners are able to pay all their private creditors in full, but nothing would be left over for transfer to the partnership estate. At Common Law, the partnership creditors' claims would rank concurrently with the unsecured private creditors' claims and would be provable in the estates of all the partners; they would be entitled to a substantial dividend. Under the Insolvency Act the partnership creditors would receive no dividend at all." *Ex parte Cohen* supra; *Cassim v The Master* supra 606; *Gardee v Dhanmanta Holdings* supra 1071; *Strydom v Protea Eiendomsagente* supra 209; *Ex parte Fernandez* supra 728.

23 *Michalow v Premier Milling Co Ltd* supra 62. Cf *Ex parte Fernandez* supra 728; *Ex parte Cohen* supra 676; *Strydom v Protea Eiendomsagente* supra 209.

24 *Michalow v Premier Milling Co Ltd* supra 63; *Cassim v The Master* supra 606; *Ex parte Fernandez* supra 728; *Ex parte Cohen* supra 677; *Strydom v Protea Eiendomsagente* supra 209; *Gardee v Dhanmanta Holdings* supra 1071; *Ferela (Pty) Ltd v Craigie* supra 169.

25 *Michalow v Premier Milling Co Ltd* supra 63:

"It follows that the statutory rule against the preferring of one creditor above another prior to sequestration *may assume for partnership creditors a greater importance than for creditors in a company and private estates*" (italics supplied).

26 *Watermeyer v Kerdel's Trustees* (1834) 3 M 424 436; *Sellar Bros v Clark* (1893) 10 SC 168 171; *Tyson v Rodger and Nicol* (1907) 10 HCG 139 154-155; *Dell v Estate Rici* (1903) 20 SC 605; *Salzburg v Patz and Saks* 1907 TH 255; *Silbert & Co v Evans & Co* supra 431 439; *Schneider v Raikin* 1954 4 SA 449 (W).

27 *Silbert & Co v Evans & Co* supra; *Strydom v Protea Eiendomsagente* supra 210.

28 ibid.

29 See *Silbert & Co v Evans & Co* supra 439.

30 De Wet and Yeats *Kontraktereg en Handelsreg* 525; but see *Strydom v Protea Eiendomsagente* supra 211.

31 *Ex parte Buttner Bros* 1930 CPD 138 140: "It seems to me that whatever the position of a partnership may be at common law, it is recognised by our insolvency law as an entity."

32 s 128.

33 *Silbert & Co v Evans & Co* supra.

34 *Strydom v Protea Eiendomsagente* supra 210; see also *Potchefstroom Dairies and Industries Co Ltd v Standard Fresh Milk Supply Co* 1913 TPD 506 512; *Still v Norton* (1838) 2 M 211; *Whitaker v Whitaker and Rowe* 1931 EDL 122 125; *Shingadia Bros v Shingadia* 1958 1 SA 582 (FC) 586; *Wessels Contract* vol 1 488; Christie *Contract* 246.

35 *Strydom v Protea Eiendomsagente* supra 211; *Muller v Pienaar* 1968 3 SA 195 (A) 203.

36 *Strydom v Protea Eiendomsagente* supra 211. See *Executors of Paterson v Webster, Steel & Co* (1881) 1 SC 350 356; n 34 supra; and as to the position in Roman-Dutch law, see par 386 ante.

37 *Standard Bank of SA Ltd v Lombard* 1977 2 SA 808 (W) 813; *Strydom v Protea Eiendomsagente* supra 209; *Standard Bank of SA Ltd v Pearson* 1961 3 SA 721 (E); but see *Muller v Pienaar* supra 202-203.

38 *Matterson Bros v Rolfes, Nebel & Co* 1915 WLD 33; *Press v Barker* 1919 CPD 243; *Sliom v Wallach's Printing and Publishing Co Ltd* 1925 TPD 650 656; *Parker v Rand Motor Transport Co* 1930 AD 353; *Muller v Pienaar* supra 202-203; *Lee v Maraisdrif (Edms) Bpk* 1976 2 SA 536 (A) 540; *Standard Bank of SA Ltd v Lombard* supra; *Strydom v Protea Eiendomsagente* supra.

39 Supreme Court Act 59 of 1959 s 26(2); Supreme Court Rules r 14(5)(h); Magistrates' Courts Rules r 40(3); *Press v Barker: Sliom v Wallachs Printing and Publishing Co Ltd* supra; *Standard Bank of SA Ltd v Pearson* supra: *Muller v Pienaar* supra 203; *Standard Bank of SA Ltd v Lombard* supra; *Strydom v Protea Eiendomsagente*

supra; *Boonzaier v Kiley* 1981 2 SA 618 (W) 619. See also the title CIVIL PROCEDURE.

40 SC Rules r 14; MC Rules r 54.

41 ibid.

42 *Rees v Feldman* 1927 TPD 884 889.

43 *Matterson Bros v Rolfes, Nebel & Co* supra; *Barrett and Glynn v Davidson* 1916 TPD 42; and see *Mennie v Lennard and Washington* 1916 WLD 8; Henning 1978 *THRHR* 8.

44 25 of 1963 s 2; see Henning 1978 *DR* 115, 1979 *MB* 45.

45 s 2(2)(c)(i).

46 Cf *Partridge v Harrison and Harrison* 1940 WLD 265 268; Henning 1978 *THRHR* 10, 1963 *Tydskrif vir Regswetenskap* 99 109.

47 *Kirsh Industries Ltd v Vosloo and Lindeque* 1982 3 SA 479 (W); *Spie Batignolles Société Anonyme v Van Niekerk: in re Van Niekerk v SA Yster en Staal Industriële Korp Bpk* 1980 2 SA 441 (NC).

48 *Noordkaap Lewende Koöp Bpk v Raath* 1977 2 SA 815 (NC) 818G.

49 *Standard Bank of SA Ltd v Pearson* supra 723C. It should, however, be noted that an action is not maintainable by a partnership in its own name against a partner, or vice versa. Such an action should be instituted by or against the other partners: *Norton's Trustees v Norden's Trustees* (1848) 3 M 330; *McLeod and Shearsmith v Shearsmith* 1938 TPD 87 92; *Shingadia Bros v Shingadia* supra 586. In this respect the rules of court should be modernized since they obviously lack sophistication when compared to the English Rules of the Supreme Court Order 81 of which r 6 provides: "(1) Execution to enforce a judgment or order given or made in —

(a) an action by or against a firm in the name of the firm against or by a member of the firm, or

(b) an action by a firm in the name of the firm against a firm in the name of the firm where those firms have one or more members in common,

shall not issue except with leave of court"; Lindley *Partnership* 982; cf *Silbert & Co v Evans & Co* supra 431 435.

50 *Strydom v Protea Eiendomsagente* supra 210. See also par 386 ante.

51 e g *Herman v Faclier* 1949 4 SA 377 (C), where it was held that though a partnership does not fall under the term "person" as defined in the Exchange Quota Regulations (GN 2385 of 1948), these regulations can apply without any difficulty to an existing partnership because it can be looked upon as a group of "persons". In *Helpmekaar (Thusano) Taxi Diens v Nasionale Vervoerkommissie* 1978 1 SA 250 (O) 255 it was held that a partnership being "an association of persons" could apply

for a motor carrier certificate under the Motor Carrier Transportation Act 39 of 1930. See also the Interpretation Act 33 of 1957 s 2 (definition of "person"). Under the Income Tax Act 58 of 1962 a partnership, unlike a company, is not regarded as a legal entity for purposes of assessment; see *Commissioner for Inland Revenue v Epstein* 1954 3 SA 689 (A) 699; *Sacks v Commissioner for Inland Revenue* 1946 AD 31 40; *ITC 1255* 39 SATC 27 29; Van Niekerk 1979 *MB* 3. Reg 34 of the Deeds Registries Act 47 of 1937 seems to imply that a partnership should be dealt with as a separate persona for registration purposes, and the Transfer Duty Act 40 of 1949 s 9(3) seems to regard partnerships as separate entities; see title DEEDS vol 7 par 142 ante.

52 See *Strydom v Protea Eiendomsagente* supra 210; and par 388 n 1 ante. An agreement by which the partners bind themselves individually to

a partnership creditor "as sureties" for partnership debts, is not invalid. There is no reason in principle why partners should not bind themselves to a partnership creditor in such a way that each partner is individually liable in solidum to the creditor for payment of the whole of the partnership debts, even during the subsistence of the partnership: "This ... was plainly the object sought to be achieved by means of the documents in question ... I can see no reason why the documents should not be valid and operative as such, even if it is to be assumed that they do not qualify as suretyships *stricto sensu*, a matter on which I need not express any firm opinion" per Botha J in *Standard Bank of SA Ltd v Lombard* supra 813H, confirmed on appeal in *Lombard v Standard Bank of SA Ltd* 1977 2 SA 806 (T). See also par 388 ante, especially n 1.

390 Conclusion Although the basic principle or general rule is that a partnership is not a legal persona,[1] the exceptions stated above[2] show that, in view of the practical convenience of dealing with a single entity[3] rather than an aggregate of individuals,[4] a partnership is treated for various purposes as an entity separate and distinct from the members composing it, albeit not as an entity endowed with all the normal attributes of legal personality or a body corporate.[5] Indeed it appears that a partnership "is so far analogous to a *persona* that it may be called a *quasi-persona*".[6]

1 See par 388 ante.
2 See par 389 ante.
3 See par 386 ante.
4 ibid.
5 *Potchefstroom Dairies and Industries Co Ltd v Standard Fresh Milk Supply Co* 1913 TPD 506 514; *Standard Bank of SA Ltd v Lombard* 1977

2 SA 808 (W) 813G; *Strydom v Protea Eiendomsagente* 1979 2 SA 206 (T) 209-210; and see par 388 n 1 ante.
6 *Potchefstroom Dairies and Industries Co Ltd v Standard Fresh Milk Supply Co* supra 514; *Silbert & Co v Evans & Co* 1912 TPD 425 441.

PARTNERSHIP PROPERTY AND SHARES IN PARTNERSHIP

PARTNERSHIP PROPERTY

391 General Common-law authorities on partnership law are silent on various important aspects concerning partnership property, e g the nature and extent of partnership property; its role *vis-à-vis* partnership creditors; ownership of partnership property, and the nature and extent of a partner's share in a partnership.[1] It would seem, however, as if partnership property did not have the same important function at common law as it has in a partnership formed under the present law. Legislation has given partnership property (or partnership funds or partnership assets as it is sometimes referred to)[2] a distinct role in a South African partnership, especially in so far as partnership creditors are concerned. In the first place, in terms of the rules of court[3] a partnership creditor who has obtained judgment against a partnership in the firm's name must first excuss the partnership assets before execution can be levied against the private estates of the individual partners. Secondly, in terms of the Insolvency Act[4] partnership property is for purposes of insolvency proceedings deemed to be a separate estate independent from the private estates of the partners in the firm. The effect of this legislation is that a partnership is, even before its sequestration is contemplated, for purposes of the Insolvency Act to be treated as having an estate separate and distinct from the personal estates of the partners,[5] and that the hypothesis must be adopted that those who deal with and grant credit to a partnership do so primarily in reliance on the partnership assets only.[6] It also follows that the individual partners in a firm have a vested interest in the partnership property in that their private estates are protected against attachment by partnership creditors to the extent that partnership assets are available to meet the creditors' claims.

The courts have not as yet had the opportunity to discuss all aspects concerning partnership assets in detail, or to fully examine all the implications of the abovementioned legislation. The result is that there are various important issues concerning partnership property which await clarification and development.

1 For an analysis of common-law authorities in this respect, see Beinart 1961 *Acta Juridica* 118; Delport 1979 *Obiter* 98.

2 The term "partnership property" appears inter alia in *SA Loan Mortgage and Mercantile Agency v Cape of Good Hope Bank and Littlejohn* (1888) 6 SC 163 and *Whiteaway's Estate v Commissioner for Inland Revenue* 1938 TPD 482. The term "partnership funds" was used inter alia in *McLeod and Shearsmith v Shearsmith* 1938 TPD 87; *Pataka v Keefe* 1947 2 SA 962 (A); *Oosthuizen v Swart* 1956 2 SA 687

(SWA); *Shingadia Bros v Shingadia* 1958 1 SA 582 (FC). The expression "partnership assets" appears inter alia in *Wegner v Surgeson* 1910 TPD 571; *Dickinson and Brown v Fisher's Executors* 1916 AD 374.

3 See the Magistrates' Courts Rules r 40(3); the Supreme Court Rules r 14(5)(h).

4 24 of 1936; see in particular ss 49(1) 92(5).

5 *Michalow v Premier Milling Co Ltd* 1960 2 SA 59 (W) 61C.

6 *Michalow v Premier Milling Co Ltd* supra 62G.

392 Description In a broad sense partnership assets include the capital held in the firm, together with all liabilities and outstanding credits, as in all business ventures.[1] More specifically, particularly in so far as the partners themselves are concerned, partnership assets can be described as all those assets which the partners intend to be partnership property. Regarding the partners inter se, the exact scope and extent of partnership property therefore rests on the intention of the partners in the firm, regardless of the question whether the property is jointly owned by the partners or not.[2] Whether property which is as between the partners looked upon as partnership property, but which is not jointly owned by them, is also partnership property *vis-à-vis* partnership creditors, is uncertain.[3] It has been held that immovable property registered in the name of one partner, but viewed by the partners inter se as being partnership property, does not form part of the partnership assets in so far as the rights of partnership creditors in terms of the Insolvency Act[4] are concerned.[5]

As a general rule, in absence of a contrary intention on the part of the partners, the property originally contributed by the partners to the firm is part of the partnership's assets.[6] Similarly, property acquired with partnership funds during the firm's existence belongs to the firm unless a contrary intention appears.[7] Profits made by the partners, together with all loans obtained by the partners for partnership purposes (whether from one of the partners or an outsider), belong to the partnership and form part of its assets.[8] The goodwill of a partnership is part of its assets unless there is an agreement to the contrary.[9] Generally speaking, all property used in the firm will be deemed to be partnership property if it is necessary for the proper functioning of the firm's business that the property should be a partnership asset.[10]

In order to determine the true intention of the partners concerning the question whether a particular asset is a partnership asset or not, reference must be made to the partnership agreement and all other surrounding circumstances.[11]

1 Beinart 1961 *Acta Juridica* 118.

2 *Ex parte Steyn* 1902 TH 184; *Whiteaway's Estate v Commissioner for Inland Revenue* 1928 TPD 482; *Fink v Fink* 1945 WLD 226; *For-*

tune v Versluis 1962 1 SA 343 (A) 357; *Muller v Pienaar* 1970 2 SA 385 (C) 390.

3 Delport 1979 *Obiter* 98 111; Beinart 144. Cf Burgess and Morse *Partnership Law and Prac-*

tice 154 especially n 5 in regard to English law.

4 24 of 1936 s 29.

5 *Michalow v Premier Milling Co Ltd* 1960 2 SA 59 (W). Furthermore, it was held in this case that even a debt due by a partner to a partnership, or a partnership claim against a partner, is not a partnership asset *vis-à-vis* partnership creditors for purposes of the Insolvency Act 24 of 1936 s 29. See also *Anstruther v Trustees in the Estates of E L Chiappini and A Chiappini & Co* (1858) 3 S 91.

6 *Fortune v Versluis* supra. Where merely the use of property is contributed, the property itself is not a partnership asset: ibid; see also *Gau v McDonald* (1874) 4 Buch 22; *SA Loan Mortgage and Mercantile Agency v Cape of Good Hope Bank and Littlejohn* (1888) 6 SC 163; *Whiteaway's Estate v Commissioner for Inland Revenue* supra. Where, however, the use of property is contributed, and the value of the property should increase as a result of the use of partnership funds, the increased value as such is a partnership asset, unless a contrary intention appears: *Fortune v Versluis* 359; *Fink v Fink* supra 244. Where services are contributed, the gains which are acquired by application of the services become partnership

property: Pothier *Partnership* 7 2 120.

7 *Fink v Fink* supra 242. Where one partner unlawfully uses partnership assets, any gain which he might obtain as a result of it would also become a partnership asset, provided that the profit-making transaction falls within the scope of the partnership objects: *Mattson v Yiannakis* 1976 4 SA 154 (W) 159D; and cf Voet *Commentarius* 17 2 5. The fact that the licence money for a business is paid out of the partnership funds does not necessarily mean that the licence, which is granted to a particular person on account of his character, becomes partnership property: *Wegner v Surgeson* 1910 TPD 571 581.

8 *Schlemmer v Viljoen* 1958 2 SA 280 (T) 287.

9 *Sherry v Stewart* 1903 TH 13 15; *Ellery v Imhof* 1904 TH 170 174; *Simon v Cramb* 1926 TPD 37 41; *Avis v Verseput* 1943 AD 331 371; *O'Kennedy v Smit* 1948 2 SA 63 (C) 65; *Robson v Theron* 1978 1 SA 841 (A) 855. The name of a partnership can be part of a partnership's assets: *Meilandt v Bell & Guyon* 1907 TH 122.

10 *Fortune v Versluis* supra 357H.

11 *Fortune v Versluis* supra 357 H; see also *Muller v Pienaar* supra 390B.

393 Distinction between partnership property and capital The capital of a partnership consists of the contributions which the partners have made for the purpose of commencement of the partnership or the carrying on of its business, and which they risk in the business.[1] Partnership capital is part of the partnership property in so far as the capital is still in existence.[2] The capital is therefore merely a portion of the partnership assets.[3]

The distinction between partnership property and a partner's capital in the firm is of particular importance when a partnership dissolves. It has been held that, in the absence of a contrary agreement, a partner's capital is to be repaid to him upon dissolution of the firm: each partner receives what he has risked in the business should there be a surplus of assets.[4] The repayment of capital therefore precedes a general division of surplus partnership assets amongst all the partners.[5]

1 Lindley *Partnership* 442.

2 *Schlemmer v Viljoen* 1958 2 SA 280 (T) 287E.

3 See Burgess and Morse *Partnership Law and Practice* 57; Lindley 442.

4 *McLeod and Shearsmith v Shearsmith* 1938 TPD 87; *Ferreira v Fouche* 1949 1 SA 67 (T) 70; *Schlemmer v Viljoen* supra 287G; *Olivier v Stoop* 1978 1 SA 196 (T) 203H; see also *Commissioner for Inland Revenue v Estate Whiteaway*

1933 TPD 486; *Whiteaway's Estate v Commissioner for Inland Revenue* 1938 TPD 482 which were decided with reference to English law.

5 See par 430 post. This was not the position at common law; see Beinart 1961 *Acta Juridica* 118. On the contribution of a partner's labour to the capital of the partnership, see *Macleod v Gron* 1940 SR 201.

394 Ownership in partnership property It is clear that since a partnership is not a legal persona, a partnership as such cannot own the partnership property as a separate entity.[1] As a general rule partnership assets are held by the partners as co-owners, that is, the partners jointly own the partnership property in undivided shares.[2]

The establishment of a partnership fund which is to be jointly owned by the partners is not one of the essentialia for constituting a partnership.[3] As such, the partnership assets need not always be jointly owned by the partners. It is therefore quite possible that a particular asset can be treated by the partners inter se as a partnership asset although, from a property law point of view, the asset is owned by one partner only.[4] It would seem, however, that the establishment of a jointly owned partnership fund is a naturale of every partnership agreement with the result that, in the absence of a contrary agreement, each partner is under an obligation to share a particular partnership asset in co-ownership with his partners.[5] It has not yet authoritatively been decided what the effect of such joint ownership would be, both in so far as third parties and the partners inter se are concerned.[6]

Before realization and distribution of the partnership assets amongst the partners, a partner is not entitled to treat any particular partnership asset as being his own, nor is any partner entitled to any specific portion of the partnership assets as a whole.[7] Regardless of the question who the owner of the partnership assets is, every partner is contractually bound towards his co-partners not to appropriate partnership assets for his own purposes or to regard it as part of his private assets.[8]

1 *Michalow v Premier Milling Co Ltd* 1960 2 SA 59 (W) 61D.
2 *Sacks v Commissioner for Inland Revenue* 1946 AD 31 40; *Muller v Pienaar* 1968 3 SA 195 (A) 202; *Robson v Theron* 1978 1 SA 841 (A) 856H.
3 See the discussion in par 371 ante; see also Smits *De Externe Gebondenheid van het Vennootschapsvermogen* 2; Delport 1979 *Obiter* 98.
4 See *Ex parte Steyn* 1902 TH 184; *Whiteaway's Estate v Commissioner for Inland Revenue* 1938 TPD 482; *Fink v Fink* 1945 WLD 226; *Fortune v Versluis* 1962 1 SA 343 (A) 357; *Anstruther v Trustees in the Estates of E L Chiappini and A Chiappini & Co* (1858) 3 S 91.
5 Delport 98; *Sacks v Commissioner for Inland Revenue* supra; see also *Anstruther v Trustees in the Estates of E L Chiappini and A Chiappini & Co* supra; *Oosthuizen v Swart* 1956 2 SA 687

(SWA) 690H.
6 It has been suggested that jointly owned partnership assets form a separate fund within a partnership, which can only be excussed by partnership creditors; and that the partners are "bound" by their joint ownership in the sense that they cannot dispose of their individual undivided shares in the common property: Smits 17 183 198; see too Asser-Kamphuisen *Verbintenissenrecht* III (part 3) 479; Delport 98. What seems to be clear is that jointly owned partnership assets can be excussed by partnership creditors and that such assets form part of the partnership estate for purposes of insolvency; see *Michalow v Premier Milling Co Ltd* supra.
7 *Sacks v Commissioner for Inland Revenue* supra.
8 See par 396 post.

395 Formation of partnership property As stated above, a particular asset becomes partnership property if the partners intend it to be part of the partnership's funds. A mere agreement amongst the partners is therefore sufficient for the creation of the partnership fund.[1] In order to establish a jointly owned partnership fund, the individual items which constitute the fund must be made the common property of all the partners. Corporeal movables initially contributed to the partnership must be delivered[2] to the partnership, whilst immovable property must be transferred to the firm.[3] Incorporeal property, such as rights, must be ceded to the partnership.[4]

Movable property acquired by a partner during the course of the partnership's business becomes the joint property of the partners ipso iure, provided that the partner acted as the partnership's agent in this respect.[5] Where a partner acquires any partnership property in his own name during the existence of the partnership, such property only becomes the joint property of the partners upon its delivery, transfer or cession (as is required) to the partnership.[6]

1 See par 392 ante.
2 Physical delivery to the partnership is not required; it is sufficient if a partner holds the particular item on behalf of the partnership: Voet *Commentarius* 17 2 6; *Berman v Brest* 1934 WLD 135 138; *Oosthuizen v Swart* 1956 2 SA 687 (SWA) 692H; *Crause v Ocean Bentonite Co (Edms) Bpk* 1979 1 SA 1076 (O) 1081.
3 *Berman v Brest* supra; *Crause v Ocean Bentonite Co (Edms) Bpk* supra.
4 Voet 17 2 6; *Berman v Brest* supra; *Oosthuizen v Swart* supra.
5 Van der Keessel *Prael* 3 21 7. Van der Keessel 3 21 7 adds that the property must be entered

into the partnership's accounts. It would seem, however, as if this is not a condition precedent for the acquired asset to become joint partnership property, but that such entry is merely evidence of the fact that the assets have been acquired for the partnership; see too Voet 17 2 6. Voet 17 2 6 furthermore suggests that incorporeal property acquired by a partner during the course of the partnership must always be ceded to a partnership before it becomes common partnership property.
6 Voet 17 2 6; *Berman v Brest* supra 139.

SHARES IN PARTNERSHIP

396 General A partner's share in a firm has a dual nature. In the first place, a partner's share comprises his proportionate interest in the partnership property after it has been realized and converted into money and all partnership creditors have been paid.[1] In this context a partner's share denotes a partner's right to claim a specific portion of the partnership assets (such as profits) when this portion is due.[2] In the second place a partner's share in a firm merely denotes his pro rata interest in the particular items of partnership assets, apart from any realization of the property as such.[3] In this context a partner's share comprises his interest in jointly owned partnership property (i e his undivided share in these assets), together with his interest in all other partnership property, including profits.

As stated above, a partner is not entitled to look upon any partnership assets as his own until the assets have been realized and the extent of his share of it determined.[4] In the absence of a contrary agreement or business practice such realization takes place at the termination of the partnership.[5] It thus follows that, as a general rule, a partner's share in the firm only becomes individualized and payable upon dissolution of the partnership.[6] In partnerships of a continuous nature it is common practice, however, for the partners to agree on a division of profits made over a period of time, usually (but not necessarily) at the end of an accounting year.[7]

It is to be noted that while the partnership property is in existence and before any realization of it, a partner's interest in the partnership assets is in itself an asset. This asset forms part of a partner's private estate, and as such it can be attached and sold in execution to satisfy the claims of a partner's private creditors.[8]

The position regarding transfer of shares is dealt with below.[9]

1 Lindley *Partnership* (13th ed) 367.
2 *Sacks v Commissioner for Inland Revenue* 1946 AD 31 40.
3 Lindley 367 and cf *Grassis and Shrewe v Lewis* 1910 TPD 533; *Liquidators of the Durban Roodepoort Mynpacht Syndicate v Blankfield* 1922 TPD 173 176.
4 See par 394 ante.
5 Noodt *Opera Omnia ad D* 17 2 65 15 (Pro So-

cio); *Fisher's Executors v Dickinson and Brown* (1914) 35 NLR 505 512.
6 *Sacks v Commissioner for Inland Revenue* supra.
7 *Sacks v Commissioner for Inland Revenue* supra. A tacit agreement to this effect can be inferred from the dealings between the partners in the past: ibid.
8 See par 413 post.
9 See pars 396 404 post.

397 Extent of partner's share There is a dearth of authority regarding the question as to what the extent of a partner's share in a partnership is before its dissolution and general realization of its property.[1] It has been held (regarding English law) that in the absence of a contrary agreement the ultimate division of the surplus assets upon a dissolution of the firm fixes the proportion of the partners' interests in the partnership whilst it is in existence.[2] A partner's share in profits which are distributable before a dissolution of the firm is determined with reference to the principles regarding the sharing of profits.[3]

The principles regarding the distribution of partnership assets upon a dissolution of the firm, and the extent of a partner's share in any surplus assets, are dealt with below.[4]

1 Cf *Whiteaway's Estate v Commissioner for Inland Revenue* 1938 TPD 482 490, where it was stated that "[t]he dearth of authority is perhaps not surprising since during the subsistence of the partnership the partnership property is dedicated to partnership needs and on dissolution the partners only divide among themselves the balance, if any, after settlement of debts, repayment of capital, etc". See too *Liquidators of the Durban Roodepoort Mynpacht Syndicate v Blankfield* 1922 TPD 173 176, where it was said that "[i]t is difficult to ascertain what a partner's interest is in any particular chattel belonging to the partnership, because that can only be ascertained after we know what the assets and liabilities of the partnership are and how the account stands between the particular partner and the other partners".

2 *Whiteway's Estate v Commissioner for Inland Revenue* supra 490.

3 See par 407 post.

4 See pars 429–431 post.

RELATIONSHIP BETWEEN PARTNERS

RIGHTS AND DUTIES OF PARTNERS

398 General The relationship between partners is primarily determined with reference to their partnership agreement. In the absence of contrary stipulations in the agreement, the partners' respective rights and duties are in addition determined by common-law principles in this respect. Since a partnership is not a legal persona, these rights and duties do not exist *vis-à-vis* the partnership, but only *vis-à-vis* the co-partners in the firm.[1]

1 *Jacobson v Norton* (1841) 2 M 218; *Sempff v Neubauer* 1903 TH 202; *Van Gend & Son's and Van Gend Bros' Trustee v G A G van Gend and H J van Gend* 1913 EDL 114 115; *Kaplan v Turner* 1941 SWA 29; *Ferreira v Fouche* 1949 1 SA 67 (T); *McLeod and Shearsmith v Shearsmith* 1938 TPD 87 92; *Oosthuizen v Swart* 1956 2 SA 687 (SWA).

399 Duty to commence and carry on business Upon the conclusion of a partnership agreement, the partners are under an obligation to carry out the terms of the agreement. A failure to commence with business in the manner and at the time agreed upon constitutes breach of contract.[1] A court will not, however, force a partner to commence with business and to act as a conscientious partner if the partner in question is unwilling to do so.[2] Damages may, however, be claimed from the latter, and in calculating the damages the court may take into account the estimated profits which the firm would have made had the agreement been properly performed.[3]

The duty to commence and carry on business also entails that each partner must make available to the partnership his contribution, as agreed upon.[4] Where the respective contributions are to be held in joint ownership, a partner is obliged to perform the necessary acts by which such joint ownership is established.[5] If services are contributed, the gains derived from those services must be accounted for.[6] A partner is also liable to bring in any fruits of the property which he has agreed to contribute.[7] Should money be contributed, a partner is liable for interest on it from the day that he is in mora.[8]

A partnership carries the risk for the accidental destruction of specific property which a partner has agreed to contribute, provided that the latter is not in mora.[9]

A partner who contributes property to a firm, gives the firm an implied warranty against eviction.[10]

1 *Lampakis v Dimitri* 1937 TPD 138.
2 See par 403 post.
3 *Lampakis v Dimitri* supra.
4 Pothier *Partnership* 7 1 110.
5 *Oosthuizen v Swart* 1956 2 SA 687 (SWA). See par 394 ante.
6 Pothier 7 1 120.
7 Pothier 7 1 115.
8 Pothier 7 1 116.

9 Pothier 110. Even where a partner is in mora in respect of his contribution, the accidental destruction of the contribution will be the firm's loss if it is clear that the property would in any event have been destroyed if it was in the firm's possession: Pothier 111.
10 Pothier 7 1 113; see also Beinart 1961 *Acta Juridica* 118 147.

400 Duty to observe good faith A partnership is a contract uberrimae fidei.[1] This means that the relationship between partners is the same as that between brothers,[2] namely one of mutual trust and confidence.[3] Where this mutual trust is destroyed, the court can order a firm's dissolution.[4]

The duty to observe good faith is not confined to partners in an existing partnership. It extends to persons negotiating for the establishment of a partnership, as well as to the parties in a partnership which has been dissolved but not finally wound up.[5]

The fiduciary duties of a partner embrace, firstly, the due acceptance and fulfilment of partnership obligations; secondly, the duty not to compete with the firm; thirdly, the duty to guard against a conflict of interest; and, fourthly, the duty of full disclosure.

(a) *Due acceptance and fulfilment of partnership obligations*

As part of the requirement of good faith every partner must accept and fulfil all the obligations imposed by the partnership agreement.[6] This connotes, inter alia, that a partner wishing to invoke against his co-partner the stringent provisions of a summary cancellation and forfeiture clause contained in the partnership agreement, must at least himself be honouring the terms of that agreement.[7] Similarly, a partner cannot complain if his other partners fail to do their duty towards him, unless he is at all times ready to do his duty towards them.[8]

(b) *Duty not to compete with the firm*

The general principle underlying this fiduciary duty is that a partner may not acquire and retain for himself any benefit or advantage which falls within the scope of the partnership business, and which it is his duty to acquire for the partnership.[9] Thus, a partner may not compete with his firm by carrying on a business of the same nature as and in rivalry with that of the partnership,[10] or by renewing a partnership lease for his own benefit during the currency of the partnership, even though the lease is only to come into operation upon termination of the partnership.[11] All benefits obtained in conflict of this duty must be shared with and accounted for to the partnership.[12] A partner cannot dissolve a partnership with the intention of overreaching his co-partners, and retain the benefits which flow from this act.[13]

It is essentially a question of fact whether a particular benefit or advantage which a partner has obtained, falls within the scope of the partnership's business. The crucial question is to determine the ambit of the partnership object,[14] since a partner is not obliged to account to the partnership for any gains which he obtains from a venture completely unconnected with the partnership's business, even if the partnership was the accidental cause of the obtainment of the benefit.[15]

(c) *Duty to guard against a conflict of interest*

A partner may not place himself in a position where his private interests may conflict with his duty towards the partnership.[16] Thus, where a third party is a debtor of a partnership as well as a debtor of a partner in his private capacity, the latter cannot obtain payment of his own debt in preference to that of the partnership: should the third party pay his debt to the partner but fail to do so to the partnership, the partner must appropriate what he receives to the credit of the partnership and himself pro rata to the amount of the respective debts.[17] Likewise, if a partner has the opportunity to sell partnership assets at a profit, he cannot instead sell his own share in the partnership for a private profit: if he does so, he must account to the partnership for what he has received in excess of what the other partners have sold their shares for.[18]

It follows from a partner's duty to avoid a conflict of interest with his partnership, that a partner cannot acquire property intimately connected with the business of the partnership, even if it may not fall directly within the scope of the firm's business, if the acquisition of such property would be detrimental to the interests of the partnership.[19]

A partner may not use information which he has obtained as a partner for his own benefit, if such action would conflict with the partnership's interests.[20]

(d) *Duty of full disclosure*

Apart from a partner's duty to render accurate accounts concerning all partnership affairs under his control,[21] a partner is also obliged to disclose to his co-partners all information affecting the partnership. Thus, if there is any prospect of profit to the partnership by the best exertions of a partner in a particular venture, the prospects should be brought to the notice of the other partners, and they should be put in a position to consider what attitude they will take up with reference to such venture.[22] Conversely, a partner may not conceal facts from his co-partners if knowledge of those facts may have an influence on the latters' decision regarding their partnership.[23]

1 *Wagner v Surgeson* 1910 TPD 571 579; *Truter v Hancke* 1923 CPD 43 49; *Purdon v Muller* 1961 2 SA 211 (A) 231E.

2 *Wegner v Surgeson* supra, quoting with approval the principle contained in *D* 17 2 63: "societas ius quodammodo fraternitatis in se habeat".

3 *Parr v Crosbie* (1886) 5 EDC 197; *De Jager v Olifants Tin "B" Syndicate* 1912 AD 505 509.

4 *Doucet v Piaggio* 1905 TH 267; *Fortune v Versluis* 1962 1 SA 343 (A) 348.

5 *Sempff v Neubauer* 1903 TH 202 216.

6 *Purdon v Muller* supra 231B.

7 *Purdon v Muller* supra 230G.

8 *Purdon v Muller* supra 231D-E.

9 *Parr v Crosbie* supra; *Ford v Abercrombie* 1904 TS 878; *Tvl Cold Storage Co Ltd v Palmer* 1904 TS 4 33; *De Jager v Olifants Tin "B" Syndicate* supra; *Mattson v Yiannakis* 1976 4 SA 154 (W). In *Mattson's* case the court referred to the question whether this principle refers to two separate inquiries or only one. Although the court left the question open, it came out openly in favour of the first mentioned viewpoint.

10 *Parr v Crosbie* supra; *Love v Hobson* 1913 EDL 400.

11 *Wegner v Surgeson* supra; *Olifants Tin "B" Syndicate v De Jager* 1912 TPD 305 320.

12 *De Jager v Olifants Tin "B" Syndicate* supra.

13 *Wegner v Surgeson* supra.

14 Cf *Mattson v Yiannakis* supra.

15 Pothier *Partnership* 7 2 120 123; *Tvl Cold Storage Co Ltd v Palmer* supra 36. See too *Goldberg v Trimble and Bennett* 1905 TS 255; *Trimble and Bennett v Goldberg* 1906 TS 1002.

16 *Tvl Cold Storage Co Ltd v Palmer* supra.

17 Pothier 7 2 121.

18 Pothier 7 2 122.

19 *Goldberg v Trimble and Bennett* supra 267-268. This decision was reversed on appeal as to the facts, but not as to the law; see *Trimble and Bennett v Goldberg* supra and cf *Bellairs v Hodnett* 1978 1 SA 1109 (A) 1127 1132G.

20 ibid.
21 See par 405 post.

22 *Nash v Muirhead* (1909) 26 SC 26 33.
23 *Doucet v Piaggio* supra 275.

401 Compensation, refunds and indemnities Under ordinary circumstances, and in the absence of any express or implied agreement to that effect, a partner is not entitled to claim remuneration for services rendered by him to the partnership.[1] There is nothing, however, preventing partners from agreeing that one of them is to receive a salary in consideration of his taking a larger or more skilled share in the management of the partnership affairs. In the absence of such an agreement each partner is expected to perform all the duties contemplated by the contract without any fee or reward.[2] If, however, a partner has performed special work beyond that performed by the others, and which was not contemplated as part of his duties under the contract, he will be entitled to claim remuneration for his services.[3] Such remuneration must be paid to a partner after payment of partnership creditors, and before a division of the net profits.[4]

A partner is not entitled to any interest on his capital contributions to the partnership, unless payment of interest has been agreed upon.[5] He is also not entitled to any rental for the use of property contributed to the firm, unless such rental has been agreed upon.[6] Where the partners have agreed on the payment of interest, the partners are not entitled to interest on such interest, unless there are special circumstances present, such as where the accrued interest is also left in the firm as capital.[7]

A partner is entitled to be refunded for expenses which he has incurred in connection with partnership affairs over and above his own share. A partner who pays a partnership creditor out of his own pocket, or who spends his own money on the maintenance of partnership property, is therefore entitled to a refund from the partnership.[8] A partner is similarly entitled to be indemnified for losses which he personally sustained whilst carrying on the business of the partnership, provided that it can be said that the risk of such losses are directly and inseparably tied up with carrying on the partnership affairs.[9] Interest on these items can also be claimed.[10]

1 Voet *Commentarius* 17 2 19; Van der Keessel *Prael* 3 21 7; *Parr v Crosbie* (1886) 5 EDC 197; *Liquidators of Grand Hotel and Theatre Co v Haarburger, Fichardt and Daniels* 1907 ORC 25; *Bell v Estate Douglas* 1909 CTR 810.
2 ibid. According to Voet 17 2 19 the partners' share in the profits to which each is entitled, is reward enough for their services. See further Pothier *Partnership* 3 4 75.
3 Voet 17 2 19; *Liquidators of Grand Hotel and Theatre Co v Haarburger, Fichardt and Daniels* supra. See too *Britannia Gold Mining Co v Yockmonitz* (1890) 7 SC 218 226, where it was held that a partner does not breach his fiduciary duty towards the partnership by receiving an honorarium for special services from his co-partners.
4 *Jameson v Irvin's Executors* (1887) 5 SC 222 251.
5 *Jameson v Irvin's Executors* supra 251; and see too Pothier 4 1 76.
6 *Jameson v Irvin's Executors* supra 251.
7 *Collier v May* (1908) 29 NLR 285 287.
8 Voet 17 2 13; De Groot *Inleiding* 3 21 7; Van der Keessel 3 21 7; Pothier 7 3 127–131; *Pataka v Keefe* 1947 2 SA 962 (A). In *Schneider*

v Raikin 1954 4 SA 449 (W) 451 it was stated that "[i]t is not clear whether *Voet*, [17 2 13] . . . is laying down a general principle that the expenses incurred by a partner over and above his own share should be refunded to him, or whether the right to a refund is to be confined to the two types of cases expressly mentioned by *Voet*, viz where the expenses are incurred to preserve property of the partnership, or where a partner has been compelled by a creditor to pay on behalf of the partnership more than his share of the joint debt". It would appear, however, as if common-law authorities did recognize a general right to a refund for all expenses incurred by a partner in partnership affairs: Delport *Gedingvoering tussen Vennote* 58–61 196–197.
9 Voet 17 2 5; Pothier 7 3 127–131. A partner cannot therefore claim damages from the partnership on the grounds that he suffered loss in his private affairs as a result of the fact that he had to give all his attention to the affairs of the partnership: Pothier 131.
10 Voet 17 2 13.

402 Sharing of profits and losses Every partner is entitled to a share in the net partnership profits.[1] Partners are free to determine the amount of each partner's share in the partnership agreement.[2] As long as it is clear that each partner receives a share of the profits, it does not matter if the formula which is used for the determination of the respective shares is complex or unusual.[3] In the absence of an agreement in this respect, profits are shared in proportion to the partners' respective contributions to the firm.[4] Where the value of the individual contributions cannot be ascertained, or where the contributions are equal in value, the profits are shared equally.[5]

Unless the partners have agreed otherwise, each partner is obliged to share in the net losses of the firm. In the absence of any contrary agreement in this respect, the general rule is that the net losses must be shared in the same proportion as the profits.[6]

Partners may refer the determination of their respective shares in the profits to a third party or even to a particular partner.[7]

1 See generally par 396 ante.
2 De Groot *Inleiding* 3 21 5; Voet *Commentarius* 17 2 8; Pothier *Partnership* 3 1 73.
3 Cf *Dickinson and Brown v Fisher's Executors* 1916 AD 374, where a partner's share in the profits was fixed on the basis of a certain percentage on his capital contribution to the firm.
4 See the authorities cited in n 2 supra, together with Pothier 1 4 15; Van der Linden *Koopmans Handboek* 4 1 11; Van der Keessel *Dictata* 3 26 9; *Fink v Fink* 1945 WLD 226.

5 Pothier 3 1 73; Van der Keessel *Prael* 3 21 7; *Shearer v Shimwell* 1910 AD 157; *Fink v Fink* supra; *Herman v Faclier* 1949 4 SA 377 (C) 398; *V (also known as L) v De Wet* 1953 1 SA 612 (O) 616. For the application of this principle to universal partnerships, see *Isaacs v Isaacs* 1949 1 SA 952 (C) 961.
6 De Groot 3 21 5; Voet 17 2 8; *Jameson v Irvin's Executors* (1887) 5 SC 222 237; *Purdon v Muller* 1960 2 SA 785 (E) 796.
7 Pothier 3 1 74.

403 Management of partnership

(a) *General*

Subject to the terms of the partnership agreement, the general rule is that every partner has a right to share in the management of the partnership,[1] and to perform management functions without the consent or co-operation of his fellow partners.[2] This means that every partner has the implied authority ("mutual mandate") to conclude transactions falling within the scope of the partnership's business and that he can bind his co-partners in this respect.[3] Unless the partners have agreed otherwise, partners stand on an equal footing regarding their say in management affairs, irrespective of their actual share in the partnership itself.[4]

It has not been authoritatively decided what the position is, should a dispute arise concerning the management of the partnership, and, in particular, whether the minority must submit to the majority.[5] It is clear, however, that a majority of partners cannot change the object of a partnership's business: this decision can only be taken unanimously, unless the power to change the partnership object is granted by mutual consent to a majority.[6] A resolution by the majority of partners is (apparently) required for the alienation of partnership assets other than the normal merchandise of the business.[7]

(b) *Contractual arrangement of management powers*

A partner's right to participate independently in the management of the partnership's affairs is a naturale of partnership and can be contractually excluded, limited or varied.

It is therefore competent for partners, for example, to entrust all or some management duties to one partner alone or even to an outsider.[8] It is also competent to agree on a sharing of specific management duties amongst the partners, in which case a partner can perform only management functions in respect of that part of the business entrusted to him.[9] Partners can also agree that all or some management rights are to be exercised jointly.[10]

Where management functions are entrusted to a sole partner, a distinction must be drawn between the case where the managing partner is appointed in terms of the original partnership agreement, and the case where his appointment is made only after conclusion of the original contract. In the latter case the managing partner is a mere mandatary of his co-partners and, unless otherwise agreed, he cannot take management decisions contrary to the wishes of the partners.[11] His mandate is as a general rule always revocable, unless he was permanently appointed as manager.[12] In the former case, the managing partner cannot be deprived of his management rights if his consent to become a partner was subject to the condition that he be appointed the managing partner.[13] In such a case the managing partner may take management decisions even contrary to the wishes of the other partners, provided that he does so in good faith.[14] The scope of his managerial powers depends, however, on the terms of his appointment.[15] In the absence of specific limitations placed upon his powers in this respect, the managing partner has the right to perform all acts which are necessary for the affairs of the partnership.[16] He may not, however, alienate the permanent assets of the partnership[17] or donate any particular partnership assets.[18]

(c) *Managerial rights regarding partnership property*
This aspect is dealt with below.[19]

(d) *Exercise of care in management affairs*
A partner is obliged to display reasonable care in managing partnership affairs. He can be held liable for damages if, due to his negligence, the partnership property is damaged or the partnership business is otherwise negatively affected.[20] In determining whether a partner acted negligently or not, account must be taken of the manner in which the partner manages his own affairs.[21] Partners cannot complain, however, merely because one partner fails to display the managerial skills which all the others do.[22]

A partner cannot set off losses he caused to the partnership against profits which he otherwise made for the partnership.[23]

1 Pothier *Partnership* 3 2 72.
2 Pothier 5 1 90.
3 Pothier 5 1 90. See par 371 ante regarding the question whether this mutual mandate is an essentiale of the partnership contract.
4 Huber *HR* 1 11 29.
5 Huber 1 11 29 contends that in partnership there is no principle that a minority must follow the wishes of the majority. He submits that every partner has the right to veto decisions of his co-partners, even if they are in the majority. Where a veto had been exercised an aggrieved partner can get leave from the court to act, provided that such action would be in the interest of the partnership and not to the opposing partners' detriment: Huber 1 11 29. Pothier 5 1 90 supports the veto right concept, but (apparently) only finds it applicable in a case where the partners are equally divided on a particular management question. See too *Lockhart v De Beer's Mining Co* (1886) 4 HCG 85 97,

where the court favoured the "ordinary rule as to the powers of the majority" in settling disputes regarding the use of partnership assets where the precise purpose for which the assets could be used, was left undefined by the partners. Cf further Voet *Commentarius* 17 2 18.
6 *Lockhart v De Beer's Mining Co* supra 96.
7 See par 367 ante.
8 Pothier 3 1 66; Voet 17 2 13; *De Villiers v Smith* 1930 CPD 219 222; *Forder, Ritch and Eriksson v Engar's Heirs* 1973 1 SA 719 (N).
9 Pothier 3 1 72.
10 Pothier 3 1 72.
11 Pothier 3 1 71.
12 Pothier 3 1 71.
13 Pothier 3 1 71.
14 Pothier 3 1 71.
15 Pothier 3 1 66; *Forder, Ritch and Eriksson v Engar's Heirs* supra.
16 Pothier 3 1 66.
17 Pothier 3 1 67.

18 Pothier 3 1 69.

19 See par 404 post.

20 Pothier 7 3 124; Voet 7 2 12; De Groot *Inleiding* 3 21 7; *Cohen v Berman* (1897) 4 OR

356; *Pataka v Keefe* 1947 2 SA 962 (A) 968.

21 Pothier 7 3 124; Voet 7 2 12.

22 Pothier 7 3 124.

23 Pothier 7 3 125.

404 Rights and duties regarding partnership property and capital

(a) *General*

Subject to the terms of the partnership agreement, each partner is entitled to enjoy the benefit of the partnership property,[1] together with free and undisturbed access to it.[2] Conversely, in the absence of a contrary agreement, one partner cannot claim exclusive possession[3] or control[4] of any particular partnership asset. Where, however, the partnership agreement provides for exclusive possession of partnership property by one partner, a co-partner commits spoliation if he should deprive that partner of possession of the property.[5]

Partners are entitled to use partnership property for partnership purposes,[6] subject to specific directions regarding its application in the partnership agreement.[7] In so applying the partnership property, the interest of the partnership as a whole must be considered, and not the interest of an individual partner.[8] A partner may therefore not use partnership property for private purposes if this would conflict with the carrying on of the partnership business.[9] Where no such conflict can arise, it seems that a partner may on occasion make limited use of partnership property for private purposes.[10] A partner who allocates partnership property for his private use must account to the partnership in respect of such use. Where partnership money is used by a partner in his private affairs, the money, together with interest, must be repaid to the firm.[11]

Where the precise purpose for which the partnership assets may be used is not outlined in terms of the partnership agreement, a majority decision is binding on all partners regarding the question whether the assets may be employed for a particular partnership venture or not.[12]

The right to use the partnership assets for partnership purposes does not include the right to alienate or encumber assets other than the partnership's merchandise,[13] unless the authority to do so is expressly or impliedly embodied in the partnership agreement, or unless a decision in its favour is taken.[14]

The risk of loss or destruction of partnership property through casus fortuitus or vis maior falls on the partnership.[15] Where the use of certain property only is contributed to the firm, the risk remains with the contributing partner.[16]

All the partners are obliged to maintain the partnership property and are liable for expenses incurred in respect of maintenance work according to their shares in the partnership.[17] A partner is, however, not entitled to make structural alterations in respect of the partnership property without all the partners' consent.[18]

A partner is not entitled to look upon any particular partnership asset as his own before a general distribution of it has taken place amongst the partners,[19] nor may he claim his proportionate interest in any item of partnership property (such as profits) whilst the partnership is in existence, unless the partnership agreement expressly or impliedly provides for a division of assets at particular points in time during the subsistence of the firm.[20] The same holds true in respect of a partner's capital in the firm: unless otherwise provided in the partnership agreement, a partner is obliged to keep his capital in the firm until the firm is dissolved.[21]

A partner cannot be compelled to increase his contribution to the firm's property over and above the extent he has initially agreed to.[22]

(b) *Transactions in respect of a partner's own share*

A partner is entitled to alienate and encumber his pro rata share in the partnership.[23] He may therefore without the consent of his co-partners take a third party as a partner in his own share in the partnership, although he cannot make him a partner in the firm without the consent of all the partners and the third party.[24]

As a partner's share in a partnership encompasses the right to claim a proportionate part of the partnership property when it is due,[25] the transfer of his share to a third party has the effect that the third party can only claim that proportionate part when it falls due.[26]

1 Cf *Wegner v Surgeson* 1910 TPD 571.
2 *De Abreu v Silva* 1964 2 SA 416 (T).
3 *De Abreu v Silva* supra.
4 *Munro v Ekerold* 1949 1 SA 584 (SWA).
5 *Shapiro v Roth* 1911 WLD 43; *De Abreu v Silva* supra.
6 Voet *Commentarius* 17 2 18.
7 Pothier *Partnership* 5 1 84.
8 Voet 17 2 18. Partners must allow one another the use of the partnership assets according to the spirit of the fraternity which exists between them: Pothier 7 3 133.
9 Voet 17 2 18; Pothier 5 1 84; Van der Linden *Koopmans Handboek* 4 1 13; *Laughton v Griffin* (1893) 14 NLR 84.
10 Pothier 5 1 84.
11 Pothier 7 2 118–119; Voet 17 2 17.
12 *Lockhart v De Beer's Mining Co* (1886) 4 HCG 85 97.
13 Pothier 5 1 89–90; *Scholtz v Registrar of Deeds* (1895) 2 OR 210; *Ex parte Steyn* 1902 TH 184; *Laughton v Griffin* (1893) 14 NLR 84; *Holmes v Schoch* 1910 TPD 700; *Pretorius v Botha* 1961 4 SA 722 (T). A managing partner cannot alienate partnership property unless express authority to do so is given or unless the selling of such property is part of the partnership's business: Pothier 3 2 67.
14 *Scholtz v Registrar of Deeds* supra; *Standard Bank v Wentzel and Lombard* 1904 TS 828; *Syrkin v Weinberg Bros* (1906) 23 SC 718 720. A majority decision (as opposed to a unanimous decision) is presumably sufficient; cf *Lockhart v De Beer's Mining Co* supra. The registrar of deeds may transfer or encumber property registered in the names of partners on a power bearing the signature of the part-

nership and of the partner who affixed that signature: GN R474 of 1963 reg 34(2).
15 See Beinart 1961 *Acta Juridica* 118 144.
16 Beinart 144.
17 Pothier 5 1 86.
18 Pothier 5 1 86.
19 *Sacks v Commissioner for Inland Revenue* 1946 AD 31 40.
20 *Sacks v Commissioner for Inland Revenue* supra 41. See also *Taylor v Barnett* 1947 1 PH A2 (N).
21 *Schlemmer v Viljoen* 1958 2 SA 280 (T) 287F.
22 Beinart 147.
23 Pothier 5 1 89, 91; Van der Linden 4 1 13; *Sacks v Commissioner for Inland Revenue* supra 43.
24 D 17 2 20; Pothier 5 1 91.
25 See par 396 ante.
26 Burgess and Morse *Partnership Law and Practice* 171. It would appear therefore that a partner cannot alienate his undivided share in jointly owned partnership property so as to make a third party a co-owner in the partnership assets: Smits *Externe Gebondenheid van Vennootschapsvermogen* 198; and cf *Langermann v Carper* 1905 TH 251 259; *Oblowitz v Oblowitz* 1953 4 SA 426 (C) 433. On the relationship between partners and a partner's partner generally, see Pothier 5 1 91–95. In terms of the regulations published under the Deeds Registries Act 47 of 1937, a partner may not register a transaction affecting his share in property registered in the partnership name until transfer has been passed to him of the share to which he is entitled: GN R474 of 1963 reg 34(3)(c).

405 Rights and duties in respect of partnership accounts Each partner who is entrusted with the management of partnership affairs is obliged to render an account of his administration of the partnership business.[1] A partner cannot be exempted from this duty in the partnership agreement, since this would amount to an agreement not to expose possible fraud.[2] Such exemption can, however, be given at the termination of the firm.[3] Where the partners entrust one partner with the duty of keeping the accounts, all the partners are obliged to make available the necessary information which must be set out in the accounts.[4]

A formal partnership account must be rendered at the times agreed upon in the partnership agreement. In the absence of an agreement in this respect, accounts must be rendered annually, or at such times which accord with usual business usage.[5] An account must also be rendered upon dissolution of the firm.[6] Unless there are special circumstances present, a court will not order the rendering of accounts at other times than those mentioned above, as this will place an intolerable burden on the managing partners.[7] Subject to the terms of the partnership contract,[8] a partner is nevertheless entitled to free access to the partnership accounts at all times and is also entitled to be given a brief summary of the state of the accounts.[9] This right continues to exist even after dissolution of the firm, unless the partners have expressly agreed otherwise.[10]

A partner who demands an account from a co-partner must be ready and willing to render an account of his own administration.[11]

A partner who is not satisfied with the accounts rendered by his co-partners is entitled to have the accounts reviewed.[12] The usual form of action in this respect is to claim an account and a debatement of it.[13] The right to challenge the correctness of the accounts in court also exists after termination of the firm.[14] A partner may waive his right to dispute the accounts if, with actual knowledge of the state of the accounts, he acquiesced therein.[15] It has also been held that partners may agree that the partnership accounts are under all circumstances to be conclusive as to the propriety and validity of charges against the business.[16]

A partner may insist that all partnership accounts be kept at the partnership's principal place of business.[17] He is also entitled to appoint a third party to interpret the accounts on his behalf if he is unable to do so correctly himself.[18]

1 Voet *Commentarius* 17 2 11; Pothier *Partnership* 7 3 135; Van der Keessel *Prael* 3 21 5; *Silver v Silver* 1934 NPD 396. All supporting documents must be produced: Voet 17 2 11.

2 Voet 17 2 11.

3 Voet 17 2 11.

4 *Purdon v Muller* 1961 2 SA 211 (A) 231.

5 Voet 17 2 11; Van der Keessel 3 21 5.

6 Voet 17 2 11. On prescription of a claim for an account upon dissolution, see *Mostert v Mostert* 1913 TPD 255; *Ensleit v Ensleit* 1952 2 SA 385 (T) 389.

7 *Tshabalala v Tshabalala* 1921 AD 311 318.

8 The right of access to the accounts may be waived: *Romersma v Buch* 1917 TPD 266; *Joubert v Jacob* 1962 1 SA 125 (T).

9 Voet 17 2 11; *Möller v Spence* (1885) 4 SC 46; *Romersma v Buch* supra; *Tshabalala v Tshabalala* supra; *Spilg v Walker* 1947 3 SA 495 (EDL); *Beiles v Glazer* 1947 2 PH A79 (W); *Setzkorn v Wessels* 1962 2 SA 218 (E).

10 See the authorities in n 8 supra.

11 Voet 17 2 11.

12 Van der Keessel 3 21 5.

13 Cf *Doyle v Fleet Motors PE (Pty) Ltd* 1971 3 SA 760 (A).

14 See *Mostert v Mostert* supra; *Love v Hobson* 1913 EDL 400; *Korb v Roos* 1948 3 SA 1219 (T). Cf, however, *Ferreira v Fouche* 1949 1 SA 67 (T), where a claim for an account and debatement after termination of the partnership was refused upon the ground that this was the function of a liquidator and that a partner cannot ask the court to act as liquidator. This decision was not followed in later cases; see *Schoeman v Rokeby Farming Co (Pty) Ltd* 1972 4 SA 201 (N); see further *Robson v Theron* 1978 1 SA 841 (A).

15 *Bowen v Daverin* 1914 AD 632 646.

16 *Bowen v Daverin* supra 646.

17 *Setzkorn v Wessels* supra.

18 *Van der Walt v Pelser* (1895) 12 SC 353; *Joubert v Jacob* supra; *Carr v Hinson* 1966 3 SA 303 (W).

406 Rights and duties upon dissolution of the firm This aspect is dealt with below.[1]

1 See pars 421 et seq post.

ENFORCEMENT OF PARTNERS' RIGHTS AND DUTIES

407 General There are in principle various remedies at the disposal of partners with which the rights and duties arising out of the partnership contract can be enforced. The principal remedy is the actio pro socio.[1] Generally speaking this action may in the first place be instituted by a partner against a co-partner during the existence of the partnership for specific performance in terms of the partnership agreement, together with fulfilment of personal obligations arising out of the partnership agreement and business.[2] Secondly, the action can be used to claim a dissolution of the partnership (where the right to dissolve exists),[3] together with its liquidation.[4] In the third place, the action can be employed after dissolution of the partnership to enforce the partners' rights and duties and to have the liquidation of the firm effected.[5] In this respect the action can be instituted for the purpose of effecting a distribution or division of partnership assets as a whole,[6] or to effect the distribution of a particular partnership asset which was by some reason or the other not included in a general distribution of all the assets.[7] A partner has no locus standi, however, to sue a co-partner after dissolution of the firm in respect of a matter for which a liquidator has been appointed.[8] A partner can neither appropriate the sole right to liquidate the firm,[9] nor institute a claim by which the court is asked to liquidate the partnership.[10]

Apart from the actio pro socio, a partner can also employ the actio communi dividundo after termination of the partnership in order to have jointly owned partnership assets divided.[11] This action can also be used to claim ancillary relief such as payment of expenses incurred in connection with the joint property.[12]

A partner may avail himself of an interdict in order to restrain a co-partner from acting in a manner contrary to his duties as a partner.[13] In appropriate cases, a declaratory order may be claimed.[14]

1 For a full discussion on the historical development of this action, see Delport *Gedingvoering tussen Vennote* 45. See too *Robson v Theron* 1978 1 SA 841 (A).
2 *Robson v Theron* supra 855 856.
3 *Robson v Theron* supra 855 856.
4 *Robson v Theron* supra 855 856.
5 *Robson v Theron* supra 855 856. See too *Truter v Hancke* 1923 CPD 43 48; *Schoeman v Rokeby Farming Co (Pty) Ltd* 1972 4 SA 201 (N), but cf *Ferreira v Fouche* 1949 1 SA 67 (T).
6 *Robson v Theron* supra.
7 *Robson v Theron* supra.
8 *Van Tonder v Davids* 1975 3 SA 616 (C).
9 *Kaplan v Turner* 1941 SWA 29.
10 *Ferreira v Fouche* supra; *Brighton v Clift (2)* 1971 2 SA 191 (R).
11 *Robson v Theron* supra 856.
12 *Robson v Theron* supra 857.
13 Cf *Spilg v Walker* 1947 3 SA 495 (EDL).
14 Cf *Munro v Ekerold* 1949 1 SA 584 (SWA).

408 Specific performance The general principles relating to a claim for specific performance are also applicable in cases concerning partnership disputes.[1] A court will therefore as far as possible give effect to a claim for specific performance, although it has a discretion to refuse the order under certain circumstances.[2] In partnership disputes there are two particular considerations in this respect. In the first place, a court will not order an unwilling partner to act conscientiously as a partner.[3] Where it is thus clear from a partner's actions that he does not wish to act as a partner in the firm, the proper remedy would be to cancel the agreement and claim damages.[4] Secondly, a court will not make an order which will have a nugatory effect. If, therefore, a partnership agreement can (and will) be terminated at any stage after the court order, the court will not make an order to commence or carry on the partnership's business, since such an order will practically have no effect.[5]

1 Delport *Gedingvoering tussen Vennote* 253.
2 *Haynes v Kingwilliamstown Municipality* 1951 2 SA 371 (A); *Diner v Dublin* 1962 4 SA 36 (N); *Oosthuizen v Swart* 1956 2 SA 687 (SWA); *Robson v Theron* 1978 1 SA 841 (A) 855.
3 *Flanagan v Flanagan* (1913) 34 NLR 452.
4 Cf *Lampakis v Dimitri* 1937 TPD 138.
5 *Cohen v Woolf* 1901 CTR 491.

409 Settlement of accounts as a condition precedent As a general rule partners are not, in so far as partnership transactions are concerned, considered as debtor and creditor inter se until the partnership is wound up or until there is a binding settlement of accounts.[1] A partner therefore has, as a general rule, no right of action against a co-partner for payment of any amounts owed to him in connection with the partnership's affairs, unless the firm's accounts are settled and there remains a credit balance due to him.[2] There are two main reasons behind this rule. In the first place, the extent of a partner's share in respect of any specific portion of the partnership assets can be determined only after a settlement of partnership accounts covering a specific time period.[3] In the second place, it should be borne in mind that partners only share in the net profits and losses of the business and not in the gross returns or expenses of each individual transaction.[4] Before the net profits or losses can be determined, a settlement of accounts is necessary.[5]

In certain instances a claim can be instituted by a partner against a co-partner without the necessity of having the partnership accounts settled. As the general rule requiring a settling of accounts is only applicable where a partner sues for the pro rata share owed to him in connection with the partnership affairs, an action can be maintained without a settlement of accounts where the claim is not one for a share owed, for example, where a partner claims that money be paid into the partnership account[6] or that a co-partner transfer property to the partners in joint ownership.[7] A claim can also be instituted without a settlement of accounts where the partners specifically agree that payment can be made to a partner regardless of the state of the partnership accounts. A settlement of accounts is naturally not required where the claim has nothing to do with the partnership affairs but concerns a private dispute between the partners.[8]

The rule that a settlement of accounts is generally required before a partner can sue his co-partner, does not mean that there must be agreement as to the correctness of the accounts.[9] In the absence of an express[10] or tacit[11] agreement as to its correctness, a dispute concerning the accounts can be brought to court by means of an action for an account and a debate.[12] A partner may also by means of an ordinary actio pro socio proceed to claim what is owed to him upon his version of the accounts. If the defendant disputes the correctness of the plaintiff's version of the accounts, a defence can be raised in the pleadings in the usual manner.[13] The court will then settle the dispute, provided that the dispute is of a limited or restricted nature.[14] Where this is not the case, such as where the dispute concerns a wide variety of issues concerning the partnership business, the latter procedure cannot be followed, and the proper action would be for a debatement of the accounts.

Disputes concerning the partnership accounts can also be settled by a third party such as a liquidator.[15]

1 *McDonald v Sutherland* (1834) 1 M 91; *Henry Fell v Thomas Goodwill* (1884) 5 NLR 265; *Nelson v Stanley* 1913 CPD 160; *Dempers v Van Rensburg* 1927 EDL 438; *Harvey v De Jong* 1946 TPD 185; *Taylor v Barnett* 1947 1 PH A2 (N); *Pataka v Keefe* 1947 2 SA 962 (A); *Shingadia Bros v Shingadia* 1958 1 SA 582 (FC); *Muller v Kaplan* 1959 2 PH F96 (O); *Dube v City Promotions* 1964 1 PH A1 (D); cf, however, *Cohen v Berman* (1897) 4 OR 356.

2 ibid; and see generally Delport 1979 *De Jure* 194.

3 Cf *Sacks v Commissioner for Inland Revenue* 1946 AD 31.

4 *Pataka v Keefe* supra; *Morewear Industries*

(Rhodesia) *Ltd v Industrial Exporters Ltd* 1954 4 SA 217 (SR).

5 ibid; and see also Huber *HR* 3 2 11, 12.

6 *Shingadia Bros v Shingadia* supra.

7 *Oosthuizen v Swart* 1956 2 SA 687 (SWA).

8 *Nelson v Stanley* supra.

9 *Dube v City Promotions* supra.

10 *Ferreira v Fouche* 1949 1 SA 67 (T); *Schoeman v Rokeby Farming Co (Pty) Ltd* 1972 4 SA 201 (N).

11 *Simon v Levin & Co* 1921 AD 49.

12 *Doyle v Fleet Motors PE (Pty) Ltd* 1971 3 SA 760 (A).

13 *Dube v City Promotions* supra.

14 *Korb v Roos* 1948 3 SA 1219 (T); *Schoeman v*

Rokeby Farming Co (Pty) Ltd supra; cf, however, Ferreira v Fouche supra.

15 Ferreira v Fouche supra; Schoeman v Rokeby Farming Co (Pty) Ltd supra.

410 Parties to the action Since a partnership is not a legal persona, a partner cannot be a debtor or creditor of the firm, but only of his co-partners.[1] It thus follows that a partner cannot claim that a co-partner must render performance to the partnership: the partnership itself does not exist apart from its members.[2] It also follows that a claim cannot be instituted against a partner in the partnership name as this would mean that the defendant partner would be both plaintiff and defendant in the same action.[3] It has been held to be possible, however, for an action to be instituted "for the benefit of the partnership"[4] as well as "for and on behalf of the partnership".[5]

As a general rule all the partners in a partnership dispute must be before the court, either as plaintiffs or defendants,[6] unless the dispute concerns some partners only.[7] A partner who has paid a partnership debt out of his private estate must sue all his co-partners for a contribution.[8]

It is possible for one partner to represent other partners in an action against a co-partner, provided that the necessary authority in this respect is given and there is no conflict of interest between the partner acting as agent and the partners who are represented.[9]

It has been held that, in cases where a partner is in breach of a contract which he has entered into with the partnership, the proper form of action is for the other partners to sue the co-partner to pay what he owes into the partnership funds.[10]

1 *Jacobson v Norton* (1841) 2 M 218; *Sempff v Neubauer* 1903 TH 202; *Van Gend & Son's and Van Gend Bros' Trustee v G A G van Gend and H J van Gend* 1913 EDL 114 115; *McLeod and Shearsmith v Shearsmith* 1938 TPD 87; *Kaplan v Turner* 1941 SWA 29; *Ferreira v Fouche* 1949 1 SA 67 (T); *Oosthuizen v Swart* 1956 2 SA 687 (SWA).
2 *Kaplan v Turner* supra; *Ferreira v Fouche* supra. Cf too *Shingadia Bros v Shingadia* 1958 1 SA 582 (FC); *De Abreu v Silva* 1964 2 SA 416 (T).
3 *Shingadia Bros v Shingadia* supra.

4 *De Abreu v Silva* supra.
5 *Oosthuizen v Swart* supra.
6 *Shingadia Bros v Shingadia* supra; *Oosthuizen v Swart* supra.
7 *Sempff v Neubauer* supra; *Jacobson v Norton* supra.
8 *J D Celliers v C F Ziervogel* 1893 H 225.
9 *De Abreu v Silva* supra and cf Nienaber 1964 *Annual Survey* 127.
10 *Shingadia Bros v Shingadia* supra; see too, in this respect, Delport *Gedingvoering tussen Vennote* 249.

411 Litigation whilst firm is in existence Common-law authorities express conflicting opinions regarding the question whether a partnership action can be maintained whilst the partnership is in existence.[1] The courts have, however, held on a number of occasions that such a possibility does exist.[2] The appellate division has also confirmed this approach in an obiter dictum.[3]

There are certain limitations on a partner's right to sue a co-partner before a dissolution of the partnership. In the first place, a court will not order the rendering of a partnership account at any stage during the partnership's existence. Since it would be inequitable to demand from a partner to render a formal account at any time during the partnership, an order will only be made for the rendering of an account upon the specific dates agreed upon, or yearly or at the dissolution of the firm.[4] The court does, however, have a discretion to order the rendering of a formal account, should the circumstances warrant such an order.[5] In the second place, a partner cannot demand payment of what is due to him at any stage during the partnership's existence. Such a claim involves the settling of the partnership accounts, and, as a general rule, such accounts are only settled upon dissolution of the firm, unless the partners agree on a settlement at specific intervals before dissolution.[6] It therefore follows that a partner can, as a general rule, only institute a claim for payment of what is due to him at specific points in time provided for in the partnership agreement and at the termination of the partnership.[7] It seems acceptable, however, that a claim for payment can be instituted at other points in time before the firm is dissolved, if such a step is equitable in the light of surrounding circumstances.[8]

Where a settlement of accounts is not a precedent for a claim by one partner against another, such as where the claim is for money to be paid into the partnership account,[9] or it involves the use of partnership assets,[10] action can be taken without asking for a dissolution of the firm.

1 For a full discussion in this respect, see Delport 1979 *THRHR* 288.
2 *Hathorn v The Salisbury Gold Mining Co (Ltd)* (1895) 16 NLR 193; *Silvert & Co v Evans & Co* 1912 TPD 425; *Cohen v Berman* (1897) 4 OR 356; *Fisher's Executors v Dickinson and Brown* (1914) 35 NLR 505; *Munro v Ekerold* 1949 1 SA 584 (SWA); *Shingadia Bros v Shingadia* 1958 1 SA 582 (FC); *Van Tonder v Davids* 1975 3 SA 616 (C); See too *Henry Fell v Thomas Goodwill* (1884) 5 NLR 265; *Hillier v Davis* (1887) 8 NLR 195; *Uren v Nelson* 1910 TPD 562; *Pataka v Keefe* 1947 2 SA 962 (A); *Taylor v Barnett* 1947 1 PH A2 (N); *De Abreu v Silva* 1964 2 SA 416 (T); cf, however,

Keefe and Keefe v Pataka 1946 WLD 551.
3 *Robson v Theron* 1978 1 SA 841 (A) 855.
4 *Tshabalala v Tshabalala* 1921 AD 311; see par 405 ante.
5 ibid.
6 See Huber *HR* 3 2 11 12; *Sacks v Commissioner for Inland Revenue* 1946 AD 31; *Taylor v Barnett* supra.
7 ibid.
8 Delport *Gedingvoering tussen Vennote* 258.
9 *Shingadia Bros v Shingadia* supra.
10 *Munro v Ekerold* supra; *Oosthuizen v Swart* 1956 2 SA 687 (SWA); *De Abreu v Silva* supra; *Van Tonder v Davids* supra.

RELATIONSHIP BETWEEN PARTNERS AND THIRD PARTIES

412 Partnership and third parties It has been stated that the law of partnership primarily regulates the relations of partners to one another and that where it deals with the relationship between the partnership and third parties it may be said to be in fact a branch of the law of agency.[1] However, one should guard against incorrect inferences about the exact role of agency or "mutual mandate" in partnership[2] from this and similar statements.[3] In any event, since a partnership does not constitute a body corporate (ultimately), the partners themselves have to bear any liability it incurs *vis-à-vis* outsiders.[4] The liability may be contractual, delictual or criminal.[5]

1 *Divine Gates & Co v African Clothing Factory* 1930 CPD 238 240; cf Gibson *Mercantile and Company Law* 262.
2 *Potchefstroom Dairies and Industries Co Ltd v Standard Fresh Milk Supply Co* 1913 TPD 506; *Muller v Pienaar* 1968 3 SA 195 (A); *Karstein v Moribe* 1982 2 SA 282 (T). On the statement in *Blumberg and Sulski v Brown and Freitas* 1922 TPD 130 138 that there must exist a mandate between the contracting parties before it can be said that the particular contract is a partnership, see par 371 ante, especially n 4 as to whether *Blumberg's* case did in fact imply that every partner should be the

agent of the partnership. For some confusion as to the exact role of agency in partnership "due to a misreading of Pothier", see Ribbens 1979 *Codicillus* 28.
3 See e g *Blumberg and Sulski v Brown and Freitas* supra; *Wulfsohn v Taylor* 1928 TPD 99; *Bain v Barclays Bank (DC&O) Ltd* 1937 SR 191; *Venter v Naude* 1951 1 SA 156 (O); *Morewear Industries (Rhodesia) Ltd v Industrial Exporters Ltd* 1954 4 SA 213 (SR); *Oblowitz v Oblowitz* 1953 4 SA 426 (C); *Eaton and Louw v Arcade Properties (Pty) Ltd* 1961 4 SA 233(T); Gibson 268–269; Story *Partnership* 4.
4 For the basic principle or general rule in the

law regarding the legal nature of partnership, see par 388 ante; for the exceptions or
quasi-exceptions to the general rule, see par

389 ante.
5 Cf Lee and Honoré *Obligations* 141.

CONTRACT

413 Contractual liability: nature and requirements in general A partner who contracts on behalf of his partnership within the limits of his authority, express or implied,
is said to act as an agent of the partnership. Since the relationship between them is that
of agent and principal, principles of the law pertaining to agency and representation
also take effect.[1] Describing the partner as an agent of the partnership is a result of the
entity view[2] which, it has been suggested, is the better one.[3]

In accordance with the aggregate view[4] partners are often styled as each other's agents.[5]
Whether they are actually agents or not, they may certainly have the power of agents.[6]
The broad principles of the law applicable to agents apply to this extent to partners.
Although partners may have the powers of agents, they are much more than agents.
The character sustained by a member of an ordinary partnership is much more complex
than merely that of an agent. He fills a double character: As principal he is bound by
what he does himself and by what each of his partners do on behalf of the partnership,
provided they act within the limits of their authority; as an agent he binds each of them
by what he does on behalf of the partnership, provided he acts within the limits of his
authority. Hence in contracting on behalf of the partnership a partner sustains the
double character of agent of his partners and principal in one and the same transaction,
and that not merely for a share, but in each capacity for the whole.[7] It has consequently[8]
been held that the liability of partners for partnership debts is joint and several[9] and, to
the same effect,[10] that partnership debts are in law the debts in solidum of all the partners[11]
and, in more refined terminology,[12] that the partners are liable singuli in solidum for
partnership debts.[13] There is now no doubt that this is the position on dissolution of a
partnership.[14] It has been stated that an individual partner was liable for his pro rata
share of a partnership debt in Roman-Dutch law.[15] Furthermore, relying on "basic principles and case law rather than common law authorities" the view was expressed that
after the dissolution of the partnership a creditor is not entitled to judgment against
some of the partners jointly and severally for the unpaid part of a partnership debt, but
seemingly only against each for his aliquot share of the debt.[16] This view has been rejected as unsound.[17] Although some doubt still remains, due to conflicting authorities,[18]
a considerable body of opinion exists that in Roman-Dutch law partners were normally
each individually liable in solidum for partnership debts.[19] In any event, the solidary
liability of individual partners as described by Van der Linden[20] and Van der Keessel[21]
has been accepted in South African law regarding the liability of partners after the dissolution of the partnership.[22] A partner is liable for the full amount of a partnership
debt as soon as the partnership is dissolved, even though the liquidation of the partnership has not been completed.[23] This being the position and since there is no reason
in principle why all partners should be sued together after dissolution of the partnership, numerous courses of action are left open to a partnership creditor, provided, of
course, that he does not recover in total more than the full amount of the debt.[24] For
present purposes only a few alternatives are mentioned: he may sue anyone of the partners individually, or some or all of them jointly and severally, for the full amount of
the debt.[25] He may sue any one of the partners individually for a lesser amount, for
instance, for a proportionate part of the debt, or some or all the partners for proportionate or equal amounts.[26] If he expressly claims or receives from one partner his proportionate part of the debt, there is authority that he thereby releases him from the

excess,[27] but it has been suggested that this is too mechanically expressed.[28] In any event, should a partnership creditor obtain a judgment ordering each of the partners to pay an aliquot part only of the debt and should it thereafter appear that one of the partners is unable to pay anything, he would, as judgment creditor, because of the nature of the court order, obviously not be able to enforce payment of the amount of that partner's aliquot part of the debt from the other partners.[29] Furthermore, if the partnership is dissolved after the accrual of the cause of action, but before the issue of summons, the creditor may sue the partnership in its name at the date of the accrual of the cause of action, in which event the action continues against the persons alleged by the creditor or stated by the partnership to be partners, as if sued individually.[30]

Stated very briefly and generally, the various statements, opinions and submissions on the nature of the liability of individual members of a partnership to partnership creditors stante societate, that is, prior to its dissolution, may be reduced to two different approaches or points of view.[31]

The first point of view may conveniently be summarized as follows: Partners are considered to be joint co-debtors during the subsistence of the partnership, either in principle or for most practical purposes. It is usually stressed, inter alia, that since a creditor is obliged to join all the partners when taking judgment against the partnership, and to levy execution on partnership assets first, partners can usually only be held liable collectively for a partnership debt, and not individually or separately for the whole or part. On dissolution the position changes. The partners then are (or become) solidary co-debtors, liable singuli in solidum for partnership debts.[32]

The other approach[33] is to place the emphasis on the joint and several liability of partners. Usually this liability is stated either with or without some qualification or explanation, or as a general principle. The explanation (if any), usually given, is that partners are rendered liable jointly and severally for partnership obligations because the contracting partner acts both as principal and as agent for his partners. Although reference is usually made to the requirement or rule that civil proceedings must in the first instance be against the partnership or all the partners jointly, not an individual member (seemingly), this is considered to be merely one of procedure. Sometimes it is emphasized that a judgment against a whole firm collectively implies judgment against each member of it, and that it may be executed on the private assets of any of the individual partners after compliance with the formal requirement of first excussing the partnership assets. Hence, though partners may shelter behind the partnership facade while all is well, in the last resort their joint and several liability may be enforced to the full extent of each partner's private resources, even during the subsistence of the partnership.[34]

These different approaches merit a brief review of the position during the subsistence of the partnership, though various aspects have been mentioned above.[35]

Although the position in Roman-Dutch law was to the contrary,[36] it is an old and established rule of South African case law that civil proceedings by or against a partnership during its subsistence must in general[37] be instituted by or against all the partners conjointly: Where a partnership sues, all the partners must appear as plaintiffs; where a partnership is sued, all partners must be joined. A creditor may not sue one or more of the individual members for payment of a partnership debt either in whole or in part. If he does, the individual partner so sued may demand that the plaintiff (creditor) join all his partners as co-defendants.[38] This rule of practice, said to be based upon considerations of convenience,[39] does not apply on dissolution of the partnership.[40]

Although the procedure described above may still be followed,[41] an alternative procedure[42] is provided by the rules of court.[43] A partnership may sue or be sued in its name.[44] The names of the partners need not be alleged, but their inclusion will not afford a defence to the partnership.[45] A plaintiff suing a partnership may by notice demand disclosure of the names and addresses of persons who were partners at the date of the accrual of the cause of action, with a view to the possible subsequent attachment and excussion of their private assets.[46]

In a successful suit, judgment must be given against the partnership and not against any of the partners individually.[47] Execution in respect of a judgment against a partnership must first be levied against the assets of the partnership. Only after these assets have been excussed may execution for the residue of the judgment debt be levied against the private assets of any person held to be, or held to be estopped from denying his status as, a partner singuli in solidum.[48] However, attachment of a partner's private assets is possible only if his name was cited in the summons or disclosure of his name was obtained under the rules of court.[49]

The arrangement of the Insolvency Act,[50] by which partnership creditors are primarily confined to partnership assets and deprived of full recourse against the partners individually the moment a partnership is sequestrated,[51] as well as the fact that where a partnership is sued a debt owed to an individual partner may not be set off,[52] provides additional support for a conclusion that the better view seems to be that partners are joint co-debtors during the subsistence of the partnership,[53] although it may be said that the partners in their private capacity have a subsidiary liability in solidum for a judgment debt of the partnership.[54] It is interesting to note that the position of the partnership in insolvency and civil practice and procedure is also referred to in another context, that is, the exceptions to the general rule concerning the legal nature of partnership.[55] In various entity jurisdictions the joint and several, or solidary liability of partners for a contractual obligation of the firm stante societate is described as subsidiary or secondary in nature, not primary.[56]

It has been held that there is no reason in principle why partners should not bind themselves to a partnership creditor in such a way that each partner is individually liable in solidum to the creditor for the payment of the whole of the partnership debts, even during the subsistence of the partnership.[57]

For an ordinary partner[58] to incur liability on a contract entered into by a partner with a third party, the requirements are that the particular partnership should have subsisted at the relevant date or held out to subsist,[59] that the contracting partner had authority to bind the partnership[60] and that he entered into the contract in the name of the partnership.[61] The different requirements will be dealt with seriatim below.

---

1 *Potchefstroom Dairies and Industries Co Ltd v Standard Fresh Milk Supply Co* 1913 TPD 506 514 per Bristowe J: "A partner is often said to be the agent of the firm. In England this expression is inaccurate, but I am not prepared to say that it is inaccurate here." Cf *Eaton and Louw v Arcade Properties (Pty) Ltd* 1961 4 SA 233 (T); *Rand Advance (Pty) Ltd v Scala Café* 1974 1 SA 786 (D) 792; De Wet and Yeats *Kontraktereg en Handelsreg* 400. For agency and representation, see title AGENCY AND REPRESENTATION.

2 For the entity theory of the nature of partnership, see par 386 ante.

3 In *Pooley v Driver* (1876) 5 Ch 458 476 Jessel MR said in part: "You cannot grasp the no-tion of agency properly speaking *unless you grasp the notion of the existence of the firm as a separate entity* from the existence of the partners ... [B]ut when you get that idea clearly you will see at once what sort of agency it is. *It is one person acting on behalf of the firm.* He does not act as agent in the ordinary sense of the word, for the others so as to bind the others; he acts on behalf of the firm of which they are members; and as he binds the firm and acts on the part of the firm, he is properly treated as the agent of the firm. *If you cannot grasp the notion of a separate entity for the firm, then you are reduced to this, that inasmuch as he acts partly for himself and partly for the others, to the extent that he acts for the others he must*

be an agent, and in that way you get him to be an
agent for the other partners, but only in that way,
because you insist upon ignoring the existence of
the firm as a separate entity" (italics supplied).
Cf Crane and Bromberg *Partnership* 274.

4 For the aggregate view of the nature of the
partnership relationship, see par 386 ante.

5 See *Potchefstroom Dairies and Industries Co Ltd
v Standard Fresh Milk Supply Co* supra 511;
Lindley *Partnership* 30; Crane and Bromberg
273.

6 A partner qua partner has authority to contract on behalf of the partnership by reason
of the partnership relationship, not by reason of an act of authorization; see *Potchefstroom Dairies and Industries Co Ltd v Standard
Fresh Milk Supply Co* supra 512; *Muller v
Pienaar* 1968 3 SA 195 (A) 201; title AGENCY
AND REPRESENTATION vol 1 ante, especially
par 119 n 12.

7 *Potchefstroom Dairies and Industries Co Ltd v
Standard Fresh Milk Supply Co* supra 511;
*Guardian Insurance and Trust Co v Lovemore's
Executors* (1887) 5 SC 205 211; *Croghan's
Executrix v Whitby and Webber* 1904 TH
101 107; *Truter v Hancke* 1923 CPD 43 48–49;
Ex parte Bester 1937 CPD 45; *Spark v Palte
Ltd (2)* 1956 3 SA 27 (SR) 30–31: "[I]n contracting with the plaintiff [he] did not do so
merely as an agent ... He was himself, as a
partner, a co-principal of the partnership,
when he contracted on behalf of the partnership he therefore contracted also as a
principal"; *Muller v Pienaar* 1968 3 SA 195
(A) 201; *Muller v Pienaar* 1970 2 SA 385
(C) 389. Cf Lindley 30; Crane and Bromberg 273; De Villiers *Encyclopedia of Forms
and Precedents* vol 13 157; Bamford *Partnership* 50.

8 in contradistinction to English law, where
the consequence is that a partner who contracts on behalf of the firm is not liable on
the contract except as one of the firm: in
other words, the contract is only binding on
him and his partners jointly. This is expressly stated in the Partnership Act of 1890
s 9, but it was settled law before that act came
into operation; see Lindley 323; Hahlo and
Kahn *Union of SA: Development of its Law and
Constitution* 701 n 89.

9 *Davis & Son v McDonald and Sutherland* (1833)
1 M 86; *McDonald v Sutherland* (1834) 1 M
91; *Simpson & Co v Fleck* (1833) 3 M 213 217;
Tedder v Greig 1912 AD 73 91–92; *Potchefstroom Dairies and Industries Co Ltd v Standard
Fresh Milk Supply Co* supra 511; *Spark v Palte
Ltd (2)* supra 31; *Sliom v Wallach's Printing and
Publishing Co Ltd* 1925 TPD 650 655; *Bester
v Van Niekerk* 1960 2 SA 779 (A) 785; *Muller*

v Pienaar 1968 3 SA 195 (A) 202–203.

10 Liability in solidum or solidary liability
means liability for the full amount of the
debt, as in joint and several liability; see *Muller
v Pienaar* 1968 3 SA 195 (A) 204; Christie
Contract 246.

11 *Hawkins v Fitzroy* (1831) 1 M 519 522;
Meintjies & Co v Simpson Bros & Co (1841) 2
M 216; *Auret's Trustee v Pienaar* (1884) 3 SC
40 41; *De Pass v The Colonial Government*
(1886) 4 SC 383 390; *Jacobson v Nitch* (1890)
7 SC 174 178; *Pienaar v Rattray* (1895) 12 SC
35; *Walker v Syfret* 1911 AD 141 165; *Harding
and Parker v John Pierce & Co* 1919 OPD
113 117; *Divine Gates & Co v African Clothing
Factory* 1930 CPD 238 241; *Baldinger v
Broomberg* 1949 3 SA 258 (C) 268; *Michalow
v Premier Milling Co Ltd* 1960 2 SA 59 (W)
61E–F; *Ex parte Fernandez* 1965 3 SA 726 (O)
727; *Muller v Pienaar* 1968 3 SA 195 (A) 204;
Ex parte Cohen 1974 4 SA 674 (W) 675; *Forder, Ritch and Eriksson v Engar's Heirs* 1973 1
SA 719 (N) 721.

12 See De Wet and Yeats 118.

13 *Niekerk v Niekerk* (1830) 1 M 452; *Colonial
Government v Fitzroy* (1830) 1 M 492; *Vos v
Vos & Co* (1836) 1 M 132; *Kidson v Campbell
and Jooste* (1844) 2 M 279 280; *Blackburn v
Meintjies* (1861) 1 R 56; *Theunissen v Fleischer,
Wheeldon and Munnik* (1883) 3 EDC 291 294;
Lamb Bros v Brenner & Co (1886) 5 EDC
152 166; *Solomon and Bradley v Millhouse* 1903
TS 607; *Estate of Stoltenhoff v Howard* (1907)
24 SC 693; *Potchefstroom Dairies and Industries
Co Ltd v Standard Fresh Milk Supply Co* supra
511; *Pienaar v Suttner Bros and Hirschfeld* 1914
EDL 416; *Joubert v Tarry & Co* 1915 TPD
277 281; *Ex parte Buttner Bros* 1930 CPD
138 147; *Lee v Maraisdrif (Edms) Bpk* 1976 2
SA 536 (A) 543F: "[E]lkeen vir die geheel."

14 In *Du Toit v African Dairies Ltd* 1922 TPD 245
a member of a partnership was sued for a
partnership debt. Mason J held that the partnership continued to exist for the purpose of
liquidating the business and that since it was
therefore not entirely dissolved, the partnership itself and not an individual member of
it should have been sued (247). De Waal J
was of the opinion that "[as] long as there are
partnership assets in existence, the partnership is still in existence, and as the partnership, therefore, was still in existence when
the action was brought, the proper party to
be sued was the partnership and not an individual member thereof" (248). Cf for similar sentiments but on different grounds:
Pienaar v Rattray supra 38; *Harding and Parker
v John Pierce & Co* supra 117; *Schiff v Ettling*
(1886) 4 HCG 230 231; *Haarhoff v Cape of*

Good Hope Bank (1887) 4 HCG 304 313; *King v Porter, Hodgson & Co* (1879) 9 Buch 117. In *Lee v Maraisdrif (Edms) Bpk* supra 541 543 Rabie JA overruled *Du Toit v African Dairies Ltd* and held that an individual member of a partnership may be sued for the full amount of the partnership debt as soon as the partnership is dissolved, even though the liquidation of the partnership has not been completed e g because there are undivided partnership assets. Cf *McDonald v Sutherland* supra; *Simpson & Co v Fleck* supra 217; *Estate of Stoltenhoff v Howard* supra; *Solomon and Bradley v Millhouse* supra; *Walker v Syfret* supra 165; *Pienaar v Suttner Bros and Hirschfeld* supra 419; *Bester v Van Niekerk* supra 783 785; *Cassim v The Master* 1962 4 SA 601 (D) 606. For a detailed discussion, see Delport 1976 *De Jure* 361; Joubert 1978 *THRHR* 297.

15 De Wet and Yeats 3d ed 577.
16 *Maraisdrif (Edms) Bpk v Lee* 1974 4 SA 696 (C) 698 702A 703B–C; cf *Haarhoff v Cape of Good Hope Bank* supra 313–314; *In re Chabaud, Luck v Chabaud* (1831) 1 M 531.
17 *Lee v Maraisdrif (Edms) Bpk* supra 544A–B.
18 espousing pro rata liability: De Groot *Inleiding* 3 1 31 and *De Iure B ac P* 2 11 13; Voet *Commentarius* 17 2 13, 16; Van Leeuwen *RHR* 5 3 11; Van Bynkershoek *Obs Tum* 2 1180, 1594. Maintaining solidary liability: De Groot *Holl Cons* 3 143; Van Wassenaer *Practyk Notariael* 2 17 5; *Holl Cons* 1 151; 1 283; 1 303; 2 235; Barels *Advysen* 2 59; 2 60; 2 61, *Handvesten van Amsterdam* 2 1 17; Verwer *Nederlants Seerechten Avaryen en Bodemereyen* 171; Van Bynkershoek *Quaest Iur Priv* 4 23; Kersteman *Woordenboek* s v "compagnieschap" and "societeit"; Lybrechts *Notaris Ampt* 2 21 2; Pothier *Partnership* 6 1 96; Van der Keessel *Thes Sel* 702 703, *Prael* 3 21 7; Van der Linden *Koopmans Handboek* 4 1 13; 1 14 9 7, ad Pothier *Contracten en Verbintenissen* 1 265 (vol 1 265–266), ad Pothier *Societeiten of Compagnieschappen* 6 1 96 (n 235–236).
19 See e g Van der Heijden *Naamloze Vennootschap* 52; Lichtenauer *Geschiedenis van het Handelsrecht* 100–101 139; Fockema Oud-Nederlandsch Burgerlijk Recht vol 1 73–75; Kohler 1907 *Zeitschrift für das gesammte Handelsrecht* 294; Van Brakel 1917 *Rechtsgeleerd Magazijn* 174; Joubert 1978 *THRHR* 292; Van den Heever *Partiarian Agricultural Lease* 26–27.
20 See n 17 supra.
21 ibid.
22 *Lee v Maraisdrif (Edms) Bpk* supra 542. See *Davis & Son v McDonald and Sutherland* supra; *McDonald v Sutherland* supra; *Hawkins v Fitzroy* supra; *Simpson & Co v Fleck* supra 217;

Solomon and Bradley v Millhouse supra; *Pienaar v Suttner Bros and Hirschfeld* supra 416; *Estate of Stoltenhoff v Howard* supra 695; *Walker v Syfret* supra 165; *Ex parte Buttner Bros* supra 147; *Divine Gates & Co v African Clothing Factory* supra 241; *Mahomed v Karp Bros* 1938 TPD 112 113; *Baldinger v Broomberg* supra 268; *Turkstra v Goldberg* 1960 1 SA 512 (T) 513–514; *Bester v Van Niekerk* supra 785; *Cassim v The Master* supra 606; *Vrystaatse Lewendehawe Ko-op Bpk v Van Jaarsveld* 1970 4 SA 292 (NC) 293; *Spie Batignolles Société Anonyme v Van Niekerk: in re Van Niekerk v SA Yster en Staal Industriële Korp Bpk* 1980 2 SA 441 (NC) 447.

23 *Lee v Maraisdrif (Edms) Bpk* supra 543–544.
24 *Lee v Maraisdrif (Edms) Bpk* supra 543H–544C; *Simpson & Co v Fleck* supra 217; *Pienaar v Suttner Bros and Hirschfeld* supra 419; *Solomon and Bradley v Millhouse* supra; *Turkstra v Goldberg* supra 513–514; *Press v Barker* 1919 CPD 243; McGregor 1909 *SALJ* 29–30 33; Joubert 296; De Wet and Yeats 119–122; Christie 249: "[P]artners . . . are jointly and severally liable. Each is liable to the creditors for the full amount of the debt and the creditor can at his option claim the full debt or any lesser amount from any of them, provided of course that he does not receive in total more than the full amount of the debt, since by definition there is only one debt due."
25 ibid.
26 *Lee v Maraisdrif (Edms) Bpk* supra 544A–C. By electing to sue one or some of the partners, the creditor does not thereby commit himself to recovering from that partner or partners alone and abandoning his right to claim against others: Christie 249; De Wet and Yeats 121–122.
27 Voet 45 2 4; De Wet and Yeats 121–122.
28 Christie 249.
29 *Lee v Maraisdrif (Edms) Bpk* supra 544A–C.
30 Uniform Rules of Court r 14(2) (7); *Spie Batignolles Société Anonyme v Van Niekerk: in re Van Niekerk v SA Yster en Staal Industriële Korp Bpk* supra 447; *Kirsch Industries Ltd v Vosloo and Lindeque* 1982 3 SA 479 (W) 484.
31 Cf De Villiers 157.
32 See e g *Estate of Stoltenhoff v Howard* supra 695; *Du Toit v African Dairies Ltd* supra 247 248; *Pienaar v Suttner Bros and Hirschfeld* supra 419; *Mahomed v Karp Bros* supra 113; *Turkstra v Goldberg* supra 514B–C; *Vrystaatse Lewendehawe Ko-op Bpk v Van Jaarsveld* supra 293: "*Stante societate* is dit sekerlik nie die geval nie en is die aanspreeklikheid van vennote dié van gesamentlike medeskuldenaars"; *Maraisdrif (Edms) Bpk v Lee* supra 701; *Lee v Maraisdrif (Edms) Bpk* supra 540G–H 544A;

Standard Bank of SA Ltd v Lombard 1977 2 SA 808 (W) 813H–814A; *Strydom v Protea Eiendomsagente* 1979 2 SA 206 (T) 209–210; *Boonzaier v Kiley* 1981 2 SA 618 (W) 619; *Karstein v Moribe* 1982 2 SA 282 (T) 293D–E: "Inasmuch as partners are joint co-debtors and creditors during the existence of the partnership" (290H); De Wet and Yeats 247 404–405; De Villiers 158; Naude 1972 *Codicillus* 2; Delport 1976 *De Jure* 363; Henning 1978 *THRHR* 4–7; Cilliers and Benade *Company Law* (3d ed) 45.

33 used as a very broad category.

34 See e g *Theunissen v Fleischer, Wheeldon and Munnik* supra 294; *Pienaar v Rattray* supra 37; *Spark v Palte Ltd* (2) supra 31; *Tedder v Greig* supra 91–92; *Joubert v Tarry & Co* supra 281; *Michalow v Premier Milling Co* supra 61E–F: "'[P]artnership' debts are in law the debts *in solidum* of all the partners. In the absence of special rules of procedure, a creditor... would be entitled to sue any individual partner for payment of the whole debt and failing satisfaction sue the other parties one by one"; *Lamb Bros v Brenner & Co* supra 166; *Ex parte Fernandez* supra 727; *Potchefstroom Dairies and Industries Co Ltd v Standard Fresh Milk Supply Co* supra 511; *Divine Gates & Co v African Clothing Factory* supra 240; *Muller v Pienaar* 1968 3 SA 195 (A) 202H–203A 204; *Bester v Van Niekerk* supra 783; Nathan *Partnership and Private Companies* 94; Gibson *Mercantile and Company Law* 273; Wille and Millin *Mercantile Law* 410; Bamford 50 63–71; Hahlo and Kahn 701 n 89; Wille *Principles* 472; Herbstein and Van Winsen *Civil Practice of the Superior Courts* 170–171; Schutz 1954 *SALJ* 396; Boberg *Persons and the Family* 5; Uys *Genootskapsooreenkoms* 110–111: "Die prosesregreël ... is dus hoogstens 'n beperking van die eiser se regte — dit is geen aantasting van die vennote se hoofdelike verpligting nie"; Lee and Honoré *Obligations* 135–141; Christie 249; Bouwer *Beredderingsproses* 198.

35 See also par 388 ante.

36 The communis opinio is that partners were liable individually for partnership debts, the point in dispute being whether the liability was pro rata or in solidum. See ns 18 19 supra.

37 For various exceptions on this rule, see Bamford 67.

38 See e g *Meintjies & Co v Simpson Bros & Co* supra 216; *Simpson & Co v Fleck* supra 217; *Walker & Co v Beeton's Trustees* (1869) Buch 38; *Official Liquidators of the Frontier Commercial Bank v Adams* (1872) 2 R 79; *King v Porter, Hodgson and Co* supra; *Bank of Africa v Kimberley Mining Board* (1883) 2 HCG 12;

Auret's Trustee v Pienaar supra 41; *Rolfes, Nebel & Co v Browne* (1889) 5 HCG 395 397; *Gubler v Peycke & Co* 1903 TH 133; *Uys v Le Roux* 1906 TS 429 431–432; *Pienaar v Suttner Bros and Hirschfeld* supra; *Matterson Bros v Rolfes, Nebel & Co* 1915 WLD 33; *Press v Barker* supra 245; *Harding and Parker v John Pierce & Co* supra 113; *Du Toit v African Dairies Ltd* 247; *Sliom v Wallach's Printing and Publishing Co Ltd* supra 655; *Parker v Rand Motor Transport Co* 1930 AD 353 357–361; *Divine Gates & Co v African Clothing Factory* supra 240; *Eting v Dembo and Lipson* 1933 1 PH A18 (T); *Mahomed v Karp Bros* supra 113; *Baldinger v Broomberg* supra; *Jacobs v Du Plessis* 1950 4 SA 25 (O) 29; *Shingadia Bros v Shingadia* 1958 1 SA 582 (FC) 583; *Geerdts v Crawford* 1953 2 SA 759 (N) 764; *Lewis v Lyons* 1958 2 PH M19 (D); *Turkstra v Goldberg* supra 513; *Michalow v Premier Milling Co Ltd* supra; *Anderson v Gordik Organisation* 1962 2 SA 68 (D) 72; *Standard Bank of SA Ltd v Pearson* 1961 3 SA 721 (E) 723A–D; *Muller v Pienaar* 1968 3 SA 195 (A) 202–203; *Vrystaatse Lewendehawe Ko-op Bpk v Van Jaarsveld* supra; *Vulcan Trading Co* (1958) *Pvt Ltd v Ayliffe* 1970 1 SA 10 (R); *Lee v Maraisdrif* (*Edms*) *Bpk* supra 540; *Standard Bank of SA Ltd v Lombard* supra; *Strydom v Protea Eiendomsagente* supra 210; *Gardee v Dhanmanta Holdings* 1978 1 SA 1066 (N) 1071; *Boonzaier v Kiley* supra 619; *Karstein v Moribe* supra 290.

39 *Muller v Pienaar* 1968 3 SA 195 (A) 203; *Divine Gates & Co v African Clothing Factory* supra 240; Henning 7; Delport *Gedingvoering tussen Vennote* 187. It has been suggested that this rule is probably of Scottish origin: McGregor 1909 *SALJ* 24; De Wet and Yeats 404 n 212. It seems that undue reliance on certain Roman-Dutch authorities regarding the availability of the beneficium divisionis to solidary debtors also played a part; see e g *Haarhoff v Cape of Good Hope Bank* supra 313–314. For the position in Scotland, see n 56 infra.

40 *Lee v Maraisdrif* (*Edms*) *Bpk* supra 542. See ns 13 22 supra; Delport 187; Joubert 296.

41 See e g *Vrystaatse Lewendehawe Ko-op Bpk v Van Jaarsveld* supra; De Wet and Yeats 406; Bamford 66–71.

42 In the Tvl by virtue of the Registration of Businesses Act 36 of 1909 s 8, a registered business partnership could sue or be sued in the registered business style of the partnership. This statutory provision has been repealed by the Revenue Laws Amendment Act 89 of 1972 s 14 with effect from 1 January 1975. A similar practice was adopted and may still be followed in Natal (see e g *Gouws v*

Venter & Co 1959 4 SA 527 (D)) even though the Registration of Firms Act 35 of 1906 of which s 15 which provided that any firm required to register under that act and which fails to register may be sued in the name under which it is carrying on business, has been repealed by the General Law Amendment Act 70 of 1968 s 1.

43 Uniform Rules of Court r 14; r 54 of the rules made under the Magistrates' Courts Act 32 of 1944 s 25. For details, see title CIVIL PROCEDURE; Nathan, Barnett and Brink *Uniform Rules of Court* 103–104; Jones and Buckle *Civil Practice of the Magistrates' Courts* vol 2: *The Rules* 400–406; Herbstein and Van Winsen *Civil Practice of the Superior Courts* 137–139. These rules do not affect the principle that while a partnership is in existence one or more of the individual members cannot be sued in respect of a partnership debt; see *Geerdts v Crawford* supra; Delport 188.

44 URC r 14(2); MCR r 54(1).

45 URC r 14(3); Bamford 63.

46 The procedures under the various rules differ. For details see the authorities referred to in n 43 supra; De Wet and Yeats 407; Bamford 67.

47 URC r 14(5)(h); MCR r 40(3); *Standard Bank of SA Ltd v Pearson* supra 723; *Standard Bank of SA Ltd v Lombard* supra 813; *Strydom v Protea Eiendomsagente* supra 210; *Sliom v Wallach's Printing and Publishing Co Ltd* supra; n 38 supra.

48 Supreme Court Act 59 of 1959 s 26(2); URC r 14(5)(h); MCR r 40(3); *Press v Barker* supra; *Sliom v Wallach's Printing and Publishing Co Ltd* supra 655; *Muller v Pienaar* supra;

Boonzaier v Kiley supra; *Theunissen v Fleischer, Wheeldon and Munnik* supra 295; *Gardee v Dhanmanta Holdings* supra 1071; *Rees v Feldman* 1927 TPD 884 887 891; *Parker v Rand Motor Transport* supra 361; *Mahomed v Karp Bros* supra 113; *Divine Gates & Co v African Clothing Factory* supra 240; De Wet and Yeats 407 n 237; Henning 4 n 18; Joubert 296; Bamford 65 n 24.

49 *Rees v Feldman* supra 889; *Xakana v Elliot Bros (Queenstown) (Pty) Ltd* 1967 4 SA 724 (E); De Wet and Yeats 407.

50 24 of 1936 s 2 definition of "debtor"; ss 3(2) 13 49 92(5) 128.

51 See par 389 ante.

52 ibid.

53 See n 34 supra.

54 See Joubert 296; Henning 4 n 18.

55 See par 389 ante; cf De Wet and Yeats 391 405; De Villiers 144–147.

56 Although the English Partnership Act of 1890 s 9 provides that in Scotland partners are jointly and severally liable, this liability is considered to be accessory and not primary in nature: Miller *Partnership* 355. According to O'Neal 1949 *Tulane Law Review* 483 the solidary liability of partners in entity jurisdictions is considered to be neither primary nor conventional, but secondary.

57 *Standard Bank of SA Ltd v Lombard* supra 813–814.

58 For extraordinary partnerships, see par 367 ante.

59 See par 414 post.

60 See par 415 post.

61 See par 416 post.

414 Existence of partnership Usually only a person who has been an ordinary partner[1] at the time the obligation was contracted is rendered liable to third parties for a partnership obligation.[2] A person cannot be a member of a partnership unless an agreement to this effect existed between all the members of the partnership.[3] The onus of proof that the particular partnership existed at the time the obligation was incurred is on the third party.[4]

A non-partner who by his words or conduct represents himself to be a partner, or knowingly allows himself to be represented as a partner, is liable as a partner to any third party who has dealt with or has given credit to the partnership on the faith of that representation. This principle of liability on the basis of holding out is an illustration of the general doctrine of estoppel by representation.[5] The doctrine of estoppel operates in favour of those third parties only who were induced to consider the non-partner a partner. It does not have the effect of rendering him liable as a partner to all partnership creditors generally,[6] or that he is recognized as a partner *vis-à-vis* the true partners.[7]

The principle of fixing a former partner with liability on the basis of holding out is not confined to the protection only of former creditors of the erstwhile partnership, who continue to deal with the remaining partners in ignorance of any change in the membership of the former partnership.[8] The fact that a creditor can show that he was a former customer of the old partnership and was given no notice of any change in the membership of that firm, is one of the commonest ways of satisfactorily proving the representation that is a necessary part of the estoppel doctrine.[9] This, however, is by no means the only way. It will always be found that the inquiry is whether the defendant has held himself out to the plaintiff in question as a partner of the firm, regardless of whether or not that plaintiff has had past dealings with the former partnership. Hence the doctrine cannot properly be restricted in such a way that it does not protect persons who have never previously dealt with the erstwhile partnership.[10]

1 For commanditarian and silent partners, see par 367 ante.
2 e g *Alcock v Mali Dyke Syndicate* 1910 TPD 567 570; *Whitelock v Rolfes, Nebel & Co* 1911 WLD 35 37–38; De Villiers *Encyclopedia of Forms and Precedents* vol 13 158.
3 See par 379 supra.
4 *Bale and Greene v Bennett* (1907) 28 NLR 361; *Berezniak v Van Nieuwhuizen* 1948 1 SA 1057 (T) 1059; *Alcock v Mali Dyke Syndicate* supra 569; *Levin v Barclays Bank DCO* 1968 2 SA 45 (A).
5 *Jelliman v SA Manufacturing Co* 1923 CPD 215 218–219; *Geikie v W Bailey and J T Button* (1882) 3 NLR 196; *Herron v Trustee of Torque Electrical Engineering Co* (1905) 22 SC 432; *S Butcher & Sons v Baranov Bros* (1905) 26 NLR 589; *Wilson and Spurgin v Burt* 1906 CTR 922; *Hall v Millin and Hutton* 1915 SR 78 80; *Dyer and Dyer v Hartwanger* 1915 EDL 398; *Bain v Barclays Bank (DC&O) Ltd* 1937 SR 191

201–202; *Estate Maibaum v Varley* 1935 NPD 396 408; *Van Dyk v Conradie* 1963 2 SA 413 (C); *Midlands Auctioneers (Pvt) Ltd v Bowie* 1975 1 SA 773 (R) 774; *Boonzaier v Kiley* 1981 2 SA 618 (W) 620. See also r 14(5)(f) (h) of the Uniform Rules of Court; De Wet *Estoppel by Representation* 71; De Villiers 161. For estoppel generally, see title ESTOPPEL.
6 *Jelliman v SA Manufacturing Co* supra 219; *Herron v Trustee of Torque Electrical Engineering Co* supra 447.
7 See par 379 supra.
8 *Midlands Auctioneers (Pvt) Ltd v Bowie* supra 775.
9 *Midlands Auctioneers (Pvt) Ltd v Bowie* supra; *Estate Maibaum v Varley* supra; *McKenzie v Dreyer & Co* 1902 CTR 282; *McKenzie v Irvine* 1902 CTR 734; *In re Paarl Bank* (1891) 8 SC 131 132.
10 *Jelliman v SA Manufacturing Co* supra 219; *Midlands Auctioneers (Pvt) Ltd v Bowie* supra.

415 Authority to bind partnership In order that an obligation may be a partnership obligation, a primary requirement is that the contracting partner must have had authority to bind the partnership.[1] The authority may be actual or ostensible.

Actual authority to enter into contracts on behalf of the partnership may be expressly granted to a partner or may be implied from the existence or customary dealing of the partnership.[2]

If a partner who has been expressly authorized to transact certain specified business on behalf of the partnership acted in terms of his mandate, the partnership will be bound even if the transaction fell outside the scope of the usual or customary business of the partnership.[3] General authority to bind the partnership may also be conferred expressly on a partner, for instance, when a partner is given complete control of the management of the business in the partnership agreement or when the partners subsequently appoint a managing partner to control the partnership business.[4] It has been suggested that unless the general authority of the managing partner expressly empowers him to conduct any business whatsoever in his discretion it would probably be construed as being subject to an implied term that he can only act on behalf of the partnership within the scope of its business.[5] Hence the partnership will usually[6] be bound only if the transaction entered into by the managing partner fell within the scope of the partnership business.[7]

One of the naturalia of a contract of partnership is that each partner is entitled to participate in management, and empowered to perform management functions without the consent or co-operation of his partners.[8] It follows that, in the absence of an agreement to the contrary, each partner has authority to perform all such acts as are necessary for or incidental to the proper conduct of the partnership business, and that such acts bind the partnership.[9] This implied authority (mutual mandate)[10] of every partner to act for the partnership and to bind it to transactions falling within the scope of the partnership business, is clearly actual authority.[11] The principle underlying the implied authority of a partner seems to be quite clear, but the real difficulty arises in its application. It is not always easy in practice to determine whether or not a particular transaction fell within the scope of the partnership business.[12] If it fell outside, the contracting partner exceeded his implied authority to bind the partnership.[13] The onus of proof to show that it fell within, lies on the third party seeking to hold the partnership liable.[14] The question whether or not the particular transaction fell within the scope of the partnership business is one of fact. The answer depends on the circumstances of each case, regard being had to, for instance, the purpose and customary dealing of the partnership, the nature of the undertaking and general commercial usage concerning similar undertakings.[15]

In the particular circumstances concerned the following acts have been held or accepted to be within the implied authority of a partner:[16] the giving of a promissory note for the purposes of a branch store opened by a partner in the name of a firm carrying on a general business and already having several other branch businesses;[17] the receipt of money on behalf of a client of the firm by an attorney where a transaction which is within the scope of the firm's business, whether strictly speaking the work of an attorney or not, involved the receipt of such money;[18] the acceptance of payment on the firm's behalf of debts due to it and the giving of valid receipts for the same, as well as the execution of a power of attorney in the firm's name for the cancellation of a mortgage bond in favour of the firm on the payment of debt secured by it;[19] where two accountants carried on business in partnership, the canvassing of votes by one partner for the appointment of the other as trustee in an insolvent estate and in particular giving a written guarantee to a creditor that he would not be required to pay into a contribution account if he gave the partner his vote;[20] guaranteeing the credit-worthiness of clients of a partnership carrying on business as bankers;[21] the purchase on the credit of an ordinary trading partnership of such goods as are or may be necessary for carrying on its business in the usual way;[22] the selling, buying, paying for and receiving of merchandise by a partner in a commercial partnership;[23] the promise to pay a debt owing by the partnership as well as the release of a partnership debt;[24] the consent to judgment on behalf of the partnership prior to its dissolution and in the absence of collusion with the creditor;[25] the application for the sequestration of the estate of a partnership debtor;[26] making an admission in connection with the business and debt of the partnership in a lawsuit against the partnership;[27] the signing of an acknowledgment of debt on behalf of a property exploiting partnership relating to the contract price of the performance of certain tests upon the soil of its immovable property with a view to the construction of an arcade upon it;[28] where a firm was brought into being for the purpose of owning immovable property, any act done by a partner on behalf of the partnership with the object of exploiting that immovable property or enhancing its value or for paying for work done with these objects in view;[29] the acceptance of bills in the name of the firm for causes appertaining to the partnership by a partner vested with the management of a trading partnership;[30] instructing an attorney to apply for a liquor licence for a restaurant business conducted by the partnership;[31] the pledging of partnership assets as security for money borrowed on behalf of the partnership business.[32] It has been submitted that a partner may have implied authority to conclude a contract of insurance.[33]

In the particular circumstances concerned the following acts have been held not to be within the implied authority of a partner:[34] drawing bills or making promissory notes in the name of the firm to pay his own private debts;[35] the signing and discounting of post-dated cheques by one partner only, on behalf of a partnership carrying on a property-owning business which receives rentals in respect of its immovable property and effects improvements from time to time;[36] the purchase of a pair of stud horses by a member of a partnership in a butchery;[37] the making of statements by a partner in a general dealer's business regarding the financial stability of a customer who has referred a third person to the firm;[38] the running up of a personal hotel accommodation and entertainment account;[39] the sale of ploughing animals where the business of the partnership was the management of a farm;[40] the purchase of another dairy business by a member of a partnership entered into for the purpose of carrying on a certain dairy business and to carry on a similar business at a place which might from time to time be agreed upon;[41] the purchase by a partner in a firm existing solely and exclusively for milling purposes of provisions of ordinary merchandise;[42] the acquiescence in a judgment against which the firm has decided to appeal;[43] the submission to arbitration of matters concerning the partnership;[44] the release from a covenant in restraint of trade favouring the partnership;[45] the direction to auditors to retain books which have been delivered to them to audit;[46] the mortgaging by only one of the partners of partnership property registered in the name of the other partner even where the whereabouts of the latter is unknown;[47] the pledging of partnership securities for a private debt.[48]

Actual authority may also be conferred with retroactive effect. If a partner professing to act on behalf of the partnership exceeds his authority, the other partners may adopt the transaction by ratifying his act, in which case they will be bound by it.[49] The effect of ratification is that the act of the unauthorized partner is regarded as though he had the requisite authority at the time the act was concluded.[50] Where a partner concludes the act in his own name, he does not profess to act for the partnership and the partners cannot by ratification acquire rights or incur obligations.[51] Ratification can be made in words or by conduct. If the partners disapprove of the act of the unauthorized partner, they should notify the other party to the contract within a reasonable time of the lack of authority. If they do not do so timeously they could be regarded as having ratified the act by their conduct.[52] Ratification by conduct should, however, not be confused with conduct justifying an inference of actual or ostensible authorization.[53]

The implied authority of a partner to act on behalf of the partnership in the conduct of its business may be varied, limited or excluded by express agreement between the partners.[54] When a partner with power thus limited exceeds his express authority and concludes a contract with a third person who is unaware of the limitation, but the partner did act within his implied or ostensible authority, the firm cannot shelter behind these secret or private instructions, but is bound by the contract.[55] This proposition was said to commend itself as being a sound one in conformity with general principles and common sense.[56] Stated differently, a third party is entitled to assume that each partner has implied authority to act on behalf of the partnership in transactions falling within the scope of the partnership business.[57] Knowledge of internal limitations on authority is not imputed to third parties.[58] A third party seeking to hold the partnership liable on a contract concluded by a partner on behalf of the partnership is not required to prove that the partner had the power *vis-à-vis* his co-partners to perform that act, but acquits himself of his onus of proof in this regard if he establishes that the act of the partner fell within the scope of the partnership business.[59]

Thus, where the partner contracted within what would have been his implied authority, but for the limitation or exclusion imposed by internal arrangement, the partners are not entitled to avoid liability on that contract by raising that partner's lack of authority against the bona fide third party, but it would be a valid defence if they are able to prove that the third party was aware of this arrangement.[60] Hence, the partnership may be liable, even though the contracting partner had no actual authority or exceeded his actual authority, and as such by way of estoppel, that is, the partners may be estopped from denying that the partner did not have the requisite authority to conclude the contract on behalf of the partnership.[61] It has been submitted, however, that this liability is not based on estoppel since all the essentials for a successful reliance on estoppel[62] need not be proved.[63] It should rather be seen as a manifestation of a rule which is basic to all kinds of associations, whether endowed with legal personality or not, and of which another illustration is the so-called *Turquand* rule of company law.[64] The basis of this rule is the protection of bona fide third parties against prejudice they may suffer as a result of the operation of private internal arrangements in the management of associations, which do not enjoy publicity.[65] On the other hand, it has been submitted that the doctrine of estoppel usually affords adequate protection to bona fide third parties dealing with individual partners acting on behalf of the partnership, although there are situations where estoppel does not suffice. The classic example is the situation where the third party is aware of limitations on the capacity of individual partners. Due to his knowledge of this internal limitation the third party may find it wellnigh impossible to prove all the essentials for a successful reliance on estoppel. Under these circumstances the bona fide third party ought to be able to rely on the *Turquand* rule.[66]

The possibility also exists that a partnership may be bound by a contract concluded by a non-partner, despite his not being authorized to act on behalf of the partnership. The partnership may be liable, on the basis of estoppel, to a bona fide third party if the partnership represented the non-partner as a partner or knowingly allowed the non-partner to represent himself as a partner.[67] In addition there seems to be no reason why partners should not in appropriate circumstances be estopped from denying that they had ratified an unauthorized act.[68]

1 Pothier *Partnership* 6 1 97; Van der Linden *Koopmans Handboek* 4 1 13; *Alcock v Mali Dyke Syndicate* 1910 TPD 567; *Meyer v Mosenthal Bros Ltd* 1925 TPD 281 284; *Forder, Ritch and Eriksson v Engar's Heirs* 1973 1 SA 719 (N) 722-723; *Cunningham & Co v Seale* 1916 SR 133; *Hugo and Hains v The Magaliesberg Prospecting and Developing Syndicate* 1893 H 248; *Eaton and Louw v Arcade Properties (Pty) Ltd* 1961 4 SA 233 (T) 240; De Villiers *Encyclopedia of Forms and Precedents* vol 13 158-159; Nathan *Partnership and Private Companies* 95; Bamford *Partnership* 52.

2 Pothier 6 1 98; *Standard Bank v Goodchild and Brittain* (1877) 7 Buch 120; *In re Paarl Bank* (1891) 8 SC 131 132; *Croghan's Executrix v Whitby and Webber* 1904 TH 101 105; *Braker & Co v Deiner* 1934 TPD 203 206; *Goodrickes v Hall* 1978 4 SA 208 (N) 211.

3 The express authorization by all the partners of such a transaction amounts to an agreement to extend the scope of the business of the partnership; see *Croghan's Executrix v*

Whitby and Webber supra 105: "[A] particular transaction may be brought within the scope of the partnership business by the fact that it has been undertaken on behalf of the partnership by consent of all the partners." De Villiers 159; Nathan 99.

4 See par 403(b) ante for a statement on the distinction between the case where the managing partner is appointed in terms of the original partnership agreement and the case where his appointment is only made subsequent to the conclusion of the original contract.

5 De Villiers 159.

6 The partnership may also be bound by the partners holding out the managing partner as having authority. See the discussion of ostensible authority below.

7 Cf *Forder, Ritch and Eriksson v Engar's Heirs* supra 721; *Paddon and Brock Ltd v Nathan* 1906 TS 158; *Contemporary Refrigeration (Pty) Ltd v Leites and Sonpoll Investments (Pty) Ltd* 1967 2 SA 388 (D) 391E-393D.

8 See Henning 1978 *MB* 191 192; par 403 ante.

9 Pothier 5 1 90; Van der Keessel *Prael* 3 21 7; Van der Linden 4 1 1 3; *In re Paarl Bank* supra; *Paddon and Brock Ltd v Nathan* supra; *Braker & Co v Deiner* supra; *De Winter v Ajmeri Properties and Investments* 1957 2 SA 297 (D) 298; *Forder, Ritch and Eriksson v Engar's Heirs* supra; *Goodrickes v Hall* supra.

10 For a discussion of the question whether mutual mandate is an additional essential of partnership or not, see par 371 ante.

11 *Forder, Ritch and Eriksson v Engar's Heirs* supra 721 724.

12 *Braker & Co v Deiner* supra.

13 e g *Meyer v Mosenthal Bros Ltd* supra; *L Stein v Garlick and Holdcroft, K Stein v Garlick and Holdcroft* 1910 TS 250; *Blaiberg v Braun* 1916 OPD 101; *Forder, Ritch and Eriksson v Engar's Heirs* supra.

14 *Meyer v Mosenthal Bros Ltd* supra; *Alcock v Mali Dyke Syndicate* supra; *Rand Advance (Pty) Ltd v Scala Café* 1974 1 SA 786 (D) 790; 1975 1 SA 28 (N); *Soref Bros (SA) (Pty) Ltd v Khan Bros Wholesale* 1976 3 SA 339 (D); *Goodrickes v Hall* supra 210-202; *Forder, Ritch and Eriksson v Engar's Heirs* supra 723.

15 *Trustee Insolvent Estate of Abdul Sumod & Co v McCubbin & Co* (1888) 9 NLR 156; *Braker & Co v Deiner* supra; *Forder, Ritch and Eriksson v Engar's Heirs* supra 722; De Wet and Yeats *Kontraktereg en Handelsreg* 401.

16 See also De Wet and Yeats 401; Nathan 97-102; Bamford 53.

17 *Niemayer and Marais v Gibson* (1884) 4 EDC 69.

18 *Croghan's Executrix v Whitby and Webber* supra.

19 Voet *Commentarius* 17 2 16; *H Scholtz v Registrar of Deeds* (1894) 1 OR 111; *Louw v The Registrar of Deeds* (1874) 4 Buch 132; *Braker & Co v Deiner* supra 207: "[O]ne partner can accept payment of a debt due to the firm and give a valid receipt for such a debt and a promise by one partner to pay a debt owing by the firm undoubtedly binds the firm. So too . . . a release by one partner of a partnership debt operates as a release by the firm." But see Bamford 54.

20 *Standard Bank Ltd v Simenhoff* 1923 2 PH C44 (A); *Holland v Simenhoff* 1923 AD 676.

21 *L Stein v Garlick and Holdcroft, K Stein v Garlick and Holdcroft* supra.

22 *Braker & Co v Deiner* supra 207 relying on Lindley *Partnership* (9th ed) 202.

23 Pothier 5 1 92; *Braker & Co v Deiner* supra 207; cf *Mattson v Yiannakis* 1976 4 SA 154 (W) 158A.

24 *Braker & Co v Deiner* supra.

25 *Braker & Co v Deiner* supra.

26 *Newton Meat Supply Co v Lang* 1929 TPD 627.

27 *Morum v Pieters* 1927 SWA 36; *Taylor v Budd* 1932 AD 326 333-334.

28 *De Winter v Ajmeri Properties and Investments* supra 298.

29 *De Winter v Ajmeri Properties and Investments* supra 298.

30 *Forder, Ritch and Eriksson v Engar's Heirs* supra 721.

31 *Goodrickes v Hall* supra 211.

32 *Syrkin v Weinberg Bros* (1906) 23 SC 718.

33 Bamford 53.

34 See n 16 supra.

35 *Standard Bank v Goodchild and Brittain* supra; *Rand Advance (Pty) Ltd v Scala Café* supra 789; *Soref Bros (SA) (Pty) Ltd v Khan Bros Wholesale* supra; *Forder, Ritch and Eriksson v Engar's Heirs* supra 721.

36 *Forder, Ritch and Eriksson v Engar's Heirs* supra 724: "The minimum requirement for implying authority on the part of G M I Engar to sign post-dated cheques alone on behalf of the partnership, is knowledge on the part of each of the partners that he was doing so . . . It cannot, in my view, be said that the other partners 'habitually allowed G M I Engar to sign and issue post-dated cheques' on behalf of the partnership unless it is proved that each one of them actually knew that he was doing so."

37 *Chalmers v Whittle, Lloyd & Co* (1884) 3 EDC 347.

38 *L Stein v Garlick and Holdcroft, K Stein v Garlick and Holdcroft* supra.

39 *Machen's Trustee v Henrey* (1884) 4 EDC 22; *Wilson and Spurgin v Burt* 1906 CTR 922.

40 *Holmes v Schoch* 1910 TPD 700.

41 *Potchefstroom Dairies and Industries Co Ltd v Standard Fresh Milk Supply Co* 1913 TPD 506 510.

42 *Meyer v Mosenthal Bros Ltd* supra 283.

43 *Grassi and Shrewe v Lewis* 1910 TPD 533.

44 *Braker & Co v Deiner* supra 208.

45 *Blaiberg v Braun* supra.

46 The auditors must return such books on demand by the other partner: *Laughton & Co v Andrews & Co* 1900 CTR 438.

47 *In re Nissen Bros* 1900 CTR 402.

48 *Zeederberg v Trustees of J Norton & Co and J D Norden & Co* (1857) 3 S 12 13.

49 For details, see title AGENCY AND REPRESENTATION.

50 See *Reid v Warner* 1907 TS 961 967; Joubert *Verteenwoordigingsreg* 162-163.

51 since an act that is ratified is an act of representation; see *Jagersfontein Garage and Transport Co v Secretary State Advances Recoveries Office* 1939 OPD 37; title AGENCY AND REPRESENTATION.

52 *Whiteside and Flanagan v Shakinowsky and Kaplan* 1924 EDL 108 110–111. See *Niemayer and Marais v Gibson* supra; *Potchefstroom Dairies and Industries Co Ltd v Standard Fresh Milk Supply Co* supra; *Taylor v Budd* supra 333–334.
53 For further statements and different consequences, see title AGENCY AND REPRESENTATION and De Wet and Yeats 402 respectively.
54 Pothier 3 2 66–72; *Goodrickes v Hall* supra 211; Henning 1978 *BM* 191 192; Oosthuizen 1977 *TSAR* 210 218; par 403 ante.
55 See Wille and Millin *Mercantile Law* 429.
56 *Goodrickes v Hall* supra.
57 Pothier 6 1 98.
58 The doctrine of constructive notice is not applicable to partnerships; see Oosthuizen 218. For a discussion of this doctrine, see Cilliers and Benade *Company Law* 51 105 121.
59 Barels *Advysen* 2 60; *Meyer v Mosenthal Bros Ltd* supra; *Rand Advance (Pty) Ltd v Scala Café* supra; Henning 192; De Villiers 161; De Wet and Yeats 402.
60 Pothier 6 1 98; *Holl Cons* 1 303; Van Bynkershoek *Obs Tum* 2 1594; *Standard Bank v Goodchild and Brittain* supra; *Forder, Ritch and Eriksson v Engar's Heirs* supra; De Villiers 161; De Wet and Yeats 402; De Wet *Estoppel by Representation* 70–71; Henning 192.
61 *Rand Advance (Pty) Ltd v Scala Café* supra 790 792; *Soref Bros (SA) (Pty) Ltd v Khan Bros Wholesale* supra; *Goodrickes v Hall* supra; De

Wet and Yeats 402; De Wet 71; Oosthuizen 218.
62 For these essentials, see title ESTOPPEL.
63 and since this liability existed in the common law prior to the reception of the doctrine of estoppel from English law: De Villiers 161; cf De Wet 71.
64 That is the so-called "rule in *Royal British Bank v Turquand*", named after the case of this name (1856) 6 E & B 327; 119 ER 886. For detailed discussion of this rule, see Cilliers and Benade 121–124 299; Oosthuizen 210–219; title COMPANIES.
65 De Villiers 161; Oosthuizen 219: "It is submitted that the Turquand rule should be seen as a general rule applicable to all societies whether endowed with legal personality or not and irrespective of the applicability of the doctrine of constructive notice; provided that the outsider has no access to the internal management of the association."
66 Oosthuizen 217–218.
67 See *Jelliman v SA Manufacturing Co* 1923 CPD 215; *Strachan v Blackbeard & Son* 1910 AD 282; *Hall v Millin and Hutton* 1915 SR 78 80; *Midlands Auctioneers (Pvt) Ltd v Bowie* 1975 1 SA 773 (R) 775; *Levin v Barclays Bank DCO* 1968 2 SA 45 (A); *Boonzaier v Kiley* 1981 2 SA 618 (W) 620; De Wet 70–71; De Wet and Yeats 402; De Villiers 160; title ESTOPPEL.
68 See title AGENCY AND REPRESENTATION.

416 In the name or on behalf of the partnership Whatever authority a contracting partner may have to bind the partnership, it is usually stated as an additional requirement that, in order to render the partnership liable, the obligation should have been contracted in the name of the partnership.[1] It has quite correctly been said that all that this amounts to is the obvious principle that the partnership incurs obligations only if it has been the intention of the contracting partner and the third party that the obligations will be incurred by the partnership and not by the contracting partner alone (i e in his personal capacity).[2] Whether this has been the intention of the partner and third party is a question of fact depending on the circumstances of each case.[3] No specific form of words is necessarily required to express this intention, but specific phrases can point to such an intention.[4] If it has been the intention of the contracting partner and the third party that the obligations will be incurred by the partnership and not the contracting partner personally, the partnership will be liable even though it derived no benefit from the contract[5] or even though the name of the contracting partner appeared on the contract without qualification.[6] Conversely, if it has been the intention that the contracting partner personally and not the disclosed partnership will incur the obligations, the partnership will not be liable, even though the contract was for the benefit of the partnership.[7] Thus, if third parties dealing with a partner choose to make him their sole debtor, with full knowledge that he is acting for his partners as well as himself, the third parties would not be justified in afterwards treating any other member of the partnership as their debtors.[8] A more difficult situation arises where the third party gives personal credit to the partner, unaware of the fact that the person he is dealing with is acting on behalf of a partnership. If considered to be purely a matter of intention and consensus, only the contracting partner and not the partnership ought to be liable, even when the third party subsequently becomes aware of the precise facts of the affair.[9] However, in view of the adoption of the doctrine of the undisclosed principal,[10] the vexed question is whether this doctrine can (and ought to) be applied to partnerships, with the result that the third party, when he subsequently discovers the undisclosed partnership, has the choice to sue either the contracting partner or the partnership, and conversely, that the undisclosed partnership can subsequently disclose itself and claim performance of the obligations which the third party has undertaken.[11] On the one hand, it was held that this doctrine cannot or should not be applied to partnerships.[12] On the other hand, it was held and submitted that it can or ought to be applied.[13] Thus, for instance, it was held in *Lotter & Co v Loubser and De Villiers*[14] that the doctrine is inapplicable and that it was even then already too late to ask the court to hold the partnership liable on the contract of a partner who has made such contract entirely in his own name on his individual credit without any reference to the firm, even though he may have in reality acted in the interests of the partnership. Fifty years later it was held that since a partner who acts on behalf of an ordinary partnership acts as an agent for the partnership, it follows logically that the doctrine of the undisclosed principal is applicable to such partnerships, but not to extraordinary partnerships.[15] Although the question of an agent acting for two undisclosed principals who will be jointly liable was left open in *Cullinan v Noordkaaplandse Aartappelkernmoerkwekers Koöp Bpk*,[16] it was subsequently stated that there seems no reason, on the basis of the ratio in that case, why the doctrine is not applicable to a situation where the principals are liable in solidum or as joint co-debtors, as in the case of partners.[17] However, the question whether the doctrine ought to be extended to partnerships was expressly left open and thus still awaits final decision.[18] It is clear, however, that even if it is assumed that it does apply, the operation of this doctrine will be excluded where it could result in prejudice to the third party, unforeseen by him at the time of entering into the contract.[19]

1 Voet *Commentarius* 17 2 13-14; Pothier *Partnership* 6 1 100-101; Van der Linden *Koopmans Handboek* 4 1 1 3; *Lamb Bros v Brenner & Co* (1886) 5 EDC 152; *Guardian Insurance and Trust Co v Lovemore's Executors* (1887) 5 SC 205 210; *Estate Davison v Auret* (1905) 22 SC 10 19; De Villiers *Encyclopedia of Forms and Precedents* vol 13 158; Bamford *Partnership* 55; cf De Wet and Yeats *Kontraktereg en Handelsreg* 403.

2 De Wet and Yeats 403; Barels *Advysen* 2 59; Van der Keessel *Prael* 3 21 7; *Lamb Bros v Brenner & Co* supra; *Guardian Insurance and Trust Co v Lovemore's Executors* supra; *Green v Green and Hansen and Schrader* (1897) 12 EDC 68; *Julaka v Duguza Abantu Butchery* 1933 TPD 634; *Berezniak v Van Nieuwenhuizen* 1948 1 SA 1057 (T); *Murray v Findlay & Co* (1904) 21 SC 144; *Sacca Ltd v Olivier* 1954 3 SA 136 (T). See also the title AGENCY AND REPRESENTATION vol 1 ante especially par 109.

3 Bamford 56.

4 See *Guardian Insurance and Trust Co v Lovemore's Executors* supra; *Sentrale Kunsmis Korp (Edms) Bpk v NKP Kunsmisverspreiders (Edms) Bpk* 1970 3 SA 367 (A) 394; title AGENCY AND

REPRESENTATION vol 1 ante especially par 109.

5 Pothier 6 1 101; see *Sacca Ltd v Olivier* supra; De Wet and Yeats 403.

6 Barels 2 59: " ... dat BRANDSTEEN, schoon in den uiterlyken schyn contraheerende *op zyn eigen naam* in de daed contraheerende voor de rekeninge van de Compagnie"; Van der Keessel 3 21 7; *Lamb Bros v Brenner & Co* supra; see also *Meter Motors (Pty) Ltd v Cohen* 1966 2 SA 735 (T).

7 Pothier 6 1 101; *Guardian Insurance and Trust Co v Lovemore's Executors* supra; see also *Torien v Horwitz* (1906) 23 SC 613; *Sellar Bros v Clark* (1893) 10 SC 168; *Alcock v Mali Dyke Syndicate* 1910 TPD 567; *Sacca Ltd v Olivier* supra.

8 *Guardian Insurance and Trust Co v Lovemore's Executors* supra 211. See also *Lotter & Co v Loubser and De Villiers* 1910 CPD 101; *Green v Green and Hansen and Schrader* supra; *Sellar Bros v Clark* supra; *Berezniak v Van Nieuwenhuizen* supra 1060.

9 De Wet and Yeats 403. See title AGENCY AND REPRESENTATION.

10 e g *Lippert & Co v Desbats* 1869 Buch 189; *O'Leary v Harbord* (1888) 5 HCG 1; *Avis v*

Highveld Supply Stores 1925 AD 410; *Cullinan v Noordkaaplandse Aartappelkernmoerkwekers Koöp Bpk* 1972 1 SA 761 (A).

11 *Karstein v Moribe* 1982 2 SA 282 (T) 293–300; see also the title AGENCY AND REPRESEN-TATION.

12 See e g *Guardian Insurance and Trust Co v Lovemore's Executors* supra; *Sellar Bros v Clark* supra; *Green v Beveridge* (1891) 8 SC 154; *Torien v Horwitz* supra; *Lotter & Co v Loubser and De Villiers* supra; *Cohen v Commissioner for Inland Revenue* 1948 4 SA 616 (T) 628; *Spark v Palte Ltd* (2) 1956 3 SA 27 (SR); see De Wet and Yeats 404; Hahlo and Kahn *Union of SA: Development of its Laws and Constitution* 701–702; Wille and Millin *Mercantile Law* 430; Nathan *Partnership and Private Companies* 102; Maasdorp *Institutes* vol 2

289.

13 See e g *Eaton and Louw v Arcade Properties (Pty) Ltd* 1961 4 SA 233 (T) 240; *Shapiro v Shapiro and Ketz's Trustee* 1907 TS 472; Bamford 57; De Villiers 158; Gibson *Mercantile and Company Law* 275; Schutz 1954 *SALJ* 395.

14 1910 CPD 101 106.

15 *Eaton and Louw v Arcade Properties (Pty) Ltd* supra 240.

16 1972 1 SA 761 (A). For a statement on the "rule in the *Cullinan* case", see title AGENCY AND REPRESENTATION vol 1 par 155 ante.

17 *Karstein v Moribe* supra 294. See also Blecher 1972 *SALJ* 286; Whiting 1971 *Annual Survey* 105.

18 *Karstein v Moribe* supra 293E–G.

19 *Karstein v Moribe* supra 299–300.

DELICT AND CRIME

417 Delictual liability There appears to be a dearth of direct authority in regard to the incidence and delimitation of the possible liability of partners for each other's delicts.[1] In an obiter dictum it was pointed out that a partner may act in many capacities for the partnership and that it depends upon the capacity in which he acts whether the partnership incurs vicarious liability or not.[2] "The mandate entrusted to a partner may be to act for the partnership as a conventional representative or to do specific work for the partnership in which latter case he would not be a servant of the partnership but rather an independent contractor."[3] It has been submitted that a partnership is liable for the delict of a partner committed while acting in the ordinary course of partnership business, or when acting with the authority of his partners.[4]

1 See McKerron *Delict* 89; De Villiers and Macintosh *Agency* 610; Elliott and Banwell *SA Notary* 229; Bamford *Partnership* 62.

2 *Rodrigues v Alves* 1978 4 SA 834 (A) 839H.

3 *Rodrigues v Alves* supra. For the concepts "servant" and "independent contractor" in this context, see De Villiers and Macintosh

538–543; but see contra McKerron 89.

4 Bamford 62; cf *Peffers v Attorneys, Notaries and Conveyancers Fidelity Guarantee Fund Board of Control* 1965 2 SA 53 (C); English Partnership Act 1890 (53 & 54 Vict c 39) ss 10 12; Lindley *Partnership* 282–284.

418 Criminal liability Since a partnership is not a legal persona, the partnership itself cannot commit an offence, cannot be prosecuted and cannot be penalized.[1] At common law a partner could be criminally liable for a crime committed by another partner only on the ground of participation in the crime or vicarious responsibility.[2] The Criminal Procedure Act[3] has, however, extended liability by providing that when a partner has committed an offence in carrying on the business or affairs of the partnership, any person who was a member of the partnership at the time of the commission of the offence is deemed to be guilty of that offence, unless it is proved that the latter did not take part in the commission of that offence and could not have prevented it. If, however, the business or affairs of the partnership are governed or controlled by "a committee or similar governing body", these provisions do not apply to any partner who was not a member of that "committee or other body" at the time of the commission of the offence.[4]

A partner can be convicted of theft of partnership property if it is clearly and positively shown that he intended to deal with it fraudulently for his own benefit and to appropriate it for himself contrary to the rights of his partner and contrary to his duty.[5]

1 *R v Levy* 1929 AD 312 322. According to the Criminal Procedure Act 51 of 1977 s 96 a reference in a charge to a partnership is sufficient if the reference is to the name of the partnership.

2 See Burchell and Hunt *Criminal Law and Procedure* vol 1 345; the title CRIMINAL LAW; Bamford *Partnership* 72.

3 51 of 1977 s 332(7). See *R v Milne and Erleigh*

(7) 1951 1 SA 791 (A) 831. For various other statutory provisions, see Bamford 72.

4 s 332(7) proviso. For the meaning of "governing body" in partnership context, see *R v Couvaras* 1946 OPD 392.

5 *R v Pretorius* 1908 TS 272 273. For Roman-Dutch law, see par 387 ante. For a detailed statement, see title CRIMINAL LAW.

DISSOLUTION OF PARTNERSHIPS

CAUSES AND FORMALITIES

419 Causes of dissolution or termination Partnerships can be dissolved through a variety of different causes, resulting in the termination of the relationship arising from the partnership agreement.[1]

(a) *Effluxion of time*

Where a partnership has been entered into for a fixed term, it will ordinarily be dissolved by the effluxion of its agreed time of duration, unless one of the partners has a just or lawful cause for its earlier dissolution, or the partners expressly or impliedly agree to continue the partnership.[2] In the latter event, although much depends upon the circumstances of the case, there is a strong presumption that the continuing partnership is a partnership at will, without any term, which can be dissolved by any of the partners at his own discretion.[3] In so far as it is consistent with the incidents of a partnership at will and subject to an agreement to the contrary, the rights and duties of the partners remain as they were at the date of expiration of the fixed term.[4]

(b) *Completion of business or undertaking*

Where the partnership has been formed with the object to carry out a certain business or specific undertaking, for instance to erect a building or to buy and sell a certain parcel of goods or to build a railway, the partnership is dissolved by the completion of the business or undertaking.[5]

(c) *Agreement of dissolution*

It is clear that a partnership, like any other agreement, can be dissolved by a subsequent agreement, express or implied, between all the partners to that effect.[6] This is probably the most common cause of dissolution.[7] If an agreement of dissolution has been procured by false representations, damages may be claimed in appropriate circumstances, but the court is not entitled to set aside the dissolution agreement and so create a general partnership during a period when none existed.[8]

(d) *Change in membership*

Any change in membership destroys the identity of the firm.[9] The partnership is dissolved by the retirement of an existing partner. If the remaining partners agree to continue the business of the partnership, a new partnership is created.[10] Since a new partner can be admitted only by agreement between him and all the existing partners, the existing partnership is dissolved and a new partnership created by the admission of a new partner.[11] Hence the reconstituted firm is in each event a new partnership, and although precisely the same business may be carried on under the style of the old firm, the business must be transferred to the new partnership.[12] As far as the transfer of liabilities are

concerned, creditors are not bound to accept the incoming partners as debtors in sub-
stitution for the members of the old firm with whom they had contracted but, as a general principle, debtors cannot object to the transfer by the old firm to the new of the
claims which the old firm had against them. Movable property will pass ipso iure but
immovable property will have to be formally transferred by registration against the title
deeds.[13]

It may be of some interest to note that in various other jurisdictions the premise that
a change in membership *inevitably* destroys the identity of the firm has been abandoned
as being too strict an application of the extreme aggregate view of partnership.[14]

(e) *Death of one of partners*

Since a partnership is constituted intuitu personae, in other words the delectus per-
sonarum is regarded as one of the main considerations on which an agreement of partnership rests,[15] the death of any one of the partners (generally) has the effect of dissolving the partnership as between all the partners[16] — the partnership does not pass to the
"universal successor"[17] of a deceased partner.[18] This rule means that not even the survivors remain (or are obliged to carry on the enterprise as) partners unless it has been
agreed to the contrary when the partnership was formed,[19] for instance where it has
been stipulated in the partnership agreement that the business will be carried on by the
surviving partners and that they will purchase the decedent's interest upon his death.[20]
A partnership agreement for the continuance of the enterprise by the survivors after
the death of a partner may have detrimental fiscal consequences and should be drafted
so as to avoid this risk, e g that the same amount would be taxable both in the hands
of the surviving partners and in the hands of the widow of the deceased.[21] Although
the "extenuated" partnership of survivors may perchance carry on precisely the same
business as the erstwhile firm, it is considered to be a new partnership.[22]

Various Roman-Dutch authorities[23] adhered to the Roman law doctrine[24] that an
agreement in a contract of partnership that the heir of a partner will succeed to the
partnership is invalid, while others[25] considered such an agreement to be valid and binding. In reliance on some of the latter it has been held that the death of one of two or
more partners will not dissolve the partnership when the contract of partnership clearly
provides for the continuation of the partnership for the benefit of the estate of the deceased partner, and the deceased partner by his will has authorized such a continuance.[26]
Although such a testamentary authorization may be express or implied,[27] it will not be
implied from the mere fact that the deceased expressed the wish that the executors should
not, in winding up the estate, embarrass the firm,[28] nor from the fact that the will allows
an extended time for the realization of the deceased's interest in the partnership business.[29] If there is no such authorization the court has no power to allow a continuance,
but there may be an exception in the case of a partnership between a husband and wife.[30]
It has been submitted, however, that if the consequence of a continuation agreement
should be that the heirs or executors of the deceased automatically become members of
the partnership, it would be in conflict with the nature of an agreement of partnership.[31]
Hence it has been suggested that a partnership is always dissolved by the death of a partner and that where the partnership contract provides for the partnership to be continued
for the benefit of the estate of the deceased partner, his executor, if so authorized in the
will, in fact concludes a new partnership on behalf of the estate with the remaining
partners.[32] The opposing views of writers and courts are the result of conflicting Roman-Dutch authorities[33] — and probably more apparent than real. Those stating that
death necessarily dissolves a partnership probably assume as their major premise that
any change in the membership of a partnership necessarily results in the formation of
a new partnership.[34] On the other hand, those asserting that death does not necessarily

dissolve a partnership which is continued by agreement after the death of a member, probably only mean that if suitable provision is made to the contrary, death does not necessarily require the immediate winding up of the enterprise so as to cause a sudden and enforced liquidation of the business, which can rarely be consummated without substantial losses both to the surviving partners and to the decedent's estate.[35] Agreements attempting to minimize this unfortunate result have taken several forms. It may, for instance, be agreed that the contribution of a deceased partner will be retained intact in the partnership for a determined period and that interim profits will accrue to his heirs, widow or estate.[36] An agreement that on dissolution of a partnership due to the death of a partner, liquidation will not take place but that the surviving partners may continue the business subject to certain conditions, does not create a pactum successorium but is valid and binding.[37] The partners can also prevent the financial disruption caused by the death of a partner by entering into a so-called buy-and-sell agreement, involving an undertaking among the partners each to sell his interest to the survivors and an undertaking by the survivors to buy the deceased's interest.[38] Usually the partners take out a joint life policy or each partner takes out a policy on his own life and cedes it to the other partners, the survivors being obliged to pay the proceeds to the deceased's estate in part or full payment of the deceased's interest.[39] Should the partners agree that in the case of dissolution due to death, all the assets and liabilities will pass to the survivor and that the first-dying's estate will receive the proceeds of a life policy in full and final settlement of his interest in the partnership, such an agreement would not be a "sale" and would not impose on the survivors any obligation to pay a "price", namely the amount of the insurance, in the event of the insurer repudiating liability on the ground that the deceased had made incorrect answers in the proposal form.[40] In any event it is clear that any partnership in which the estate is involved must necessarily be of limited duration so that it does not delay the winding-up of the deceased partner's estate.[41] It has been suggested that this difficulty may be overcome if provision is made for a new partnership to exist between the administrator or trustee of a trust created by the deceased partner, rather than his executor, and the surviving partners, as the deceased's executor can then perform his duty to liquidate and distribute the estate irrespective of the new partnership.[42] Again, the fiscal consequences of the various "continuation agreements" should be borne in mind.[43] If an agreement of partnership provides that the partnership will not be terminated by a partner's death, but that the deceased's share in the partnership will be administered by an administrator, the registrar of deeds may endorse the title deed of any immovable property held by the partnership to the effect that the deceased's share must be administered in terms of the Administration of Estates Act of 1965.[44] [45] Should the deceased partner's death have occurred before 2 October 1965 his share would be administered in terms of the Administration of Estates Act of 1913,[46] and the registrar would then not have been empowered to require that a trust should have been created on the deceased partner as he would have been if the provisions of the Administration of Estates Act of 1965[47] were applicable.[48]

(f) *Sequestration*

A partnership is dissolved by the sequestration of the estate of the partnership,[49] and by the sequestration of the private estate of a partner.[50] The liquidation of a company which is a partner will also dissolve the partnership.[51] The sequestration of the estate of a partner does not necessarily mean that the estate of the partnership has to be sequestrated,[52] but where the estate of a partnership is sequestrated the estate of each partner (other than a partner *en commandite* or a special partner)[53] is simultaneously sequestrated[54] unless the partner undertakes to pay the debts of the partnership and gives security for such payment.[55]

(g) *Partner declared mentally ill*

When any member of a partnership is declared mentally ill by the court, the court may, by the same or by any subsequent order, dissolve the partnership or make such order as in the circumstances may seem just.[56]

(h) *Partner becoming alien enemy*

Although alien friends may lawfully contract a partnership, alien enemies are disabled during war from entering into any partnership with each other, as indeed they are from entering into any commercial contract.[57] Hence the basic principle is that "an antecedent partnership existing between persons domiciled in different countries, is dissolved by the breaking out of war between these countries; for the whole rights, duties, obligations, relations and interests of the partnership, as such become changed thereby, and the objects of the partnership are no longer legally attainable, or capable of execution".[58] The same result follows if, after the outbreak of war, an alien partner becomes resident in enemy territory, for instance, where he is repatriated.[59] The declaration of war furnishes the necessary legal notice of such dissolution, and no recourse to the court for a dissolution order is necessary in such circumstances.[60] If there is no declaration of war, but a de facto state of war exists between the two countries, the same result probably follows, but the court should be approached to declare a dissolution.[61] Where a partner is an enemy subject but not resident in enemy territory, the partnership is not automatically terminated,[62] although the other partners may apply for an order dissolving the partnership.[63]

Usually legislation is enacted to regulate the confiscation of enemy property.[64]

(i) *Frustration*

A partnership is dissolved if it becomes objectively impossible to achieve its business purpose through the occurrence of events beyond the control of the partners. This is merely an application of the ordinary rules of frustration of contract.[65]

(j) *Notice of dissolution*

A partnership formed for an indefinite duration, without any term, is a partnership at will — an agreement to act as partners until one of them no longer desires to do so.[66] Any one of the partners can dissolve the partnership at his own discretion, even against the wishes of all the other partners, by giving notice to them that he no longer intends to continue the partnership. This notice of dissolution must be given in good faith and not at an unreasonable or inconvenient time.[67] The notice of dissolution is not given in good faith where the partner renounces the partnership in order to secure for himself alone some benefit or advantage the partners had proposed to make when they entered into the partnership. He will have to share the profits of that benefit with his former partners, even though they would not be obliged to share in the losses resulting from the failure of his venture.[68] If a partner renounces the partnership unseasonably so as to benefit himself and injure his partners, he will be liable to them in damages for the loss caused thereby.[69] In determining the reasonableness of a renunciation, regard must be had to the interests of the partnership as a whole and not merely the interests of those partners opposed to the dissolution of the partnership.[70] A renunciation may be made to the other partner or his agent and, either expressly, in writing or orally, or tacitly.[71] A contract of a partnership terminable at will may require that a withdrawing partner has to give his partners notice of a specified period before he dissolves the partnership.[72] Should the prescribed period not be observed by the withdrawing partner, it seems that the partnership will nevertheless be dissolved by his notice of dissolution although he would be liable in damages for the loss caused by his premature renunciation.[73]

(k) *Just or lawful cause*

Whether or not there is a definite period specified for the duration of the partnership, and even though the partnership agreement expressly prohibits withdrawal,[74] a partner may unilaterally terminate the agreement, and obtain a court order dissolving the partnership against the wishes of the other partners,[75] if his conduct is justifiable and reasonable.[76] A partner wishing to invoke against another partner the stringent provisions of a summary cancellation and forfeiture clause contained in the partnership agreement must at least himself be honouring the terms of that agreement.[77] The repudiated partner again, is entitled to insist on the normal process of liquidation and the preservation of his right as a partner to remain in possession of the partnership assets until a liquidator is appointed.[78] What constitutes iusta causa is a factual question which depends on the circumstances of each case. But, in general any event or conduct which irreparably destroys mutual trust and confidence between the partners and/or which makes good co-operation between the partners impossible, may afford just ground for dissolution.[79] Among the various grounds that have been held or stated to be sufficient to justify dissolution are the following: the complete disappearance and prolonged absence of a partner;[80] the breach of a material term of the partnership agreement by a partner;[81] the incapacity of a partner by reason of illness, or of an inveterate infirmity, substantially to perform his duties under the partnership agreement,[82] in which case it is not necessary to show that the incapacity is permanent,[83] the partners being unable to carry on business owing to quarrellings, bickerings and loss of confidence not largely due to the applicant,[84] although minor quarrels or frictions or neglects of duty will not in themselves constitute sufficient cause for dissolution;[85] gross and persistent negligence[86] or a serious violation of duty[87] on the part of a partner, for instance where a partner in spite of warnings persistently and continuously failed to attend early in the morning and late in the evenings when important duties of supervising had to be done;[88] a dispute as to the retention of a bookkeeper, the giving of credit to a contractor and the purchase of offices, rendering mutual co-operation impossible;[89] the failure of a partner carrying on the business to keep proper books of account and notwithstanding repeated requests to furnish proper account of the business to the other partners and, though not dishonest, being very careless and having no business knowledge;[90] where a husband and wife carried on business in partnership and the mutual co-operation and trust between the partners had been destroyed by the institution of divorce proceedings on the ground of the wife's adultery;[91] the relations between the partners becoming so strained that it is impossible to continue the partnership with benefit to either partner;[92] the occurrence of a deadlock between two brothers in partnership;[93] the secret employment of the attorney of the partnership to act as a spy on the other partner constituting a breach of the duty of uberrima fides;[94] a partner obtaining a loan, without the knowledge of the other partner, from a third party on terms which involved his endeavouring to expel the other partner and if successful entering into a new partnership with the lender;[95] the fulfilment of a condition for instance, where the partnership agreement provided that if either partner became addicted to drink, the other partner could dissolve the partnership, and one partner did become so addicted;[96] the commission of adultery by one partner with the wife of the other;[97] where mutual co-operation and trust were no longer possible between the partners and no reasonable expectation existed that the business would be carried on at a profit;[98] carelessness in the conduct of the business by a managing partner, though not in itself amounting to gross negligence, when coupled with a refusal to attend to the legitimate complaints of another partner;[99] where there is no reasonable expectation of a profit being made and where the partnership business cannot be carried on at all because its substratum has fallen away;[100] the surreptitious and illegal appropriation of profits by a partner to himself.[101] The onus of proving on a balance of probabilities that a partner has been guilty of misconduct irreparably destroying mutual trust and good faith between the partners, is on the partner who alleges it as a ground for his repudiation of the agreement.[102]

Should the renunciation be unjustifiable or unreasonable, the remaining partners have their remedy in damages, but the bonds of the partner's further association for the objects of the partnership are thus dissolved: a partner cannot as a rule be compelled by a decree of specific performance to continue the partnership relationship.[103] It has been submitted, however, that the mere fact that the guilty partner cannot be forced to continue to implement the partnership agreement, does not imply that he cannot be restrained from acting adversely to the provisions of the partnership agreement, and that there is ample authority for the granting of an interdict restraining the breach of a partnership agreement.[104]

1 For various expositions, see De Wet and Yeats *Kontraktereg en Handelsreg* 409; De Villiers *SA Encyclopedia of Forms and Precedents* vol 13 162; Bamford *Partnership* 75; Wille and Millin *Mercantile Law* 432. Even aggregate jurisdictions, when faced with the problem of the termination of the contract of partnership, is forced to concede that there is something to be dissolved, namely the association among those individual partners, although what is in law dissolved or terminated is a contractual relationship only; see Miller *Partnership* 435-436.

2 Felicius *Tractatus de Societate* 34 4; De Groot *Inleiding* 3 21 4; Van Leeuwen *RHR* 4 23 11; Huber *HR* 3 11 18; Voet *Commentarius* 17 2 24; Pothier *Partnership* 8 1 139; Van der Keessel *Prael* 3 21 8; Van der Linden *Koopmans Handboek* 4 1 14; *Wegner v Surgeson* 1910 TPD 571; *Fortune v Versluis* 1962 1 SA 343 (A) 348; cf *Robson v Theron* 1978 1 SA 841 (A) 856B.

3 *Wegner v Surgeson* supra 576.

4 Cf *Wegner v Surgeson* supra; *Volk v Brown* 1925 1 PH A27 (C); Bamford 75.

5 Felicius 34 1-2; De Groot 3 21 8; Huber 3 11 23; Voet 17 2 26; Pothier 8 2 143; Van der Linden 4 1 14; *Agostino v Subat and Marinelli* (1914) 35 NLR 270; *Harvey v De Jong* 1946 TPD 185; *Stewart v Schwab* 1956 4 SA 791 (T); *Dube v City Promotions* 1964 1 PH A1 (D).

6 Van Leeuwen *RHR* 4 23 11; Kersteman *Woordenboek* s v "*compagnieschap*"; Pothier 8 4 149; e g *Hitchins v Chapman* 1932 NLR 255; *Kaplan v Turner* 1941 SWA 29; *Fink v Fink* 1945 WLD 266 247; *Latham v Sher* 1974 4 SA 687 (W); *Robson v Theron* supra 856; *Van Tonder v Davids* 1975 3 SA 616 (C); *Narayanasamy v Venkatrathnam* 1979 3 SA 1360 (D) 1361; *Spie Batignolles Société Anonyme v Van Niekerk: in re Van Niekerk v SA Yster en Staal Industriële Korp Bpk* 1980 2 SA 441 (NC).

7 Cf De Villiers 162; Wille and Millin 432.

8 *Latham v Sher* supra 690. For criticism on the view expressed by the court (690E) that the cancellation of a dissolution agreement could have the effect of continuing or reviving a partnership in a single asset or a particular

source of income, see De Wet and Yeats 409.

9 *Executors of Paterson v Webster, Steel & Co* (1881) 1 SC 350 355: "There can be no doubt that, as a general principle, the Court can only recognise the members of which the firm consists, and that any change among them destroys the identity of the firm"; *Standard Bank v Wentzel and Lombard* 1904 TS 828 833-834; *Wagstaff and Elston v Carter and Talbot* 1909 TS 121; *Whitelock v Rolfes, Nebel & Co* 1911 WLD 35 37-38; *Divine Gates & Co v African Clothing Factory* 1930 CPD 238 240; *Goldberg v Di Meo* 1960 3 SA 136 (N) 142; *Kirsh Industries Ltd v Vosloo and Lindeque* 1982 3 SA 479 (W) 480-481 483.

10 *Executors of Paterson v Webster, Steel & Co* supra; *Essakow v Gundelfinger* 1928 TPD 308; *Divine Gates & Co v African Clothing Factory* supra.

11 *Executors of Paterson v Webster, Steel & Co* supra; *Whitelock v Rolfes, Nebel & Co* supra; *Wagstaff and Elston v Carter and Talbot* supra; *Standard Bank v Wentzel and Lombard* supra; *Kirsh Industries Ltd v Vosloo and Lindeque* supra.

12 *Essakow v Gundelfinger* supra; *Goldberg v Di Meo* supra; *Whitelock v Rolfes, Nebel & Co* supra.

13 *Executors of Paterson v Webster, Steel & Co* supra; *Whitelock v Rolfes, Nebel & Co* supra; *Standard Bank v Wentzel and Lombard* supra; *Pienaar and Marais v Pretoria Printing Works* 1906 TS 654; *Foss v Beningfield & Son* (1907) 28 NLR 284; *Essakow v Gundelfinger* supra; *De Jager v Bethlehem Trading Co* 1916 OPD 3; *Walker v Standard Bank of SA Ltd* 1923 AD 438; *Berman v Brest* 1934 WLD 135; *Goldberg v Di Meo* supra 142-143 145; *Joubert v Jacob* 1962 1 SA 125 (T); Deeds Registries Act 47 of 1937 reg 34(3)(b).

14 This premise of inevitable dissolution is said to be dependent on delectus personae and the non-transferability of interests in partnership. But both these are considered to be matters of partnership agreement which can be varied by agreement. Accordingly this premise does not prevail in these jurisdictions when the partners expressly agree to

the changes and during the dissolution; Crane and Bromberg *Partnership* 444: "Today the older view has little support in theory or in practice... Partnerships have evolved with the economy. Concepts which were appropriate in a simpler day for 2-or-3 man firms without written agreements need modification today for larger firms with elaborate structures and continuity agreements... [W]e recognize in this respect, as we do in many others, that a partnership is what the partners make it." Heenen *International Encyclopedia of Forms and Precedents* vol 1 3 61. See also *Harding and Parker v John Pierce & Co* 1919 OPD 113 116: "Now the transaction complained of was a transaction with the old firm, or rather the firm with the old *personnel*."

15 "Society by consent is finished... by the death... of any of the partners, for it being one individual contract of the whole, and not as many contracts as partners, it is like a sheaf of arrows bound together with one tie, out of which, if one be pulled, the rest will fall out, and the personal humour and industry of the partners are so chosen, that it is not supposed to be communicated to their heirs": Stair *Institution* 1 6 5 cited in Miller 17.

16 Gaius *Inst* 1 152; 3 25 5; *D* 17 2 35; 17 2 52 9; 17 2 59; 17 2 63 10; 17 2 65 9; De Groot 3 21 8; Van Leeuwen *RHR* 4 23 11, *Cens For* 1 4 23 31; Huber 3 11 21–22; Voet 17 2 23; Kersteman *Woordenboek* s v *"societeit"*, *"compagnieschap"*; Van Bynkershoek *Quaest Iur Priv* 2 14 (333); Van Wassenaer *Practyk Notariael* 2 17 11; Pothier 8 3 144–146; Van der Keessel *Dictata* 3 26 10, *Prael* 3 21 8; Van der Linden 4 1 14; *Torbet v Executors of Attwell* (1879) 9 Buch 195 200; *Soeker's Executrix v Lawrence* (1897) 14 SC 210; *Ex parte Estate of the late J C Niemeyer* 1902 TS 20 24; *McKay v McKay* 1903 CTR 428; *Ex parte Naggs* 1904 CTR 20; *Bell v Estate Douglass* (1906) 23 SC 661; *Ex parte Duncan's Executor* 1910 TPD 886 887; *Vigne's Executor v Mackenzie* 1913 TPD 42; *Blumberg and Sulski v Brown and Freitas* 1922 TPD 130 135; *McLeod and Shearsmith v Shearsmith* 1938 TPD 87 89; *Ex parte Weinrich's Executors* 1939 CPD 37 41; *Gouws v Venter & Co* 1959 4 SA 527 (D); *Ex parte Whaley* 1962 4 SA 164 (SR) 167; *Maraisdrif (Edms) Bpk v Lee* 1974 4 SA 696 (C) 698; *D'Angelo v Bona* 1976 1 SA 463 (O) 466–467; *Van der Merwe v Sekretaris van Binnelandse Inkomste* 1977 1 SA 462 (A) 473F 479 481; *Erasmus v Havenga* 1979 3 SA 1253 (T) 1257; De Wet and Yeats 409; De Villiers 162; Lee and Honoré *Obligations* 144; Fuller 1940 *Yale Law Journal* 202.

17 See the conclusions of Van Zyl *Universele*

Opvolging in die SA Erfreg (LLD thesis University Stellenbosch 1981) 348–351 as to the "universal successor" in Roman law, in Roman-Dutch law and in SA law.

18 ibid.

19 ibid.

20 e g Huber 3 11 22; Pothier 8 3 146; *Van der Merwe v Sekretaris van Binnelandse Inkomste* supra.

21 See *Van der Merwe v Sekretaris van Binnelandse Inkomste* supra 482; Van Niekerk 1979 *MB* 3; Piek 1977 *THRHR* 302.

22 Should the premise that a change in membership destroys the identity of the firm be consistenly applied, see under (d) above; *Maraisdrif (Edms) Bpk v Lee* supra; *D'Angelo v Bona* supra 466; *Van der Merwe v Sekretaris van Binnelandse Inkomste* supra 479 481; De Villiers 162; Van Niekerk 3; but see contra *Harding and Parker v John Pierce & Co* supra 116; n 14 supra.

23 De Groot 3 21 8; Van Leeuwen *RHR* 4 23 11, *Cens For* 1 4 23 31; Huber 3 11 21; Voet 17 2 23; Van Wassenaer 2 17 11; Van Bynkershoek 2 14 (333), *Obs Tum* 2 1866; 3 2271; 3 2557; 4 3259; Pauw *Obs Tum Nov* 1 124; 1 128; Van der Keessel *Dictata* 3 26 10 and cf *Prael* 3 21 8 (uncertain); see De Wet and Yeats 409–410.

24 Gaius *Inst* 1 152; *I* 3 25 5; *D* 17 2 35; 17 2 52 9; 17 2 59; 17 2 63 10.

25 Kersteman s v *"societeit"*, *"compagnieschap"*; Van Bynkershoek *Quaest Iur Priv* 3 10 (450), *Obs Tum* 2 1190; 3 2757; Pauw 1 295; 1 445; *Holl Cons* 3 332 (667 n 7); Pothier 8 3 145; Van der Linden *ad Pothier Societen* 8 3 145 (129n), *Koopmans Handboek* 4 1 14, *Notarisambt* 5 23 6 (257–258 280–281); cf Van der Keessel *Prael* 3 21 11 and 3 21 8 (uncertain):"Illud sane frequenti usu probutum esse socio, ut socii paciscantur de continuanda societate post mortem socii cum vidua eius"; see also De Wet and Yeats 409.

26 *Torbet v Executors of Attwell* supra 197–198 200–201. See also *Liquidators of Union Bank v Kiver, Widow and Executrix of Hofmeyr* (1891) 8 SC 146 148; *Ex parte Duncan's Executor* supra 888; *Dickinson and Brown v Fisher's Executors* 1916 AD 374 388 399; *Ex parte Weinrich's Executors* supra 40; *Ex parte Becker's Executors* 1939 CPD 496 497; *Ex parte Wolman* 1946 CPD 672 675; *Ex parte Whaley* supra 169; *Blumberg and Sulski v Brown and Freitas* supra 135; *Harding and Parker v John Pierce & Co* supra 116.

27 *Ex parte Weinrich's Executors* supra; *Ex parte Wolman* supra.

28 *Ex parte Duncan's Executor* supra; *Ex parte Weinrich's Executors* supra.

29 ibid.
30 *Ex parte Duncan's Executor* supra; *Ex parte Weinrich's Executors* supra; *Ex parte Wolman* supra.
31 De Wet and Yeats 409.
32 De Villiers 162. See also *McLeod and Shearsmith v Shearsmith* supra 89 94; *Maraisdrif (Edms) Bpk v Lee* supra 699; *D'Angelo v Bona* 466.
33 See ns 24 25 supra.
34 See n 22 supra; Fuller 220–221.
35 See De Wet and Yeats 410, especially ns 254 255; Fuller 220–221. But see contra *Torbet v Executors of Attwell* supra; *Harding and Parker v John Pierce & Co* supra.
36 See *Van der Merwe v Sekretaris van Binnelandse Inkomste* supra; De Wet and Yeats 410.
37 *D'Angelo v Bona* supra 467. See also *Van der Merwe v Sekretaris van Binnelandse Inkomste* supra 478; *Erasmus v Havenga* supra 1257.
38 Lee and Honoré 144. Cf *Erasmus v Havenga* supra 1256A.
39 ibid.
40 *Grobbelaar v Bosch* 1964 3 SA 687 (E) 690.
41 De Villiers 175.
42 De Villiers 175. See also *McLeod and Shearsmith v Shearsmith* supra.
43 Van Niekerk 3; Piek 302.
44 66 of 1965 s 40.
45 Deeds Registries Act 47 of 1937 reg 34(3)(d).
46 24 of 1913 s 61.
47 66 of 1965 s 40.
48 See title DEEDS vol 7 par 142 ante.
49 *Simpson & Co v Fleck* (1833) 3 M 213; *In re P D Johnson* (1885) 6 NLR 92; *Tobias & Co v Woolfe and Brown* 1915 OPD 60; *Cassim v The Master* 1962 4 SA 601 (D) 606.
50 De Groot 3 21 8; Voet 17 2 26; Pothier 8 3 148; Van der Keessel *Prael* 3 21 8; *SA Loan, Mortgage and Mercantile Agency Ltd v R C Birkett* (1885) 6 NLR 77; *Estate Stoltenhoff v Howard* (1907) 24 SC 693; *Hirsch, Loubscher & Co Ltd v Jacobson and Goldberg* 1915 CPD 452; *Intermares Corp (Pty) Ltd v Seinsch* 1971 2 SA 570 (SWA). See also par 389 ante.
51 *Pavie v The French Bakery Co Ltd* 1903 TH 5 10.
52 *Ferela (Pty) Ltd v Craigie* 1980 3 SA 167 (W). See also par 389 ante.
53 See the Insolvency Act 24 of 1936 s 13(1) for definition of "special partner", and par 367 ante. For additional exceptions, see title INSOLVENCY. For the provisions of the Moratorium Act 25 of 1963 concerning partners on military service, see title DEFENCE vol 7 pars 276–289 ante.
54 Insolvency Act 24 of 1936 s 13(1).
55 s 13(1) proviso. See further the title INSOLVENCY.
56 Mental Health Act 18 of 1973 s 59; cf C

4 37 7.
57 Story *Partnership* 14.
58 Story 15 approved in *Stern & Co v De Waal* 1915 TPD 60 66. See also Van der Keessel *Prael* 3 21 8; *In re Liebermann, Bellstedt & Co* 1916 CPD 5; *Monhaupt v Minister of Finance* (1918) 39 NLR 47; *Enseleit v Enseleit* 1952 2 SA 385 (T); Henning 1970 *Meditationes Medii* 50.
59 *Enseleit v Enseleit* supra.
60 *Enseleit v Enseleit* supra.
61 See Nathan *Partnership and Private Companies* 129; n 58 supra.
62 *The Treasury v Gundelfinger and Kaumheimer* 1919 TPD 329.
63 *In re Liebermann, Bellstedt & Co* supra.
64 e g the Trading with the Enemy Act 39 of 1916. For other legislation, see Henning 51–53; title WAR AND EMERGENCY.
65 D 17 2 63 10; Huber 3 11 23; Pothier 8 2 140–142; Van der Linden *Koopmans Handboek* 4 1 14; *Curtis and Curtis v Beart* 1909 TH 141 144; *Welverdiend Diamonds v H & B Syndicate* 1928 1 PH A39 (W); De Villiers 163; Bamford 77.
66 C 4 37 5; *Wegner v Surgeson* supra 577.
67 D 17 2 4 1; 17 2 65 4; 17 2 17 2; Voet 17 2 24; Huber 3 11 17; Van Leeuwen *Cens For* 1 4 23 31; Kersteman s v "*compagnieschap*"; Pothier 8 4 150–151; Van der Keessel *Prael* 3 21 8; Van der Linden *Koopmans Handboek* 4 1 14; *Parr v Crosbie* (1886) 5 EDC 197; *In re M C Camrooden & Co* (1890) 20 NLR 171; *Wegner v Surgeson* supra: *Mackay v Naylor* 1917 TPD 533 538; *P Patlansky v J and B Patlansky* 1917 WLD 7; *De Kock and Kessel Ltd v Modern Packaging Co (Pty) Ltd* 1943 WLD 216; *Purdon v Muller* 1961 2 SA 211 (A) 230–231; Du Plessis 1979 *De Jure* 368.
68 e g De Groot 3 21 8; Voet 17 2 24; Pothier 8 4 150; *Parr v Crosbie* supra; *Wegner v Surgeson* supra; *Wiehahn v Marais* 1965 1 SA 398 (T).
69 e g Pothier 8 4 151; *Wegner v Surgeson* supra; De Villiers 164.
70 Pothier 8 4 151.
71 Voet 17 2 24; Huber 3 11 20; *Maloney v Venter and Currie* 1923 1 PH A22 (G); Bamford 82.
72 *Hitchins v Chapman* supra 260; *Wiehahn v Marais* supra; *Brighton v Clift* 1970 4 SA 247 (R).
73 See *Wiehahn v Marais* supra; *Brighton v Clift* supra; De Villiers 163; Wille and Millin 436; Gibson *Mercantile Law* 278; Bamford 81; According to Nienaber 1964 *Annual Survey* 129 despite the fact that the partner cannot as a rule be compelled by a decree of specific performance to implement the partnership

agreement, there is ample authority for granting an interdict restraining the breach of a partnership agreement; cf *Hitchins v Chapman* supra; *Adams v Willcox* 1940 2 PH A55 (W); *Spilg v Walker* 1947 3 SA 495 (EDL).

74 A clause in a partnership contract prohibiting renunciation of the partnership before the expiry of the definite period fixed for its duration is regarded as being unenforceable; see D 17 2 14; De Groot 3 21 8; Pothier 8 4 152; Van der Keessel *Prael* 3 21 8; *Wiehahn v Marais* supra 401; *Brighton v Clift* supra 248.

75 See also par 420 post.

76 D 17 2 14–17; Voet 17 2 24; Pothier 8 4 152; Van der Keessel *Prael* 3 21 8; *Wiehahn v Marais* supra; *Brighton v Clift* supra; *Maloney v Venter and Currie* 1923 1 PH A23 (G); *Fortune v Versluis* supra 348; see also Du Plessis 370; Bamford 82; n 73 supra.

77 *Purdon v Muller* 1961 2 SA 211 (A) 230.

78 i e in the event of the mere extrajudicial repudiation by one partner on the gound of alleged misrepresentation on the part of another partner as to his professional earning capacity: *Brighton v Clift* supra.

79 See e g *Curtis and Curtis v Beart* supra 144; *Fortune v Versluis* supra; *Woomack v Commercial Vehicle Spares (Pvt) Ltd* 1968 3 SA 419 (R); De Wet and Yeats 411; n 76 supra. Cf *Emphy v Pacer Properties (Pty) Ltd* 1979 3 SA 363 (D) 366; *Erasmus v Pentamed Investments (Pty) Ltd* 1982 1 SA 178 (W) 182–185; title COMPANIES vol 4 par 394 ante.

80 D 17 2 16; Voet 17 2 24; Pothier 8 4 152; *In re Coch v Nicholson* (1884) 1 SAR 201; *Coch v Lichtenstein* 1910 AD 178 187.

81 D 17 2 14; Voet 17 2 24; Pothier 8 4 152; *Strachan v Prinsloo* 1925 TPD 709; *Reidy v Dromery* 1923 1 PH A40 (N); see also *Purdon v Muller* supra.

82 Pothier 8 4 152; *Pelunsky v Pastoll* 1920 WLD 32.

83 *Pelunsky v Pastoll* supra 35.

84 *Armstrong v Wallwork* 1913 CPD 978 980; *Franckenburg v Peetz* 1934 NPD 162; *Fortune v Versluis* supra; *Woomack v Commercial Ve-*

hicle Spares (Pty) Ltd supra 422; *Wilson v Garrard* 1911 SR 115. Cf *Emphy v Pacer Properties (Pty) Ltd* supra 368; *Erasmus v Pentamed Investments (Pty) Ltd* supra 183.

85 *Purdon v Muller* 1960 2 SA 785 (E) 797; 1961 2 SA 211 (A).

86 *Curtis and Curtis v Beart* supra.

87 *Strachan v Prinsloo* supra.

88 *Strachan v Prinsloo* supra.

89 *J L Schurink Sr v T L Schurink Jr* (1895) 2 OR 46 48. Cf *Marshall v Marshall (Pty) Ltd* 1954 3 SA 571 (N); *Emphy v Pacer Properties (Pty) Ltd* supra 366.

90 *Bailey, Nourse and Marais v Barratt* (1899) 6 OR 295.

91 *Warrington v Warrington* 1916 WLD 46 47.

92 *Gildemeister v Machachlan* 1906 CTR 899; cf *Emphy v Pacer Properties (Pty) Ltd* supra.

93 *Hare v Hare* 1910 CTR 199. Cf *Emphy v Pacer Properties (Pty) Ltd* supra.

94 *Hutton v Steinweiss* 1905 TS 43.

95 *Douchet v Piaggio* 1905 TH 267.

96 *Holshausen v Cumming* 1909 EDC 33.

97 *Salter v Haskins* 1914 TPD 264; cf *Lawrence v Lawrich Motors (Pty) Ltd* 1948 2 SA 1029 (W).

98 *Armstrong v Wallwork* supra.

99 *Curtis and Curtis v Beart* supra.

100 *Curtis and Curtis v Beart* supra; cf *Erasmus v Pentamed Investments (Pty) Ltd* supra 185.

101 *Woolmack v Commercial Vehicle Spares (Pvt) Ltd* supra 423E; *Versluis v Greenblatt* 1973 2 SA 271 (NC).

102 *Fortune v Versluis* supra; cf *Erasmus v Pentamed Investments (Pty) Ltd* supra.

103 *Wiehahn v Marais* supra 401; *Brighton v Clift* supra 249. If a partner has purported to terminate a partnership concluded for a definite term without just cause he is not entitled to any profit made by his partners after the date of his renunciation although he remains liable to bear his share of the losses: Voet 17 2 24; Pothier 8 4 154. See also *Robson v Theron* supra 855H–856A for instances where action may be instituted by a partner for specific performance in terms of the partnership agreement.

104 Nienaber 129.

420 Formalities of dissolution If the dissolution of a partnership cannot be effected by agreement and it appears that the renunciation itself or certain aspects thereof will be contested by the other partners, the partner who made the renunciation should approach the court for an order to effect or confirm the dissolution.[1] If, for example, the facts are not clear or there is a likelihood of such a conflict of evidence that it would be preferable to have oral evidence, procedure should be by way of action rather than notice of motion.[2] In the event of the deed of partnership containing an arbitration clause which covers the question of dissolution, the court will stay dissolution proceedings brought before it, pending a reference to arbitration.[3]

Where the partnership is dissolved by agreement, the consequences do not follow unless the dissolution was bona fide. Hence, notwithstanding publication of dissolution in the *Gazette*, the partners will continue to be de facto partners after the purported date of dissolution, if there was no genuine dissolution of partnership on that date.[4]

Former partners may be estopped from asserting as against bona fide third parties the prior dissolution of the partnership where the latter have not been warned of the dissolution.[5] The dissolution of the partnership should, therefore, be given sufficient publicity. Partners should, in particular, give special notice of the dissolution to former customers who traded with them on the strength of their collective credit.[6] Publication in the *Gazette* and *Dunn's Gazette* is not sufficient to relieve former partners from liability where it is proved that actual knowledge of the dissolution did not reach the creditors concerned.[7] Any one of the former partners is entitled to notify customers and creditors of the dissolution. The notice should not, however, contain any misrepresentation regarding the dissolution and should not in any way damage the interests of the former partnership.[8]

Statutory provisions in the Transvaal which required that notice of any change in the style, constitution, personnel or premises of business partnerships must be advertised and that written notice of dissolution must be given to the licensing officer,[9] have been repealed.[10]

Taking a new partner into a partnership business is an alienation of the business from the old partnership to a new partnership and may (apparently) be regarded also as an alienation by one of the partners of the old partnership.[11] Consequently the requirements of the Insolvency Act[12] regarding alienation of a business are of relevance.[13] If a trader[14] alienates any business belonging to him or the goodwill of such business, or any goods or property forming part of it (except in the ordinary course of that business) and does not publish notice of that intended alienation in the *Gazette* and in two issues of an English and in two issues of an Afrikaans newspaper circulating in the district where the business is carried on, within not less than 30 and not more than 60 days before the date of alienation, that alienation will be void as against his creditors for a period of six months after such alienation, and will be void against the trustee of his estate, if his estate is sequestrated at any time within the six-month period.[15] No specific form for the notice is prescribed.[16]

1 Pothier *Partnership* 8 4 154; *Brighton v Clift* 1970 4 SA 247 (R) 249; and see e g *Gildemeister v MacLachlan* 1906 CTR 899; *Armstrong v Wallwork* 1913 CPD 978; *Cridlan v Schmitz* 1936 WLD 41; *Chapman v Karsten* 1939 CPD 498; *Robson v Theron* 1978 1 SA 841 (A) 856B-D. The court is not bound to decree a dissolution where it has already occurred de facto: *Ex parte Johnson and Smith* 1899 CTR 127.

2 *Ex parte Cowen* 1909 TH 18; *Chapman v Karsten* supra; *Cridlan v Schmitz* supra; *Ewing v Bosomworth* 1923 SR 139; *Goodman v Lunn* 1947 1 SA 445 (C) 448.

3 *Blotnick v Turecki* 1944 CPD 100. See title ARBITRATION.

4 *Shapiro v Shapiro and Kelz's Trustee* 1907 TS 472 476.

5 See e g Voet *Commentarius* 17 2 25; Pothier 9 157; *In re Paarl Bank* (1891) 8 SC 131 132

134–135; *McKenzie v Irvine* 1902 CTR 734; *Midlands Auctioneers (Pvt) Ltd v Bowie* 1975 1 SA 773 (R) 774-775.

6 ibid.

7 *Estate Maibaum v Varley* 1935 NPD 396 409. See also *In re Paarl Bank* supra; *McKenzie v Irvine* supra; *Bain v Barclays Bank (DC&O)* 1937 SR 191 200.

8 *Wiehahn v Marais* 1965 1 SA 398 (T) 401; *Brighton v Clift* supra 250.

9 Tvl Registration of Businesses Act 36 of 1909 ss 3 8(3) 9. For discussion, see De Villiers *SA Encyclopedia of Forms and Precedents* vol 13 166-167; Wille and Millin *Mercantile Law* 438-439.

10 Revenue Laws Amendment Act 89 of 1972 s 14. The repealing section was brought into operation by Proc 16/1975 (*Gazette* 4557 of 10 January 1975) with effect from 1 January 1975.

11 *Whitter v Berman* 1932 WLD 71.
12 24 of 1936 s 34.
13 Cf De Wet and Yeats *Kontraktereg en Handelsreg* 467; Mars *Insolvency* 228.
14 For definition of "trader", see the Insolvency

Act 24 of 1936 s 2; *Scott-Hayward v Habibworths (Pty) Ltd* 1959 1 SA 202 (T).
15 Insolvency Act 24 of 1936 s 34(1).
16 See title INSOLVENCY.

GENERAL CONSEQUENCES

421 Introduction The dissolution of a partnership, like its formation, has consequences which affect not only the relationship between the partners, but also that between partners and third parties. Although the partnership has been dissolved, it has not yet been liquidated.[1] It has often been stated, but not without criticism,[2] that after dissolution the partnership continues for the purpose of liquidation and distribution of assets.[3] However, the view that a partnership is (necessarily) not dissolved until its liquidation has been completed with the consequence that, until such time, the proper party to be sued, is the partnership and not an individual member of it,[4] has been rejected as erroneous.[5] Furthermore, upon dissolution of the partnership and in the absence of an agreement to the contrary a partner has a right to demand that the partnership must be liquidated.[6] This consequence of dissolution may conveniently be dealt with separately.[7]

1 *Ferreira v Fouche* 1949 1 SA 67 (T) 70. The partners may agree, however, that the partnership will only be dissolved after the liquidation and/or distribution of the partnership assets have been completed; see Joubert 1978 *THRHR* 297. A liquidation need not always be resorted to.

2 See *Maraisdrif (Edms) Bpk v Lee* 1974 4 SA 696 (C) 698–699.

3 *Haarhoff v Cape of Good Hope Bank* (1887) 4 HCG 304 313; *In re Paarl Bank* (1891) 8 SC 131 132; *Solomon and Bradley v Millhouse* 1903 TS 607; *Pretoria Hypothec Mpy v M and D Golombick* 1906 TH 51 52; *Blumberg and Her v Shapiro and Ketz* 1907 TH 65 66; *Barker & Co v Blore* 1908 TS 1156 1160–1161; *Pienaar v Suttner Bros and Hirschfeld* 1914 EDL 416 419; *Du Toit v African Dairies Ltd* 1922 TPD 245 247 248; *Essakow v Gundelfinger* 1928 TPD 308 312; *Kaplan v Turner* 1941 SWA 29 31–32; *Ferreira v Fouche* supra; *Cloete v Senekal and Roux* 1950 4 SA 132 (C) 134; *R v Levitan* 1958 1 SA 639 (T) 646; *Goldberg v Di Meo* 1960 3 SA 136 (N) 145; *Dube v City Promotions* 1964 1 PH A1 (D); *Stellenbosch Farmers' Winery Ltd v Pretorius* 1970 3 SA 234 (SWA) 235; *Schoeman v Rokeby Farming Co (Pty) Ltd* 1972 4 SA 201 (N) 205; *Lee v Maraisdrif (Edms) Bpk* 1976 2 SA 536 (A) 543C; *Narayanasamy v Venkatrathnam* 1979 3 SA 1360 (D) 1362; *Spie Batignolles Société Anonyme v Van Niekerk: in re Van Niekerk v SA Yster en Staal Industriële Korp Bpk* 1980 2 SA 441 (NC) 446; *Kirsh Industries Ltd v Vosloo and Lindeque* 1982 3 SA 479 (W) 484.
In most civil and common-law jurisdiction dissolution puts an end to the partnership, but

only as regards new operations. In nearly all cases dissolution does not result ipso facto in the disappearance of the partnership. This "extension" of the partnership for purposes of liquidation and winding-up is considered to be further proof that it is not possible to reduce the institution to a simple contract even in those countries where the existence of the partnership as legal entity is not recognized: Heenen *International Encyclopedia of Comparative Law* vol 13 52 94 151; Miller *Partnership* 435–436; Mohr *Van Maatschap, Vennootschap onder Firma en Commanditaire Vennootschap* 192. Hence a sharp distinction is also drawn between the terms "dissolution" and "termination". "Dissolution" is used to designate the change in relation of the partners caused by any of the partners ceasing to be associated in the carrying on, as distinguished from the winding up, of the business. "Termination" is described as the point in time when all the partnership affairs are wound up: Crane and Bromberg *Partnership* 416.

4 *Du Toit v African Dairies Ltd* supra.

5 *Maraisdrif (Edms) Bpk v Lee* supra 701–702: "Ek kon nêrens enige aanduiding vind dat ... 'ontbinding' eers na likwidasie plaasvind nie ... In die verweerdaresse se verweerskrif is beweer dat ... ontbinding eers plaasvind wanneer daar geen vennootskapsbates meer is nie ... Hierdie verweer het ek reeds verwerp"; *Lee v Maraisdrif (Edms) Bpk* supra. However, the view that a partnership "is not dissolved until its affairs have been liquidated" has subsequently been reiterated without any qualification in *Kirsh Industries*

Ltd v Vosloo and Lindeque supra 484.
6 Pothier *Partnership* 9 161; Van der Linden
  Koopmans Handboek 4 1 14; *Barker & Co v Blore*
  supra; *McLeod and Shearsmith v Shearsmith* 1938
  TPD 87 91; *Kaplan v Turner* supra 32; *Meiss-*
  ner v Joubert 1946 CPD 618 621; *Ferreira v*
  Fouche supra; *Purdon v Muller* 1961 2 SA 211

(A) 232; *Wegner v Surgeson* 1910 TPD 571
577; *Geo Anderson v M Royce* (1895) 2 OR
266; *Brighton v Clift* 1970 4 SA 247 (R) 249;
Robson v Theron 1978 1 SA 841 (A) 856; *Na-*
rayanasamy v Venkatrathnam supra; cf *Karstein*
v Moribe 1982 2 SA 282 (T) 302.
7 See par 426 post.

422 Consequences for partners inter se As far as the relationship between the partners is concerned, the primary consequence of dissolution of the partnership is that their
implied authority (mutual mandate)[1] is terminated.[2] Consequently, subject to a number
of exceptions,[3] all new transactions entered into by a partner, which are unconnected
with the liquidation or not necessarily consequential to transactions which occurred
during the existence of the partnership, do not bind his former partners but are for his
own account alone.[4] Although the bonds of the partners' further association are dissolved the relationship between the partners is finally terminated only when the liquidation of the firm is completed.[5] Unless the contrary appears[6] from the agreement of
partnership or the dissolution agreement, no provision of the partnership agreement is
binding after dissolution.[7] If the dissolution is made dependent on a condition, the rights
and duties of the partners remain unchanged until the condition is fulfilled.[8] Where
the dissolution has been procured by misrepresentation, the court is not entitled to res-
urrect a general partnership which was in fact dissolved so as to impose on the parties
the reciprocal rights and obligations of such partnership for a period during which they
were in fact not partners.[9] During the course of the winding-up of the affairs of the
partnership a partner is still entitled to expect perfect fairness and good faith from his
former partners.[10] Thus the former partner does not on dissolution lose his right to examine and inspect the books of the partnership, in order to have them examined by
qualified auditors in suitable circumstances.[11] He will be entitled to exercise this right
irrespective of his motive, unless he has expressly or impliedly waived or renounced
it.[12] If one of the former partners improperly appropriates a partnership asset and uses
it for his own benefit, he will be obliged to account to his erstwhile partners for their
interest and for their share of the profits of such use.[13] This does not mean, however,
that the partnership agreement is regarded as extending beyond the dissolution so as to
include the period of such improper use.[14] Similarly, if on dissolution of a partnership
the business is continued by one or more partners without realization and distribution,
they are liable to account to the outgoing partners for that portion of the profits which
are fairly attributable to the use of the capital contributed by the latter.[15] Former partners are also entitled to their share of the profits and their share of the losses arising
from transactions which are a necessary result of transactions commenced or concluded
prior to dissolution.[16]

A written lease definitely expressed for a fixed term, by which a partner lets property
to his partnership, embodies a somewhat anomalous relationship, but it is not necessarily terminated by the dissolution of the partnership.[17] However, if there is no lease
and the partnership is dissolved the owner can eject his former partners without notice
to quit.[18]

Property contributed quoad usum can on dissolution of the partnership immediately
be reclaimed in whole by the contributing partner. It is not subject to sale and division
between the partners. Compensation for fair wear and tear cannot be claimed, but the
contributing partner is entitled to the fruits and any appreciation in value of such property.[19] Property contributed quoad dominium falls for division between the partners on
dissolution. It remains common property and each partner normally has the right to
continue in joint possession for the purpose of liquidation.[20]

Dissolution does not put an end to the debts of each of the former partners to the partnership or to those of the partnership to each of the former partners, or to their obligation of respectively accounting for them on the winding-up of the partnership.[21] The general rule is that partners are not considered as debtors and creditors inter se until there has been a final or prior binding settlement of accounts and that a partner has no right of action against another partner for payment of any amount owed to him in connection with partnership affairs unless the firm's accounts are settled and a credit balance remains due to the partner.[22] Hence actual repayment of money taken by a partner from the partnership funds is necessary on dissolution of the partnership only when the partner's liability to the firm exceeds what is due out of the partnership fund to him, and then only to the extent of the excess.[23] However, a partner has no locus standi to sue a former partner after dissolution of the partnership in respect of a matter for which a liquidator has been appointed.[24] If a liquidator has not been appointed a partner does have locus standi subject to the limitation that he can neither appropriate the sole right to liquidate the partnership, nor institute a claim by which the court is requested to liquidate the partnership.[25]

Deeds of partnership often contain provisions which are intended to apply after dissolution,[26] for instance, provisions restraining a former partner from trading,[27] arbitration clauses relating to disputes arising from the dissolution and/or liquidation of the partnership,[28] clauses regulating the manner of liquidation of the partnership[29] and provisions concerning the continuation of the business and the succession to the rights and liabilities of the partnership on its dissolution.[30] Provisions such as these will in general remain effective notwithstanding the termination of the partnership,[31] but it has been suggested that it would be advisable to ensure that the partnership agreement contains an express provision to this effect.[32]

1 For implied authority, see par 415 ante.
2 Voet *Commentarius* 17 2 25; Pothier *Partnership* 9 155; Van Wassenaer *Practyk Notariael* 2 17 13; *In re Paarl Bank* (1891) 8 SC 131 134; *Bosman v Registrar of Deeds and The Master* 1942 CPD 302 307.
3 For circumstances where partners would nevertheless be liable to third parties, see par 423 post.
4 Pothier 9 155; Van der Linden *Koopmans Handboek* 4 1 14; *Davis & Son v McDonald and Sutherland* (1833) 1 M 86; *Birkenruth v Shaw, Hoole & Co* (1850) 1 S 39 45; *Western Province Bank v Du Toit Smith & Co* 1892 CTR 22; *In re Paarl Bank* supra; *Barker & Co v Blore* 1908 TS 1156 1159; *Bosman v Registrar of Deeds and The Master* supra; *Holliday qq Wise v W G Anderson qq Anderson Sr* (1835) 3 M 452; *R v Levitan* 1958 1 SA 639 (T); but cf *Maraisdrif (Edms) Bpk v Lee* 1974 4 SA 696 (C) 698C-E.
5 *In re Paarl Bank* supra; *Barker & Co v Blore* supra; *Du Toit v African Dairies Ltd* 1922 TPD 245; *Kaplan v Turner* 1941 SWA 29 31; *Meissner v Joubert* 1946 CPD 618 621; *Ferreira v Fouche* 1949 1 SA 67 (T) 70; *R v Levitan* supra; *Dube v City Promotions* 1964 1 PH A1 (D); *Lee v Maraisdrif (Edms) Bpk* 1976 2 SA 536 (A) 543B-E; *Brighton v Clift* 1970 4 SA 247 (R) 248-249; *Narayanasamy v Venkarath-*

nam 1979 3 SA 1360 (D) 1362. It has been said that the relationship between the partners as such is for all intents and purposes terminated on dissolution and that after dissolution their relationship is merely that of co-owners of joint property or of a joint estate: *Maraisdrif (Edms) Bpk v Lee* supra 698C-G; cf in this regard also Pothier 8 3 146; 9 161; Van der Linden 4 1 14 where the term "*societeit*" used prior to dissolution, is subsequently replaced by "*gemeenschap*"; *Latham v Sher* 1974 4 SA 687 (W) 690-691.
6 This may be implied; see *Scriven Bros v Rhodesian Hides and Produce Co Ltd* 1943 AD 393 401.
7 *Rogers v Mathews* 1926 TPD 21; *Beiles v Glazer* 1947 2 PH A79 (W).
8 *Aronstein v Maisel* 1904 CTR 601.
9 *Latham v Sher* supra 691.
10 *Sempff v Neubauer* 1903 TH 202 216.
11 *Beiles v Glazer* supra; *Romersa v Buch* 1917 TPD 266 270; *Spilg v Walker* 1947 3 SA 495 (EDL) 503.
12 ibid.
13 e g *Wegner v Surgeson* 1910 TPD 571 584; *Parr v Crosbie* (1886) 5 EDC 197; *Latham v Sher* supra 691.
14 *Latham v Sher* supra.
15 *Monhaupt v Minister of Finance* (1918) 39 NLR

47 51–52; *Ellery v Imhof* 1904 TH 170; cf *Treasury v Gundelfinger and Kaumheimer* 1919 TPD 329.

16 Voet 17 2 23; Pothier 9 155; *Nash v Muirhead* 1909 CTR 64; *Davis & Son v McDonald and Sutherland* supra; cf *Simon v Levin & Co* 1921 AD 49.

17 *Whitaker v Whitaker and Rowe* 1931 EDL 122 125–127.

18 *Whitaker v Whitaker and Rowe* supra 125–127.

19 Felicius *De Societate* 39.2; De Groot *De Iure B ac P* 2 12 24; Kersteman *Woordenboek* s v *"societeit"*; Pothier 9 158; cf *Fortune v Verslius* 1962 1 SA 343 (A); Beinart 1961 *Acta Juridica* 118 146.

20 Voet 17 2 27; Pothier 9 160; *Brighton v Clift* supra 249; Beinart 146.

21 Pothier 9 160; Nathan *Partnership and Private Companies* 131.

22 For a full statement on the general rule and exceptions, see par 407 ante; Delport *Gedingvoering tussen Vennote* 264–268.

23 *McLeod and Shearsmith v Shearsmith* 1938 TPD 87.

24 *Van Tonder v Davids* 1975 3 SA 616 (C).

25 *Kaplan v Turner* supra 29; *Ferreira v Fouche* supra; *Brighton v Clift* supra; Delport 259–260; see par 426 post.

26 Cf De Villiers *SA Encyclopedia of Forms and Precedents* vol 13 168; Bamford *Partnership and Voluntary Association* 93 110.

27 Such a provision is subject to the ordinary rules of enforceability of contracts in restraint of trade; see *Savage and Pugh v Knox* 1955 3 SA 149 (N) 155; *Malan v Van Jaarsveld* 1972 2 SA 243 (C); De Villiers 169–170; title CONTRACT.

28 e g *Van Heerden v Sentrale Kunsmis Korp (Edms) Bpk* 1973 1 SA 17 (A) 30; *Pennant v Kelly* 1908 TH 97 99; *Meyerowitz v Lieberman* 1940 WLD 40; *Blotnick v Turecki* 1944 CPD 100; see title ARBITRATION.

29 See e g *Robson v Theron* 1978 1 SA 841 (A); par 428 post.

30 See par 419(d)–(e) ante; cf Bamford 110–113; De Villiers 174–175.

31 See ns 6–7 26–30 supra.

32 De Villiers 168.

423 Consequences regarding relationship between partners and third parties On dissolution partners are liable singuli in solidum for partnership debts.[1] The rule of practice that civil proceedings must in general be instituted against all the partners conjointly and not against an individual member[2] does not apply on dissolution of the partnership.[3] The meaning of the expression "dissolution of the partnership", however, was previously uncertain.[4] Due to conflicting decisions it was a matter of some doubt whether the expression designated the occurrence of an event causing dissolution[5] or meant that the affairs of the partnership have been wound up.[6] The first designation has prevailed.[7] The consideration that after its dissolution the partnership continues for the purpose of its liquidation does not entail the postponement of the individual liability of partners until the liquidation of the partnership has been completed. Hence, a partner is individually liable for the full amount of a partnership debt as soon as the partnership is dissolved, even though the liquidation of the partnership has not been completed, for instance, where there are still undivided partnership assets.[8] This being the position on dissolution, numerous courses of action are left open to a partnership creditor. He may sue the partnership or any one of the partners or all the partners.[9] Various alternatives have already been mentioned above.[10] However, a partnership creditor suing one or some of the individual partners must allege and prove that the partnership has been dissolved.[11] A claim against one partner on a partnership obligation contained in a written document on the ground that the partnership has been dissolved is not a liquid claim capable of supporting a claim for provisional sentence.[12] The dissolution of a partnership is not a "simple condition" upon which such a claim arises within the meaning of that term,[13] that is, "a condition or event of a kind unlikely, in the nature of things, to give rise to a dispute, or where it is disputed, is inherently capable of speedy proof by means of affidavit evidence".[14] Hence, it is not permissible to attempt to prove in provisional sentence proceedings the truth of a disputed allegation that a partnership has been dissolved and so obtain a provisional judgment against an individual partner.[15]

If a former partner pays a debt of the erstwhile partnership in full, the obligation is extinguished by performance and he may recover the proportionate share of such payment from his former partners.[16]

It was held that dissolution does not in any manner affect the efficacy and validity of past contracts and transactions with the partnership and that a dissolved partnership remains in existence, in so far as creditors are concerned, until their claims have been discharged.[17] Thus the estate of a partnership can be sequestrated after its dissolution, even though it only became insolvent after it was dissolved and either on the ground that it was in fact insolvent or because of an act of insolvency, which includes an act of insolvency subsequent to its dissolution;[18] judgment can be given against a dissolved partnership;[19] and a dissolved partnership may be sued in its name at the date of the accrual of the cause of action.[20] The partnership may extinguish its obligations by due performance or by delegation to, for instance, a new partnership formed to take over its business.[21] Novation by delegation is effected by express or implied agreement between the old partnership, the creditor and the new partnership.[22] Hence, the consent of each creditor is necessary for the old partnership to be released of its obligations, and the new partnership will not be liable to a creditor of the old partnership unless such an agreement (novatio inter easdem personas) is established.[23] A creditor may refuse his consent, or consent on certain conditions and hold the old partnership liable if these conditions are not fulfilled.[24]

Although the implied authority (mutual mandate) of partners is terminated on dissolution with the consequence that subsequent transactions entered into by a partner normally do not bind his former partners,[25] a partner's implied authority nevertheless continues for the purpose of liquidating the affairs of the partnership.[26] Consequently his former partners will be bound if a partner completes transactions begun but unfinished at the time of dissolution, which would include receiving payment of a partnership debt,[27] or enters into transactions which are necessary consequences of transactions concluded during the existence of the partnership.[28] They will also be bound if they acquiesce in or adopt his acts,[29] or if he enters into transactions relative to the partnership business having good reasons for being ignorant of the dissolution of the partnership, for instance, where the death of a partner which effected the dissolution had not yet come to his knowledge.[30] As stated above,[31] former partners may be estopped from asserting as against bona fide third parties the prior dissolution of the partnership where the latter have not been warned of dissolution.[32]

Dissolution does not as a rule terminate the rights of a partnership.[33] This follows from the fact that all rights can be freely ceded unless expressly or impliedly the right was exercisable only by the partnership.[34] Consequently a lease to a partnership does not automatically terminate on dissolution of the partnership.[35] The mere fact that the dissolution of the partnership is followed by one of the partners remaining in possession of the premises by arrangement with the other does not operate as an assignment for which the lessor's consent is required.[36] An agreement to assign a partner's interest in the partnership lease to his co-partner in terms of the deed of dissolution followed by the giving up of personal occupation does not amount to an actual assignment in breach of an express prohibition in the lease.[37] However, a sole surviving partner is not entitled to exercise a right of renewal contained in a partnership lease on his own behalf and for his own benefit where he is the executor dative of the deceased partner's estate.[38] A grant of exclusive trading rights does not lapse on dissolution of a partnership, and the rights may be ceded to and enforced by one of the partners after dissolution.[39] A former partner can acquire a right of action from a partnership which has ceased to exist, only if such right has been duly ceded to him by the partnership.[40]

Dissolution of the partnership does not result in a third party being exposed to more than one independent cause of action.[41] Consequently, unless a particular partner has acquired the right of action by cession[42] or has been authorized to act on behalf of the other partners also,[43] all the former partners should join in a claim to enforce a right acquired by the partnership before dissolution.[44] Since the implied authority of a partner continues for purposes of liquidation, he may sue in the firm's name to recover debts due to the partnership if it had been dissolved without any agreement as to a liquidator, at least where his co-partner is outside the jurisdiction.[45]

1 *Lee v Maraisdrif (Edms) Bpk* 1976 2 SA 536 (A) 543. See pars 413 ns 10 14 and 421 ante.

2 See par 413 text to n 36 ante.

3 *Lee v Maraisdrif (Edms) Bpk* supra 542. See par 413 n 38 ante.

4 Cf par 421 n 3 ante.

5 See par 419 ante.

6 For various decisions as to the previous conflicting positions on death and on sequestration, see par 413 n 14 ante. Cf Joubert 1978 *THRHR* 297; Delport 1976 *De Jure* 361. For an agreement dissolution made dependent on the condition that liquidation and distribution must be completed prior to dissolution, see par 421 n 1 ante; cf par 422 n 8 ante.

7 *Du Toit v African Dairies Ltd* 1922 TPD 245, in which the second designation of the term was preferred, was overruled in *Maraisdrif (Edms) Bpk v Lee* 1974 4 SA 696 (C); *Lee v Maraisdrif (Edms) Bpk* supra. See pars 413 n 14 421 n 5 ante.

8 *Lee v Maraisdrif (Edms) Bpk* supra; see also par 413 n 22 ante.

9 e g *Pienaar v Suttner Bros and Hirschfeld* 1914 EDL 416 419; *Lee v Maraisdrif (Edms) Bpk* supra; *Spie Batignolles Société Anonyme v Van Niekerk: in re Van Niekerk v SA Yster en Staal Industriële Korp Bpk* 1980 2 SA 441 (NC) 447.

10 See par 413 text to ns 24–30 ante.

11 *Turkstra v Goldberg* 1960 1 SA 512 (T); *Boonzaier v Kiley* 1981 2 SA 618 (W).

12 *Turkstra v Goldberg* supra 514.

13 *Turkstra v Goldberg* supra 514.

14 *Rich v Lagerwey* 1974 4 SA 748 (A) 755G.

15 *Boonzaier v Kiley* supra 621.

16 *McDonald v Sutherland* (1834) 1 M 91; *Uren v Nelson* 1910 TPD 562; *Simon v Levin & Co* 1921 AD 49. His claim would be subject to the general rule that settlement of accounts is a condition precedent; see par 409 ante.

17 e g *Haarhoff v Cape of Good Hope Bank* (1887) 4 HCG 304 313; *Essakow v Gundelfinger* 1928 TPD 308 312; par 421 n 3 ante.

18 e g *Blumberg and Her v Shapiro and Ketz* 1907 TH 65; *Hunt, Leuchars and Hepburn v Steedman & Co* (1915) 36 NLR 189; *Essakow v Gundelfinger* supra 312; *Ex parte Zausmer* 1938 CPD 449; *Cloete v Senekal and Roux* 1950 4 SA 132 (C); *Stellenbosch Farmers' Winery Ltd*

v Pretorius 1970 3 SA 234 (SWA); see also par 421 ns 3 5 ante.

19 e g *Pretoria Hypothec Mpy v M and D Golombick* 1906 TH 51; *Blumberg and Her v Shapiro and Ketz* supra.

20 e g *Goldberg v Di Meo* 1960 3 SA 136 (N) 145; *Spie Batignolles Société Anonyme v Van Niekerk: in re Van Niekerk v SA Yster en Staal Industriële Korp Bpk* supra; *Kirsh Industries Ltd v Vosloo and Lindeque* 1982 3 SA 479 (W) 484. In such event the action continues against the persons alleged by the plaintiff or stated by the partnership to be partners, as if sued individually: r 14(7) of the Uniform Rules of Court.

21 *Executors of Paterson v Webster, Steel & Co* (1881) 1 SC 350 355; *Whitelock v Rolfes, Nebel & Co* 1911 WLD 35 38; *Walker v Standard Bank of SA Ltd* 1923 AD 438; *Joubert v Jacob* 1962 1 SA 125 (T).

22 The contract between the former partners and the creditor is substituted by an express or implied contract between the former partners, the creditor and the new partners, whereby the obligations of the former partners are extinguished and the new partners acquire similar but new obligations in their stead. The right to delegate may be a term of the original contract, which is not uncommon in the case of leases; see *Hughes v Rademeyer* 1947 3 SA 133 (A) 139; Cilliers and Benade *Company Law* 65.

23 See n 20 supra.

24 *Walker v Standard Bank of SA Ltd* supra.

25 See par 422 n 2 ante.

26 Pothier *Partnership* 9 155; Van der Linden *Koopmans Handboek* 4 1 14; *Davis & Son v McDonald and Sutherland* (1833) 1 M 86; *Birkenruth v Shaw, Hoole & Co* (1850) 1 S 39 45; *Western Province Bank v Du Toit, Smith & Co* 1892 CTR 22; *In re Paarl Bank* (1891) 8 SC 131 134; *Barker & Co v Blore* 1908 TS 1156 1159; *Bosman v Registrar of Deeds and The Master* 1942 CPD 302 307; *R v Levitan* 1958 1 SA 639 (T).

27 *R v Levitan* supra.

28 Pothier 9 155; *In re Paarl Bank* supra; *R v Levitan* supra.

29 *Birkenruth v Shaw, Hoole & Co* supra; *Ermelo*

Trading Co v Umbilo Bottle Exchange 1925 2 PH A4 (T).

30 Voet *Commentarius* 27 2 23; Pothier 9 156.

31 See par 420 ante.

32 See pars 414 420 ante.

33 Pothier 9 172; *Nanabhay v Potchefstroom Municipality* 1926 TPD 483 489: "[I]t cannot be laid down as a general proposition that a right granted to a partnership ceases when the partnership is dissolved"; *Ogden v Darling and Derry* 1903 TH 417; *Executors of Paterson v Webster, Steel & Co* supra; *Blumberg v Buys and Malkin and Margolis* 1908 TS 1175 1180; *Baldinger v Broomberg* 1949 3 SA 258 (C) 268; *Raulstone v Place* 1959 4 SA 241 (N) 242; cf *Whitaker v Whitaker and Rowe* 1931 EDL 122; *Berman v Brest* 1934 WLD 135.

34 Pothier 9 172; *Blumberg v Buys and Malkin and Margolis* supra; *Executors of Paterson v Webster, Steel & Co* supra 355–356; *Nanabhay v Potchefstroom Municipality* supra 489; *Baldinger v Broomberg* supra; *Raulstone v Place* supra.

35 *Baldinger v Broomberg* supra; cf *Whitaker v Whitaker and Rowe* supra; *Raulstone v Place* supra.

36 *Baldinger v Broomberg* supra.

37 *Royal Hotel (Kokstad) Ltd v Burton* 1938 CPD 25.

38 *Raulstone v Place* supra 242: "In any event, the applicant ... is entitled to say that, as there were two lessees in the original lease, who undertook to be jointly and severally liable to him for the performance of their obligations under the lease, and as he agreed to grant the renewal of the lease to both lessees, he is not prepared to permit one of them alone to renew the lease."

39 *Blumberg v Buys and Malkin and Margolis* supra.

40 *Berman v Brest* supra.

41 See *Karstein v Moribe* 1982 2 SA 282 (T) 293E; *Pretoria Private Detective Agency v Orkin* 1925 TPD 292; *Ex parte The Matabele Syndicate* (1894) 1 OR 168; *De Wet and Yeats Kontrakereg en Handelsreg* 414–415; *De Villiers SA Encyclopedia of Forms and Precedents* vol 13 173, but see contra Pothier 9 172.

42 *De Jager v Bethlehem Trading Co* 1916 OPD 3; *Berman v Brest* supra; *McCreadie v Dodgson* 1962 3 SA 333 (W).

43 *Kilian and Stein v Norden Executor of Horn* (1845) 3 M 530.

44 *Pretoria Private Detective Agency v Orkin* supra.

45 *Barker & Co v Blore* supra.

424 Relevant statutory provisions In addition to those mentioned above,[1] the following selected statutory provisions are of relevance on dissolution of a partnership.

If a firm of auditors has been appointed to hold the office of auditor of a company,[2] a building society,[3] a banking institution,[4] an insurer,[5] a pension fund[6] or a co-operative[7] respectively, such appointment will not lapse by reason of a change in the composition of the members of the partnership, provided that not less than half the persons who were partners as at the date when the firm was last appointed continue to be partners.[8]

If a person is apprenticed to a partnership, his contract of apprenticeship is not terminated by reason of the death or retirement of any partner if the business of the partnership is continued by another person or partnership, but the rights and obligations of the employer under the contract are in such case deemed to be transferred to the person or partnership continuing the business.[9]

In the event of one or more of the partners retiring from the partnership or dying before 31 December in any year in respect of which a licence was issued to the partnership, the remaining partner or partners may, on payment of the prescribed transfer fee, carry on the trade or occupation in respect of which such licence was issued for the unexpired term of the licence.[10] However, any licence issued to a partnership lapses when a new partner is admitted.[11]

Any person, except a practising attorney, who for or on expectation of any fee, gain or reward, direct or indirect, to himself or any other person, draws up or prepares or causes to be drawn up or prepared any agreement, deed or writing relating to the dissolution of any partnership or any variation of its terms, is guilty of an offence.[12]

If a creditor and debtor are partners and the debt is one which arose out of the partnership relationship, the period of prescription will not be completed before a year has elapsed after the day on which the partnership relationship has ceased to exist.[13]

In the case of a licence to deal in arms and ammunition issued to persons trading in partnership, the licence must, if any partner retires from the partnership or dies, be transferred to the remaining partner or partners jointly by endorsement of the licence by the commissioner of the South African Police, on application of the remaining partner or partners and payment of the prescribed transfer fee in the prescribed manner. If a new partner is admitted the licence may be so transferred by the commissioner in his discretion.[14]

The above is not intended as a numerus clausus of all relevant provisions and for all intents and purposes. For details the appropriate titles should be consulted.

1 See pars 419(d)–(h) 420 421 ante.
2 Companies Act 61 of 1973 s 274(2).
3 Building Societies Act 24 of 1965 s 67(10).
4 Banks Act 23 of 1965 s 35(7).
5 Insurance Act 27 of 1943 s 9(1)bis.
6 Pension Funds Act 24 of 1956 s 9(5).
7 Co-operatives Act 91 of 1981 s 146(2).
8 For notification of any change in the name, constitution or adress of such firm, see Public Accountants' and Auditors' Act 51 of 1951 s 26bis.

9 Manpower Training Act 56 of 1981 s 22 (5)(a). See s 22(5)(b) as to the lodgment of the contract for registration of the transfer.
10 Licences Act 44 of 1962 s 5(2).
11 s 5(3).
12 Attorneys Act 53 of 1979 s 83(8)(a)(iv).
13 Prescription Act 68 of 1969 s 13(1)(d); see also Pothier *Partnership* 9 1 166.
14 Arms and Ammunition Act 75 of 1969 s 20(2).

LIQUIDATION AND DISTRIBUTION OF ASSETS

425 General Upon dissolution of a partnership each partner has a right against his co-partners to have the partnership property applied in payment of the partnership debts and to have the surplus assets, if any, applied in payment of what may be due to him after deducting what may be due by him to the firm.[1] This usually entails that the partnership must be liquidated, that is, a realization of assets, payment of creditors and distribution of assets must take place. A liquidation need not, however, always be resorted to. Where, for example, partners agree that the dissolved partnership's assets and liabilities are to be taken over by a new firm, and an outgoing partner is to be paid a fixed sum representing his share in the firm, a general liquidation of the partnership is not required.[2]

1 *McLeod and Shearsmith v Shearsmith* 1938 TPD 87 91; *Brighton v Clift* (2) 1971 2 SA 191 (R) 192.

2 *Meissner v Joubert* 1946 CPD 618; *D'Angelo v Bona* 1976 1 SA 463 (O).

LIQUIDATION

426 Initiation of liquidation Where partners agree, either in the partnership agreement or at a later stage, on the manner in which the partnership is to be liquidated upon dissolution, any partner can, upon dissolution of the firm, employ the actio pro socio to claim specific performance of such an agreement.[1] In the absence of an agreement to this effect, the actio pro socio may in general be brought by a partner to have the partnership liquidated and wound up.[2] It is not, however, the function of the court to act as liquidator, and an action cannot be brought against a co-partner which will cast this duty upon the court.[3] Neither can a partner appropriate the sole right to liquidate the partnership.[4] As a general rule therefore, in the event of disputes arising between the partners concerning the liquidation, the proper procedure is to appoint a liquidator to realize the partnership assets for the purpose of liquidating the partnership debts and to distribute the balance of the assets or their proceeds amongst the partners.[5] This procedure is nevertheless not mandatory in all cases.[6] Thus, in appropriate cases a partner may, for purposes of liquidating the partnership, claim an account from his co-partner together with a debate on it and payment of what is found to be due.[7] A partner may also present an account to his co-partners and claim from them what is allegedly due to him in terms of that account: if the correctness of the account is disputed, the court will settle the account, provided that the issues between the parties are restricted and properly defined.[8] Furthermore, if, after a distribution of assets and payment of creditors, a partner retains possession of a particular partnership asset or assets which have not been included in the distribution, a partner may institute the actio pro socio to claim a distribution of these assets.[9] Where the partners cannot agree on the method of dividing a particular jointly owned partnership asset, or where a partner should retain possession of such an asset after dissolution, a partner can, as co-owner of the asset, institute the actio communi dividundo to claim a division of that asset.[10]

1 *Robson v Theron* 1978 1 SA 841 (A) 856A; see also *Van der Post v Vortman* 1913 AD 236.
2 ibid.
3 *Ferreira v Fouche* 1949 1 SA 67 (T); *Brighton v Clift (2)* 1971 2 SA 191 (R).
4 *Kaplan v Turner* 1941 SWA 29.
5 *Robson v Theron* supra; *Ferreira v Fouche* supra; *Olivier v Stoop* 1978 1 SA 196 (T) 203.
6 *Vigne's Executor v Mackenzie* 1913 TPD 42; *Truter v Hancke* 1923 CPD 43 48; *Schoeman v Rokeby Farming Co (Pty) Ltd* 1972 4 SA 201

(N).
7 *Truter v Hancke* supra; *Korb v Roos* 1948 3 SA 1219 (T); and see too *Love v Hobson* 1913 EDL 400; *Mostert v Mostert* 1913 TPD 255. The procedure in this respect is laid down in *Doyle v Fleet Motors PE (Pty) Ltd* 1971 3 SA 760 (A); cf, however, *Ferreira v Fouche* supra.
8 Cf *Dube v City Promotions* 1964 1 PH A1 (D); *Schoeman v Rokeby Farming Co (Pty) Ltd* supra.
9 *Robson v Theron* supra.
10 ibid.

427 Appointment of liquidator A liquidator may, upon dissolution of the firm, be appointed by the partners jointly.[1] As such they may appoint either one or some of the partners as liquidator, or even a third party.[2] A provision in the partnership agreement (or a subsequent agreement) regarding the appointment of a liquidator will be enforced by the court, unless such an appointment will prejudice a partner's interests in the liquidation process.[3] Partners may agree to refer the appointment of a liquidator to a third party.[4]

Where the parties are unable to agree on the appointment of a liquidator, the court may be approached to make an appointment.[5] The court has a discretion to appoint a liquidator. Although it will often do so upon application by the partners, it has the right to refuse the application[6] when, for example, the existence of the partnership is in dispute.[7] The court may appoint a third party to act as liquidator,[8] for example, the partnership's accountant.[9] A partner may nominate a liquidator, but the court is not obliged to accept the nomination[10] or name the liquidator, and may leave the decision on whom to appoint to someone else, for instance the master of the supreme court.[11]

In appropriate cases an interim liquidator may be appointed.[12]

1 Apparently unanimous consent is required: *Kilian and Stein v Norden Executor of Horn* (1845) 3 M 530 537.
2 *Kaplan v Turner* 1941 SWA 29; *Ferreira v Fouche* 1949 1 SA 67 (T); *Olivier v Stoop* 1978 1 SA 196 (T).
3 *Putnam v Redfield* (1874) 4 Buch 79 85.
4 *Stewart v Dickson* (1864) 5 S 10.
5 *Olivier v Stoop* supra; *Robson v Theron* 1978 1 SA 841 (A). The magistrate's court has jurisdiction in this respect: *Olivier v Stoop* supra;

see also *Ex parte Jeppe* 1907 TS 440.
6 *Truter v Hancke* 1923 CPD 43 48.
7 *Cridlan v Schmitz* 1936 WLD 41 42.
8 *Welverdiend Diamonds v H&B Syndicate* 1928 1 PH A39 (W). See too *Young v Young* (1918) 39 NLR 460 465.
9 *Brighton v Clift (2)* 1971 2 SA 191 (R).
10 *Brighton v Clift (2)* supra and see *Olivier v Stoop* supra.
11 *Young v Young* supra; *Olivier v Stoop* supra.
12 Cf *Cridlan v Schmitz* supra.

428 Rights and duties of liquidator A liquidator's rights and duties are governed by the terms of his appointment.[1] He is usually empowered to wind up the partnership's affairs, to realize the firm's assets, to collect the debts due to it, to pay its liabilities, to prepare a final account between the parties and to divide the surplus partnership assets amongst the partners.[2] As it is not the court's function to act as liquidator, it will not, when appointing a liquidator, anticipate problems which may present themselves to the liquidator at a later stage and give directions in that regard.[3] Should difficulties arise regarding the liquidation, the liquidator must decide which course to take and may seek the partners' concurrence in that respect.[4] Where the partners do not agree with the liquidator's decisions, a court may be approached to give directions on the matter.[5]

In the absence of any contrary agreement between the partners or any particular direction in this respect, the liquidator must take control of all the partnership assets as they stand on dissolution of the firm,[6] including the goodwill.[7] For this purpose he may sue the partnership's debtors in its name[8] and claim partnership assets which are in the possession of one of the partners.[9]

As a general rule, and in the absence of any contrary agreement between the partners or any other directions in this respect, the liquidator must convert all partnership property into money by means of a sale, usually a public auction.[10] This is not, however, mandatory and a court may be approached to give alternative directions regarding the mode in which the assets are to be valued and distributed.[11] A liquidator may not purchase partnership assets at a public auction himself without the partners' consent.[12] Without prior agreement the liquidator cannot sell the partnership assets to any individual partner.[13]

A liquidator must draw up an account showing the firm's assets and liabilities and the separate position of each partner.[14] Objections to the account may be brought to court which may refer them to the master.[15]

As a matter of practice a liquidator must give security for the proper performance of his duties.[16]

In the absence of any contrary agreement or court order, a liquidator is entitled to the commission usually allowed to liquidators of the particular kind of business, even where the liquidator is one of the partners appointed by agreement between the parties.[17]

A liquidator is discharged if he has duly accounted to the partners in the erstwhile partnership.[18] A court will not order his release where this has not been done.[19]

1 See *Sherry v Stewart* 1903 TH 13; *Bockris v Bockris* 1910 WLD 182; *Brighton v Clift (2)* 1971 2 SA 191 (R).
2 ibid.
3 *Brighton v Clift (2)* supra.
4 *Brighton v Clift (2)* supra.
5 *Brighton v Clift (2)* supra.
6 *Van Tonder v Davids* 1975 3 SA 616 (C); and see par 392 ante regarding the contents of partnership assets.
7 *Robson v Theron* 1978 1 SA 841 (A).
8 *De Vries en Marais v Hollins* (1882) 1 SAR 25; *Barker & Co v Blore* 1908 TS 1156.
9 After his appointment the liquidator alone has locus standi to institute an action for the protection of partnership assets: *Van Tonder v Davids* supra. As to what can be claimed from a partner, see *Ellery v Imhof* 1904 TH

170; *O'Hea v Quin* 1905 TH 54; *Parr v Crosbie* (1886) 5 EDC 197; *Nash v Muirhead* (1909) 26 SC 26; *Wegner v Surgeson* 1910 TPD 571; *Monhaupt v Minister of Finance* (1918) 39 NLR 47; *Fink v Fink* 1945 WLD 226; *Latham v Sher* 1974 4 SA 687 (W).
10 *Sherry v Stewart* supra; *Young v Young* (1918) 39 NLR 460.
11 ibid; and see *Robson v Theron* supra and par 429 post.
12 *Naturman v Preskovsky and Fluxman* 1935 WLD 36.
13 *Re Quin and O'Hea* 1904 TH 77; *Ellery v Imhof* supra.
14 Pothier *Partnership* 9 1 167 et seq.
15 Cf *In re Charles Lloyd and Samuel Nathan* (1891) 12 NLR 133.
16 *Woolf v Norrie* 1910 WLD 43.

17 *O'Hea v Quin* supra.
18 *Re Davidson* 1904 TH 52.

19 *Re Davidson* supra.

DISTRIBUTION

429 Court's approach As a general rule all partnership assets must on dissolution of the firm be converted into money by means of a sale and each partner be given his pro rata share.[1] There may however, be special circumstances warranting another mode of distribution.[2] If the partners cannot agree on the mode of distribution a court may be approached for directions. In this respect a court has a wide equitable discretion, having regard inter alia to the particular circumstances, and what is most to the partners' advantage and preference.[3] Thus, where the court finds it impossible, impracticable or inequitable to physically divide a particular asset between the parties or to cause it to be auctioned and to have the proceeds divided between them, it may arbitrio iudicis place a valuation on that asset with due regard to the particular circumstances concerning its value at the date of dissolution of the partnership. The court may then award the asset to one partner and order him to pay the others their shares.[4]

1 *Sherry v Stewart* 1903 TH 13: *Young v Young* (1918) 39 NLR 460.
2 *Young v Young* supra.
3 *Robson v Theron* 1978 1 SA 841 (A).

4 *Robson v Theron* supra 858. For a discussion of the various modes of distribution (referred to with approval in *Robson v Theron*), see *Pothier Partnership* 9 1 167–178.

430 Manner of distribution On dissolution of the partnership the partnership assets must be distributed in accordance with any agreement which the partners may have concluded in this respect. In the absence of a contrary agreement, partnership debts, which include loans made by the partners to the firm,[1] are repaid first.[2] If there is a shortfall, the partners must contribute the loss in the proportion in which losses are shared.[3] If a surplus remains after payment of creditors, each partner is repaid rateably what he has contributed to the partnership in capital.[4] Any surplus is then shared between the partners in proportion to the amounts contributed by each of them.[5] Where the value of the different contributions cannot be ascertained the surplus is shared equally.[6]

Where a partner has contributed the use of a certain asset to the partnership, such an asset does not form part of the assets to be distributed amongst the partners: a partner is entitled to a return of such property prior to partnership creditors' claims against the estate.[7]

1 *Schlemmer v Viljoen* 1958 2 SA 280 (T) 287.
2 *Schlemmer v Viljoen* supra 287; and see also *Commissioner for Inland Revenue v Estate Whiteaway* 1933 TPD 486; *McLeod and Shearsmith v Shearsmith* 1938 TPD 87; *Olivier v Stoop* 1978 1 SA 196 (T) 203.
3 See par 423 ante; and cf *Liquidator of the Owl Syndicate v Bright* (1909) 26 SC 12.
4 *Commissioner for Inland Revenue v Estate Whiteaway* supra; *Whiteaway's Estate v Commissioner for Inland Revenue* 1938 TPD 482 (both cases decided in terms of English law);

Ferreira v Fouche 1949 1 SA 67 (T); *Schlemmer v Viljoen* supra; *Olivier v Stoop* supra. This was not, however, the position at common law: see Beinart 1961 *Acta Juridica* 118.
5 *Monhaupt v Minister of Finance* (1918) 39 NLR 47 50. See also Voet *Commentarius* 17 2 27; *Whiteaway's Estate v Commissioner for Inland Revenue* supra 490 (decided in terms of English law).
6 Beinart 118.
7 Beinart 146; Pothier *Partnership* 7 3 126.

431 Relationship between partners after liquidation The relationship amongst the partners is terminated as soon as the liquidation of the firm is completed.[1] If it then appears that one partner has appropriated partnership funds during the existence of the partnership without accounting for it, a partner can claim his share without applying to court for the appointment of a liquidator.[2] If a partner consents to a dissolution, and it appears after liquidation that his consent had been obtained through a misrepresentation made to him concerning the state of the partnership, damages may be claimed on the grounds of misrepresentation.[3] A court cannot, however, set aside the agreement to dissolve the partnership and thus by a fiction deem the parties to have continued the partnership when in fact they did not do so.[4]

1 *Lee v Maraisdrif (Edms) Bpk* 1976 2 SA 536 (A) 543.
2 *Muller v Kaplan* 1959 2 PH F96 (O). See also *Uren v Nelson* 1910 TPD 562.
3 Cf *Latham v Sher* 1974 4 SA 687 (W).

4 *Latham v Sher* supra 690G. Presumably the court would be entitled to set the liquidation accounts aside and order the parties to draw proper accounts.

BIBLIOGRAPHY

Abbreviations

DR — De Rebus Pretoria Association of Law Societies of the Republic of South Africa 1979–

MB — Modern Business Law Durban Butterworth 1979–

SALJ — South African Law Journal Cape Town Juta 1901–

THRHR — Tydskrif vir Hedendaagse Romeins-Hollandse Reg Durban Butterworth 1937–

TSAR — Tydskrif vir Suid-Afrikaanse Reg Johannesburg Rand Afrikaans University 1976–

Andrea(e), S J F *Oud Nederlandsch Burgerlijk Recht* Haarlem 1906
Arangio-Ruiz, V *La Società in Diritto Romano* Napoli Jovene 1965
Asser, C *Handleiding tot de Beoefening van het Nederlands Burgerlijk Recht* Zwolle Lillink v 3 dl 3 *Verbintenissenrecht: Bijzondere Overeenkomsten* 3d print (Kamphuisen and Van Andel) 1960
Baker, J H "The Law Merchant and the Common Law before 1700" 1979 *Cambridge Law Journal* 295
Bamford, B R *Bamford on the Law of Partnership and Voluntary Association in South Africa* 3d ed Cape Town Juta 1982
Barels, J M *Aanmerkingen over eenige onzer aloude Gebruiken in die Rechtsoeffeninge: Beschouwing van de Statutaire Gemeenskap: Ondersoek over de Pandingen binnen Amsterdam* Amsterdam 1780
Barels, J M *Advysen over den Koophandel en Zeevaart mitsgaders verscheidene Turbes, Memorien, Resolutien, Missives enz daar toe behoorende* Gartman 1780–1781 2v
Barrett, J M and Seago, E *Partners and Partnerships: Law and Taxation* Charlottesville (Virginia) Michie 1956
Bates, C *Law of Limited Partnership* New York 1886
Bauer, C *Unternehmung und Unternehmungsformen im Spaetmittelalter und in der beginnenden Neuzeit* Jena Fischer 1936
Beinart, B "Capital in Partnership" 1961 *Acta Juridica* 118
Bergstedt, T M "Partnership in Commendam — Louisiana's Limited Partnership" 1961 *Tulane Law Review* 815
Blecher, M D "Undisclosed Principals and General Principles" 1972 *SALJ* 286
Boberg, P Q R *The Law of Persons and the Family* Cape Town Juta 1977
Boey, Th *Woorden-tolk, of verklaring der voornaamste onduitsche en anderen Woorden, in de hedendaagsche en aalönde rechtspleginge voorkomende* Den Haag Gaillard 1773
Bouwer, A P J *Beredderingsproses van Bestorwe Boedels* 2d ed Pretoria Van der Walt 1978
Buckland, W W *A Text-book of Roman Law from Augustus to Justinian* 3d ed (Stein) Cambridge University Press 1963
Buckland, W W and McNair, A D *Roman Law and Common Law: a Comparison in Outline* 2d ed (Lawson) Cambridge Cambridge University Press 1965

Burchell, E M and Hunt, P M A   *South African Criminal Law and Procedure General Principles of Criminal Law* Cape Town Juta 1970

Burdick, F M   *The Law of Partnership including Limited Partnerships* 3d ed Boston Little Brown 1917

Burgerlijk Wetboek; met een inleiding van B L Bakels 9de dr Kluver 1976

Burgess, R and Morse, G   *Partnership Law and Practice in England and Scotland* London Sweet and Maxwell 1980

Burns, A R   Partnership In *The Encylopedia of the Social Sciences* v 12 New York Macmillan 1948

Christie, R H   *The Law of Contract in South Africa* Durban Butterworths 1981

Cilliers, H S and Benade, M L   *Company Law* 4th ed Durban Butterworths 1982

Code Civil des Francais: Edition originalle et seule officielle Paris 1804

Code Napoleon adapté à la Hollande — Wetboek Napoleon ingerigt voor het Koningrijk Holland Amsterdam Allart 1809

Cooke, C A   *Corporation Trust and Company: an Essay in Legal History* Manchester Manchester University Press 1950

Corbett, P   "Partnership in Roman and English Law" 1887 *Law Magazine and Review* 219

Corpus Iuris Civilis I and II   (Mommsen, T and Krueger, P) Dublin/Zürich Weidmann Verlag 1968

Crane, J A   "The Uniform Partnership Act — A Criticism" 1915 *Harvard Review* 762

Crane, J A and Bromberg, A R   *Crane and Bromberg on Partnership* St Paul Minn West Publishing Company 1968

Crook, J A   *Law and Life in Rome* London Thames and Hudson 1967

Daube, D   "Societas as Consensual Contract" 1938 *Cambridge Law Journal* 381

De Groot, H   *De Jure Belli ac Pacis Libri tres in quibus jus naturae et gentium juris publici praecipua explicantur* Amsterdam 1651

De Groot, H   *Inleidinge tot de Hollandsche Rechtsgeleertheyd* 's-Gravenhage 1631

De Villiers, S W L   Partnership In: *South African Encyclopaedia of Forms and Precedents other than Court Forms* v 13 Durban Butterworths 1976

De Villiers, J E and Macintosh, J C   *Law of Agency in South Africa* 3d ed (Silke) Cape Town Juta 1981

De Wet, J C   "*Estoppel by Representation*" *in die Suid-Afrikaanse Reg* LLD University of Stellenbosch 1939

De Wet, J C and Yeats, J P   *Die Suid-Afrikaanse Kontraktereg en Handelsreg* 3d ed Durban Butterworths 1964 4th ed (De Wet and Van Wyk) Durban Butterworths 1978

Delport, H J "Gedingvoering met die actio pro socio tydens die bestaan van die vennootskap" 1979 *THRHR* 288

Delport, H J   *Gedingvoering tussen Vennote* LLD University of Pretoria 1977

Delport, H J   "Lee en 'n Ander v Maraisdrif (Edms) Bpk 1976 (2) SA 536 (A)" 1976 *De Jure* 361

Delport, H J   "Mede-eiendom en die Vennootskapsvermoë 1979 *Obiter* 98

Domat, J   *The Civil Law and its Natural Order*; translated by W Strahan Boston 1850

Drake, J H   "Partnership Entity and Tenancy in Partnership: the Struggle for a Definition" 1917 *Michigan Law Review* 609

Du Plessis, P A   "Kennisgewing van Uittrede uit Vennootskappe" 1979 *De Jure* 368

Duff, P W   *Personality in Roman Private Law* Cambridge Cambridge University Press 1938

Elliott R C and Banwell, E   *The South African Notary* 5th ed (Elliott) Cape Town Juta 1977

Felicius, H   *Tractatus de Societate ab Angelo Felicio* Gorinchemi 1666

Fuller, W   "Partnership Agreements for the Continuation of an Enterprise after the Death of a Partner" 1940 *Yale Law Journal* 202

Gaius *Institutiones*: Text with Critical Notes and Translations by F de Zulueta Oxford 1953

Gaius *Institutiones: The Institutes of Gaius* Oxford Clarendeon Press 1958-1963 2v

Gibson, J T R and Comrie, R G   *South African Mercantile and Company Law* 4th ed Cape Town Juta 1977

Gillooly, T C   "The taxation of partners" 1981 *DR* 383

Gilmore, E A   *Handbook on the Law of Partnership* St Paul Minnesota 1911

Goldschmidt, L   *Universalgeschichte des Handelsrechts* Stuttgart Enke 1891

Gower, L C B   *Gower's Principles of Modern Company Law* 4th ed (Gower, Cronin, Easson, Wedderburn) London 1979

Hahlo, H R   *Company Law through the Cases: a Collection of leading English and South African Cases on Company Law* 2d ed Cape Town Juta 1969

Hahlo, H R   *The South African Law of Husband and Wife* 3d ed Cape Town Juta 1969 4th ed 1975

Hahlo H R and Kahn, E   *The Union of South Africa: the Development of its Laws and Constitution* Cape Town Juta 1960

Heaton, H   *Economic History of Europe* New York; London Harper and Row 1948

Heenen, J   Partnership and other Personal Associations for Profit In: *International Encyclopedia of Comparative Law* v 13 Tübingen J C B Mohr (Paul Siebeck); The Hague Mouton [1973?]

Henning, J J   "Die Leeuevennootskap: Aspekte van 'n Deelname in Wins en Verlies deur Vennote" 1980 *MB* 143

Henning, J J "Die Moratoriumwet, 1963" 1976 *Tydskrif vir Regswetenskap* 99

Henning, J J   "Die Moratoriumwysigingswet: Ingekorte en Uitgebreide Sivielregtelike Beskerming vir Militêre Dienspligtiges" 1979 *MB* 45

Henning, J J   "Sivielregtelike Beskerming van Militêre Dienspligtiges" 1978 *DR* 115

Henning, J J   "Vennootskap en Moratorium — die Regsposisie van die Vennoot op Militêre Diens en sy Vennote" 1978 *THRHR* 2

Henochsberg, E S   *Henochsberg on the Companies Act* 3d ed (Milne, Nathan, Smith and Meskin) Durban Butterworths 1975

Herbstein, J and Van Winsen, L de V   *The Civil Practice of the Superior Courts in South Africa* 3d ed (Van Winsen, Eksteen and Cilliers) Cape Town Juta 1979

Higgins, P F P   *The Law of Partnership in Australia and New Zealand* Wellington 1963

Hildesheimer, E E   *Das jüdische Gesellschaftsrecht* Frankfurt Kaufmann 1930

Holdsworth, *Sir* W S   "Early History of the Commercial Societies" 1916 *Juridical Review* 308

Holdsworth, *Sir* W S   *A History of English Law* 7th ed (Goodhart and Hanbury) London Methuen 1956-1966 16v

Hollandsche Consultatiën Utrecht; Amsterdam 1728-1747 5v

Huber, U   *Heedendaegse Rechtsgeleerdtheyt, soo elders, als in Friesland gebruikelik* Amsterdam 1742

Jensen, A L   "Is the Partnership under the Uniform Partnership Act an Aggregate or an Entity?" 1963 *Vanderbilt Law Review* 377

Jones, P S T and Buckle, H O   *The Civil Practice of the Magistrates' Courts* 7th ed (Baker, Erasmus, Farlam) Cape Town Juta 1979-1980

Joubert, D J   "Aspekte van die Aanspreeklikheid van Vennote" 1978 *THRHR* 291

Kaser, M   *Roman Private Law;* translated by R Dannenbring 2d ed Durban Butterworths 1968

Kersteman, F L   *Hollandsch Rechtsgeleert Woorden-Boek* Amsterdam 1768-1773

Kniep, F   *Societas Publicanorum* Jena Fischer 1896

Kohler, J "Niederländisches Handelsrecht in der Blutezeit des Freistaates" 1907 *Zeit-schrift für das gesammte Handelsrecht* 293

Le Gall, J *French Company Law* London Oyez 1974.

Lee, R W *Elements of Roman Law* 3d ed London Sweet and Maxwell 1952

Lee, R W and Honoré, A M *The South African Law of Obligations* 2d ed (Newman and McQuoid-Mason) Durban Butterworths 1978

Lehmann, K *Lehrbuch des Handelsrechts* 3d ed (Hoeniger) Berlin and Leipzig Walter de Grunter & Co 1921

Levy, E "Neue Brüchstücke aus den Institutionem des Gaius" 1934 *Zeitschrift der Sa-vigny Stiftung für Rechtsgeschichte* (Romanistische Abteilung) 258

Lewis, W D "The Uniform Partnership Act — A reply to Mr Crane's Criticism" 1916 *Harvard Law Review* 158

Lichtenaur, W F *Geschiedenis van de Wetenschap van het Handelsrecht in Nederland tot 1809* Amsterdam Noord-Hollandsche Uitgevers 1956

Lindley, N L *Lindley on the Law of Partnership* 14th ed (Scamell and I'Anson Banks) London 1979

Little, P *Law of Partnership Taxation* JSD Dissertation, New York University 1979

Lybrechts, A *Redenerend Vertoog over't Notaris Ampt* Amsterdam 1968

Maasdorp, A F S *Institutes of South African Law* v 3 8th ed (Hall) Cape Town Juta 1970

Maeijer, J M M *Vennootschapsrecht in Beweging* Brussels 1976

Maine, H J S *Lectures on the early History of Institutions* London Murray 1875

Mars, W H *The Law of Insolvency in South Africa* 7th ed (Waters and Jooste) Cape Town Juta 1980

McGregor, A J "The Case of Simpson & Co v Fleck; being a Note on the Liability of Partners — after Dissolution of Partnership" 1909 *SALJ* 15

McKerron, R G *The Law of Delict* 7th ed Cape Town Juta 1971

Meyer, M A "Formation and Nature of Partnership" 1971 *Tulane Law Review* 347

Miller, J B *The Law of Partnership in Scotland* Edinburgh Green 1973

Mitchell, W *Early Forms of Partnership* In *Select Essays in Anglo-American Legal History* v 3 Boston Little Brown 1909 3v

Mohr, A L *Van Maatschap Vennootschap onder Firma en Commanditaire Vennootschap* Arn-heim Gouda Quint 1976

Morice, G T *English and Roman-Dutch Law; being a Statement of the Differences between the Law of England and Roman-Dutch Law as prevailing in South Africa and some other of the British Colonies* 2d ed Grahamstown The African Book Company 1905

Muirhead, J S *An Outline of Roman Law* 2d ed London; Edinburgh; Glasgow 1947

Muller-Gügenberger, C Bemerkunzur "Societas Leonina" In *Gedächtnisschrift für Jurgen Rödig* (Ramm, Rittner and Schmiedel) Berlin 1978

Nathan, C J M, Barnett, M and Brink, A *Uniform Rules of Court* 2d ed (Nathan and Barnett) Cape Town Juta 1977

Nathan, M *The Common Law of South Africa; a Treatise based on Voet's Commentaries on the Pandects, with References to the leading Roman-Dutch Authorities, South African Decisions and Statutory Enactments in South Africa* 2d ed Johannesburg 1913 4v

Nathan, M *The South African Law of Partnership and Private Companies* 2d ed Johannes-burg Hortors 1938

Naude, S J "Bamford: The Law of Partnerships and Voluntary Associations in SA" 1972 *Codicillus* 2

Nienaber, P "Partnership" 1964 *Annual Survey* 124

Noodt, G *Opera Omnia* Lugdunum Batavorum 1735

O'Neal, F H "An Appraisal of the Louisiana Law of Partnership" 1949 *Louisiana Law Review* 450

Oosthuizen, M J   "Die Turquand-reël as reël van die Verenigingsreg" 1977 *TSAR* 210

Partnership In *Corpus Juris Secundem* v 68 St Paul Min West 1950

Pauw, W   *Observationes Tumultuariae Novea* (Fischer et al) Haarlem Willink 1964–1972 3v

Piek, J N   "Van der Merwe v Sekretaris van Binnelandse Inkomste 1977 1 SA 462 (A)" 1977 *THRHR* 302

Planiol, M   *Treatise on the Civil Law* by M Planiol with the collaboration of G Ripert translated by the Louisiana State Law Institute Paris 1939

Pollock, Sir F   *Digest of the Law of Partnership* 15th ed (Gower) London Stevens 1952

Pothier, R J   *Oevres, contenant les Traités du droit Francais: Traité du Contrat de Société* Paris 1768–1778

Pothier, R J   *Pandectae Justinianeae, in novem ordinem digestea: cum legibus Codicis, et Novellis quae jus Pandectarum confirmant, explicant et abrogant* Lugduni 1782 3v

Pothier, R J   *Traité des Obligations* Paris 1813

Pothier R J   *A Treatise on the Contract of Partnership with the Civil Code and the Code of Commerce relating to that Subject in the same order;* translated from the French with Notes referring to Decisions of the English Courts by O D Tudor London Butterworths 1854 Reprint Durban Butterworths 1970

Pothier, R J   *Verhandeling van Contracten en andere Verbintenissen,* met aanmerkingen door J van der Linden Leiden 1804–1806 2v

Pothier, R J   *Verhandeling van het Recht omtrent Sociëteiten of Compagnieschappen en andere Gemeenschappen;* naar het Fransch door J van der Linden Leiden 1802

Ribbens, D S   "Legal Personality and Partnership — Quo Vadis?" 1978 *Codicillus* 7

Ribbens, D S   "Legal Personality and Partnership — Quo Vadis?" 1979 *Codicillus* 25

Roberts, A A   "Colonia Partiaria" 1942 *SALJ* 236

Salin, E   Usury In *The Encyclopedia of the Social Sciences* v 15 New York Macmillan 1948

Schiffres, I J   Partnership In: *American Jurisprudence* 2d ed Rochester, New York Lawyers Co-operative Publishing Co v 59–v 60

Schmoller, G   "Die geschichtliche Entwicklung der Unternehmung" 1890 *Zeitschrift für Wirtschafts und Sozialwissenschaften* 93

Schorer, W and Van Wijn, H   *Dertig Rechtsgeleerde Vraagen uit de Inleidinge tot de Hollandsche Regtsgeleerdheid van H de Groot, beneven antwoorde* 'sGravenhage 1777

Schulz, F   *Classical Roman Law* Oxford Clarendon Press 1951

Schulz, W P   "Liability of Partner for Partnership Debts" 1954 *SALJ* 395

Smits, P R   *De Externe Gebondenheid van het Vennootschapsvermogen* Deventer Kluwer 1969

Sohm, R   *Institutionen: Geschichte und System des römischen Privatrechts;* translated by T C Ledlie 3d ed Oxford Oxford University Press 1907

Stein, P   "The Mutual Agency of Partners in the Civil Law" 1959 *Tulane Law Review* 595

Story, J   *Commentaries on the Law of Partnership, as a Branch of Commercial and Maritime Jurisprudence, with occasional illustrations from the Civil and Foreign Law* 5th ed Boston Little Brown 1859

Sugarman, R R   *The Law of Partnership* New York 1937

Szlechter, E   *Le Contrat de Société en Babylone, en Grèce et a Rome* Paris 1947

Teetor, P R   "England's Earliest Treatise on the Law Merchant: the Essay on Lex Mercatoria from *The Little Red Book of Bristol* (circa 1280 AD)" 1962 *American Journal of Legal History* 178

Thomas, J A C   *Textbook of Roman Law* Amsterdam; New York; Oxford 1976

Troplong, R T   *Commentaire sur le Contrat des Sociétés Civiles et Commerciales* (Book 3 tit 9) Brussels 1843

Underhill, A   *Underhill's Principles of the Law of Partnership* 11th ed (Hardy, Ivamy and Jones) London Butterworths 1981

Uys, J F   *Die Genootskapsooreenkoms* LLD Rijksuniversiteit Leiden 1961

Van Brakel, S   "Vennootschapsvormen in Holland gedurende de Zewentiende Eeuw"
    1917 *Rechtsgeleerd Magazijn* 175
Van Bynkershoek, C   *Observationes Tumultuariae* (Meijers et al) Haarlem Willink
    1926–1962 4v
Van Bynkershoek, C   *Quaestionum juris privati* Lugduni Batavorum Van Kerckhem 1744
    facsimile ed Amsterdam Rodopi 1969
Van den Heever, F P   *The Partiarian Agricultural Lease in South African Law* Cape Town
    Juta 1940
Van der Heyden, E J J   *De Ontwikkeling van de Naamloze Vennootschap in Nederland voor
    de Codificatie* Amsterdam Van der Vecht 1908
Van der Keessel, D G   *Dictata ad Justiniani: Institutionum* (Beinart, Hijmans and Van War-
    melo) Amsterdam Balkema 1967 2v
Van der Keessel, D G   *Praelectiones Iuris Hodierni* (Van Warmelo, Coertze, Gonin and
    Pont) Cape Town Balkema 1961–1975
Van der Keessel, D G   *Theses Selectae Iuris Hollandici et Zelandici* Leiden 1800
Van der Linden, J   *Rechtsgeleerd Practicaal en Koopmans Handboek* Amsterdam Allart 1806
Van der Linden, J   *Verhandeling van het Notarisambt in Frankryk* 2d print Amsterdam 1825
Van der Merwe, S W J   *Die Juridiese Versekeringsbegrip met besondere verwysing na die Risiko*
    LLD University of South Africa 1975
Van Leeuwen, S   *Censura forensis* Lugduni Batavis 1741
Van Leeuwen, S   *Het Rooms-Hollandsch Recht* Leiden-Rotterdam 1664
Van Leeuwen, S   *Het Rooms-Hollands-Recht* 12de dr op nieuws overgezien en met aan-
    tekeningen uitgebreid door C W Decker Amsterdam 1780–1783 2v
Van Niekerk, A F   "Die Vennootskap in die Inkomstebelastingsreg" 1979 *MB* 3
Van Oven, J C   *Leerboek van Romeinsch Privaatrecht* 3d ed Leiden E J Brill 1948
Van Schilfgaarde, P and Van Solinge, P   *De Vennootschap volgens het ontwerp B W, pre-
    adviezen uitgebracht voor de Vereeniging "Handelsrecht"* Zwolle Tjeenk Willink 1974
Van Warmelo, P   "Aspects of Joint Ownership in Roman Law" 1957 *Tydschrift voor
    Rechtsgeschiedenis* 150
Van Warmelo, P   "Die Geskiedkundige Ontwikkeling van die Mede-eiendom in die
    Romeinse en Romeins-Hollandse Reg" 1950 *THRHR* 205
Van Wyk, A H   *The Power to Dispose of the Assets of the Universal Matrimonial Community
    of Property; a Study in South African Law, with Excursions on the Laws of Brazil and the
    Netherlands* LLD University of Leiden 1976
Van Zyl, D H   *Geskiedenis en Beginsels van die Romeinse Privaatreg* Durban Butterworths
    1977
Van Zyl, F J   *Universele Opvolging in die Suid-Afrikaanse Erfreg* LLD University of Stel-
    lenbosch 1981
Verwer, A   *Nederlants See-rechten; Avaryen en Bodemeryen* Amsterdam Boom 1711
Vinnius, A   *In Quator Libros Institutionum Imperialium Commentarius Academicus et Forensis*
    Lugduni Batavorum 1726
Voet, J   *Commentarius ad Pandectas* Den Haag De Hondt 1698–1704
Wassenaer, G van   *Practyk Notariael* Utrecht Van Zijl 1661
Watson, A   *The Law of Obligations in the later Roman Republic* Oxford Clarendon Press
    1965
Wessels, Sir J W   *History of the Roman-Dutch Law* Grahamstown African Book Com-
    pany 1908
Whiting, R C   "Law of Agency" 1971 *Annual Survey* 96
Wieacker, F   *Societas, Hausgemeinschaft und Erwerbsgesellschaft* Weimar 1936
Wille, G   *Principles of South African Law; being a Text-book of the Civil Law of the Union*
    7th ed (Gibson) Cape Town Juta 1977
Wille, G and Millin, P   *Mercantile Law of South Africa* 17th ed (Coaker and Schultz)
    Johannesburg Hortors 1975 Reprint 1980

TABLE OF STATUTES

This table of statutes is arranged alphabetically under the short titles of the statutes. Reference to colonial (republican) acts, provincial ordinances and foreign acts follow after the alphabetical table and are set out in chronological order.

TABLE OF CASES

A

B

PAR.

Q

INDEX

References are to paragraph numbers

References are to paragraph numbers

References are to paragraph numbers

References are to paragraph numbers

partnership agreement – *continued*
  extent of 365
  indicia 376
  intention 374
  lawfulness 363 378
  legal relationship arising from 361
  minor 379
  name given to 375
  natural person, with 379
  naturalia 415
  outsider, with 379
  party 379
  preparation of 382
  rescission 377
  signed 380
  stamp duty 382
  survivor, continuance by 419
  termination 408
    unilateral 419
  terms 373
    variation of 382
  third party –
    as against 373
    with 379
  true intention 374
  unilateral termination 419
  unlawful, performance in terms of 378
  valid 365 377
  void 378
  woman married in community of property 379
  written 380
    signing of 380 383
partnership asset, *see* partnership property
partnership capital 375 376 392 404
  contribution, interest on 376
  right and duty 404
partnership contract, *see* partnership agreement
partnership creditor 387 389
  course of action left open to 413
  individual partner 387
  liability of partner 389
  own funds, partner paying out of 401
  partnership property *vis-à-vis* 391 392
  preference 389
    assets, over 387
partnership debt 365 389
  creditor suing for 413
  in solidum 413
    singuli in solidum 413
  joint and several 365
  liability 365 389
  paid out of private estate 410
  partner as surety 389
partnership fund 391 394
  account for 431
  appropriation 431
  joint ownership 394 395
  partner claimant of 370
partnership lease –
  assignment of 423
  own benefit, for 400
  renewal 423
partnership money, use of 404

partnership obligation –
  actual 415
  due acceptance and fulfilment 400
  ostensible 415
partnership property 365n 391–395 413
  alienation 404
  appropriated for own purposes 394
  capital and, distinction between 393
  cession, on 395
  contribution, increase in 404
  court's approach 429
  creditor *vis-à-vis* 391 392
  description 392
  destruction, accidental 399
  distribution 396 429
    court's approach 430
    dissolution, on 396
    manner 430
    retention after 426
  division 404
    jointly used 426
  exclusive possession 404
  function 395
  future 365n
  insolvency, on 391
  intention 395
  joint, expenses incurred 407
  joint ownership 394 395 396
  legislation 391
  liquidation, on 428
  loss or destruction 404
  maintenance work 404
  majority decision 404
  new firm, taken over by 425
  ownership 386 391 393 404
  partner –
    ownership, relating to 404
    private use by 404
    vested interest in 391
  partnership debt, applied in payment of 425
  partnership funds, acquired with 392
  present 365
  private use by partner 404
  proportionate interest 396
  public auction 428
  quoad usum or quoad dominium, contributed 422
  retention after distribution 426
  right and duty 404
  single piece, in 365n
  structural alteration 404
  theft 418
  transfer, on 395
  true intention 392
  types of 395
  use 404
passing-off 381
performance 410
  specific 408 426
personnel, change in, notice of 420
premises, change of, notice 420
presumption 419 424
principal –
  joint co-debtor 416
  liability in solidum 416

References are to paragraph numbers